The Emergence of Leadership

The second half of the twentieth century witnessed the emergence of the most complex global organizations humans have ever known. This book focuses on leadership – the key factor which sustains them. Leadership in organizations is currently understood primarily from a perspective based on systems thinking that underlies theories of organizational culture, practice and learning. Leadership is understood as an attribute of both the individual and the learning organization – but this argument eliminates and ignores the paradoxical and emergent nature of leadership.

Increased complexity in organization has occurred in human history many times before: for example, the Greek "polis" of Athens; the military defence of large areas of land by aristocracy and monarchy; and national states with democratic elections and representative bodies. Accompanying these changes there has always been intense debate resulting in new understandings of leadership and ethics. *The Emergence of Leadership* argues that we are at such a point today, and explores in detail the implications for leadership in such theories as culture, the learning organization, living systems and complex adaptive systems. All of these are found to depend on systemic self-organization and traditional rationalist thought before and apart from action.

Arguing for an ethics of participative self-organization, the author holds that this will mean the end of "business ethics" as we know it today. In the past we have focused on individual leaders, but since ethics can no longer be viewed simply as rational choice in planning and action, we are faced today with the challenge of understanding self-organization in terms of the emergence of personal identity – as well as freedom and innovative change – in social interaction. This will necessarily entail understanding more about the nature of risk and conflict, spontaneity and motivation and the emergence of diversity.

Douglas Griffin is Visiting Professor and Associate Director of the Complexity and Management Centre at the University of Hertfordshire. He has worked for most of the last 20 years as an independent consultant in the areas of cross-cultural teamworking and organization development. During this time he has also been employed by 3M Germany in strategic personnel development and organizational learning services.

Complexity and Emergence in Organizations

Series Editors:
Ralph D. Stacey, Douglas Griffin and Patricia Shaw
Complexity and Management Centre, University of Hertfordshire

The books in this series each give expression to a particular way of speaking about complexity in organizations. Drawing on insights from the complexity sciences, psychology and sociology, this series aims to develop theories of human organization, including ethics.

Titles in this series include:

Complexity and Management
Fad or radical challenge to systems thinking?
Ralph D. Stacey, Douglas Griffin and Patricia Shaw

Complex Responsive Processes in Organizations
Learning and knowledge creation
Ralph D. Stacey

The Paradox of Control in Organizations
Philip J. Streatfield

Complexity and Innovation in Organizations
José Fonseca

The Emergence of Leadership
Linking self-organization and ethics
Douglas Griffin

Changing the Conversations in Organizations
A complexity approach to change
Patricia Shaw

The Emergence of Leadership

Linking self-organization and ethics

Douglas Griffin

London and New York

First published 2002
by Routledge
11 New Fetter Lane, London EC4P 4EE

Simultaneously published in the USA and Canada
by Routledge
29 West 35th Street, New York, NY 10001

Reprinted 2002

Routledge is an imprint of the Taylor & Francis Group

© 2002 Douglas Griffin

Typeset in Times by Wearset Ltd, Boldon, Tyne and Wear
Printed and bound in Great Britain by The Cromwell Press, Trowbridge, Wiltshire

British Library Cataloguing in Publication Data
A catalogue record for this book is available from the British Library

Library of Congress Cataloging in Publication Data
Griffin, Douglas
　The emergence of leadership : linking self-organization and ethics /
　Douglas Griffin.
　　p. cm. – (Complexity and emergence in organizations)
　Includes bibliographical references and index
　1. Leadership. 2. Executives–Conduct of life. 3. Self-organizing systems.
　4. Business ethics. I. Title. II. Series.

　HD57.7 .G745 2001
　174'.4–dc21
　　　　　　　　　　　　　　　　　　　　　　　　　　　　　　2001052007
ISBN 0–415–24916–3 (hbk)
ISBN 0–415–24917–1 (pbk)

I would like to dedicate this book – the work, friendship and intensely alive conversation from which it has emerged – to the family from which I have emerged,

to my mother Rose, and to the memory of my father Dallas

and to my brother and sisters. From the perspective on ethics I have taken in this book families can also be seen as on-going emerging conversations in the middle of which we appear on the scene, very much in the sense of Shakespeare's reference to the world as a stage, naïvely finding ourselves in the first conflicts, and begin to find our selves in the world.

Contents

Illustrations

Series preface
Complexity and Emergence in Organizations

The aim of this series is to give expression to a particular way of speaking about complexity in organizations, one that emphasizes the self-referential, reflexive nature of humans, the essentially responsive and participative nature of human processes of relating and the radical unpredictability of their evolution. It draws on the complexity sciences, which can be brought together with psychology and sociology in many different ways to form a whole spectrum of theories of human organization.

At one end of this spectrum there is the dominant voice in organization and management theory, which speaks in the language of design, regularity and control. In this language, managers stand outside the organizational system, which is thought of as an objective, pre-given reality that can be modelled and designed, and they control it. Managers here are concerned with the functional aspects of a system as they search for causal links that promise sophisticated tools for predicting its behaviour. The dominant voice talks about the individual as autonomous, self-contained, masterful and at the centre of an organization. Many complexity theorists talk in a language that is immediately compatible with this dominant voice. They talk about complex adaptive systems as networks of autonomous agents that behave on the basis of regularities extracted, from their environments. They talk about complex systems as objective realities that scientists can stand outside of and model. They emphasize the predictable aspects of these systems and see their modelling work as a route to increasing the ability of humans to control complex worlds.

At the other end of the spectrum there are voices from the fringes of organizational theory, complexity sciences, psychology and sociology who are defining a participative perspective. They argue that humans are themselves members of the complex networks that they form and are drawing attention to the impossibility of standing outside of them in order to objectify and model them. With this intersubjective voice people speak as subjects interacting with others in the co-evolution of a jointly constructed reality. These voices emphasize the radically unpredictable aspects of self-organizing processes and their creative potential. These are the voices of decentred agency, which talk about agents and the social world in which they live as mutually created and sustained. This way of thinking weaves together relationship psychologies and the work of complexity theorists who focus on the emergent and radically unpredictable aspects of complex systems. The result is a participative approach to understanding the complexities of organizational life.

This series is intended to give expression to the second of these voices, defining a participative perspective.

Series editors
Ralph D. Stacey, Douglas Griffin, Patricia Shaw
Complexity and Management Centre,
University of Hertfordshire

1 Introduction: how we have come to think of ourselves as victims of systems

- Systemic self-organization: the elimination of paradox
- Participative self-organization: the reappearance of paradox
- Complex responsive processes and the question of ethics
- Outline of the book

A widely prevalent way of thinking about leadership and ethics in relation to today's corporations is epitomized by a popular film genre. These films narrate the struggle of some heroic individual against a large organization. For example, there is the story of a large utility on the West Coast of the USA. Over a number of years, acids from one of the utility's plants leaked into the ground water used by adjacent residential communities. Many of the residents developed multiple forms of cancer and some of them claimed that this was due to drinking the polluted water. However, they were completely unsuccessful in their attempts to connect the cancer with the operations of the neighbouring plant. Then, by chance, a young assistant in a law office noticed that there were a number of cancer cases that seemed to be related to the plant, a pattern no one had so far noticed. She took up the cause and in her heroic struggle, as the leader, she united the residents in taking a joint action suit against the corporation. When a former employee supplied her with relevant documents from his basement, they were able to win the case, which turned out to be the largest settlement against an American corporation up to that time. Some of the top executives were found guilty of negligence and the young woman, the heroic leader, received a bonus of two million dollars from her law firm. Typically, after such a film, there is an air of excited triumph in the crowd as people leave the cinema. Someone finally took revenge on one of those big corporations, triumphing against "the system"!

Throughout the film, the characters talk about the corporation as an "it", which has intentionally leaked the acid, allowed the pollution of ground water and caused the cancer. This is typical of the everyday way in which we speak of large organizations, consisting of thousands of employees, as acting with culpable intention and being ethically responsible. When we talk in this way, we are talking "as if" an inanimate, nebulous entity called a corporation, or a "system", can have intention but in doing this we tend to forget the "as if". We slide automatically into talking about the "system" as having intention and being ethically responsible. However, in law, the corporation can only be found guilty of criminal intent if it can be proved that individuals in it acted intentionally to cover up the facts concerning the on-going leakage. In other words, it must be proved that individuals acted wilfully against the good of the community. Here, ethical responsibility is ascribed to the autonomous individual. It is *both* the corporation as "the system" *and* the autonomous individual, each in their own way, who are ethically responsible. We derive satisfaction from finding *both* the corporation *and* the individual guilty. The basis for thinking about ethics these days, therefore, has a "*both . . . and*" structure. We take it for granted that ethical responsibility is located separately in *both* the corporation *and* the autonomous individual and, in doing so, we forget the "as if" conjecture applied to the corporation. We tend not to sense anything contradictory, that is, paradoxical, about this way of thinking.

In automatically obscuring any paradox and forgetting the "as if" intention ascribed to the organization as a "system", we slip into thinking about the corporation as having a mind of its own, as setting its own purposes and acting with the freedom that only human beings in fact have. This way of thinking affirms an ethically passive stance in which most of us, as victims of the system, feel that the cause of unethical behaviour, such as the on-going leakage and the subsequent cancers of the residents, has been found, guilt allocated and justice served. It is the "system" and a few powerful individuals who are to blame, and the heroic individual leader has delivered us.

But has the cause of the unethical action really been found? Certainly, in the film described, key elements of a cover-up are identified. However, there is an important question about causality that is not even being asked. Indeed, the question is completely obscured by the way of thinking about ethical responsibility described above. The important question is: how could on-going damage to the environment of such a serious nature, over such a long period, happen in the complex daily interaction of thousands of employees working in the corporation and living in the surrounding community? Presumably, all of these people were acting with purpose as autonomous human beings and no one intended the result because, after all, they all lived in the community they were polluting. Presumably, they were all ethically responsible as human beings. However, the only causes of, and ethical responsibility for, the pollution are identified as *both* the corporation with its "as if" intention *and* senior individual managers. The rest are simply passive victims with no ethical responsibility for what happened, despite the fact that they were working daily with the leaky processes. Surely they had something to do with what happened? But we do not usually take this as a matter for examination and explanation.

Richard Sennett, in his book *The Corrosion of Character* (1998), explores how corporations, both large and small, have been affecting the surrounding communities in which their employees live. His book eloquently and persuasively argues that the qualities of community and of individual identity in the workplace have been deteriorating in the USA for decades. He presents evidence for the corrosion of individual character in: the gradual loss of community; the transition to more flexible concepts of working time; a different work ethos; and the superficial nature of role relationships among members of teams. He holds that the new capitalism and the indifference of corporations to their employees are responsible for this. The passion of his argument gives the book the urgency of an ethical "j'accuse!". However, I would argue that the ethical basis of his argument is the same as the film plot described above. The "system" of new capitalism and indifferent corporations carries out its intentions and is implicitly taken to be morally responsible for "its" actions, which destroy communities and corrode character. In the film, there are both the few criminal individuals and the criminal "system", and Sennett points to both the many individual victims and the morally culpable "system". Notice how this "both . . . and" way of thinking focuses ethical responsibility on a few managers and the corporation as perpetrators, while relegating most people to the passivity of helpless victims of the "system" without ethical responsibility for what they do.

To emphasize the point, I am arguing that nowadays we locate ethical responsibility in both the "system", simply taking it for granted that a "system" can be ethically responsible, and in a few individuals. In doing this, we adopt a particular view of leadership in which it is individual leaders who are blamed and punished when things go wrong, or praised and rewarded when things go right. The rest of us are allocated to passive roles as victims of "the system", and of manipulative leaders, and our salvation lies in the actions of heroic leaders. In thinking in this way, we are obscuring how we are all together involved in the dangerous situations that arise. Perhaps this is why we find ourselves repeatedly exposed to these dangerous situations. It then becomes a matter of great importance to understand just how we have come to think in this "both ... and" way in which we ascribe an "as if" intention to the "system".

Systemic self-organization: the elimination of paradox

In the first volume of this series, *Complexity and Emergence in Organizations* (Stacey, Griffin and Shaw, 2000), my co-authors and I examined the origins of "both ... and" thinking, over two centuries ago, in the work of the German philosopher Immanuel Kant. The collapse of the metaphysical systems of thought of the Middle Ages left thinkers facing an enormous paradox. In the emerging scientific approach of that time, humans were thought of as a part of nature and, therefore, subject to its deterministic, "if–then" causality. But in philosophy and theology, humans were thought of as exercising freedom of choice in the use of their rational powers and, therefore, not subject to the notions of causality and time to be found in thinking about nature. Kant found a way to eliminate this paradox of humans being part of nature, on the one hand, and superior to it, on the other. He introduced, for the first time in the history of thought, what has become the "both ... and" way of thinking about causes and time, now so taken for granted by us. In three volumes over a number of years, Kant laid the basis for a way of thinking that avoids settling for either the extreme of scientific empiricism, which denies rational choice, or dogmatic rationalism, which focuses entirely upon it. He argued that humans are *both* subject to the laws of nature *and* free to set their own goals. However, he did not see this view as being at all paradoxical because of the separate theories of causality he proposed for nature, on the one hand, and human action, on the other. Since rational humans can understand the causality of nature, they are free to rationally choose goals in relation to it.

Systems thinking

To support this contention, Kant developed the basis for what I will be referring to in this volume as *systemic self-organization*. Kant held that we are truly human in setting on-going goals for our actions, but that we can also think about nature using a particular understanding of the causality of on-going goal setting. That particular understanding amounts to an "as if" way of thinking. Kant suggested that we could hypothesize goals in nature as "regulative ideas". He adopted a dynamic way of looking at nature as a system. The system dynamically unfolds a form, a goal of its own, namely, to realize a mature form of itself. But that is not to say that the dynamic is setting the goal. It is the human scientist observing and hypothesizing who is thinking and testing *"as if" the system were setting and unfolding such a goal itself.* In arguing for this way of thinking, Kant was motivated by his admiration for the scientific method as initially developed by Newton, but he thought that basing it solely on causality of the "if–then" kind was not enough. Hence he developed the notion of nature as system in which internal interactions between its parts display a self-generating, self-organizing dynamic in which the whole emerges as the realization of the "as if" goals hypothesized for it. Organisms are thought of as developing from simple initial forms, such as a fertilized egg, into a mature adult form, all as part of an inner coherence expressed in the dynamic unity of the parts. An organism thus expresses a nature with no purpose other than its own form and Kant described this as "purposive", that is, displaying a unified form in itself. The parts of an organism exist because of, and in order to sustain, the whole as an emergent property. Nature, then, is to be understood as a system dynamically unfolding a goal ascribed to it by a human. Human freedom is thus retained when nature is understood as systemic self-organization because it is the human who is postulating the "as if" goal of the system and because, within that understanding of nature, humans can rationally choose goals for their own actions.

It would be hard to underestimate the importance of Kant's move in eliminating paradox through the introduction of "both . . . and" thinking with its notion of nature as system moving dynamically "as if" having purpose. It is especially difficult for us to understand this because Kant thought not only in terms of "if–then" causality, as we do today, but also in terms of three other kinds of causality, in the tradition going back to Aristotle. The other three kinds of causality are: material cause, meaning that a thing is what it is because of matter; formal causality, meaning that a thing is what it is because it has the form it has; and on-going goal striving causality which moves to achieve ends in which the end motivates the striving. The latter is referred to as teleological cause from "telos", the Greek word for goal, or as final cause, from "finis", the Latin word for end state. For Kant, it was important to retain the notion of teleological causality, hence the idea of nature as dynamic systems with formal cause incorporating subordinated, "as if" on-going goal striving causality. This view of nature moving in an "as if" goal-striving way, was consistent with human goal striving, so enabling Kant to eliminate the paradox of humans being subject to nature and free of nature at the same time. Instead of a paradox, there was the view of humans both subject to nature and free of it through their rational ability to understand it from an objective, observing position. This way of looking at nature is of the essence of our world today. It is, therefore, important to try understand some of the advantages and disadvantages of the move to "both . . . and" thinking and why it can lead to developing the habit of not even noticing the potential for paradox.

There is no denying that thinking in terms of systemic self-organization is far superior to taking only the perspective of simple "if–then" cause and effect. For example, consider the way we speak with medical personnel about our bodies and healing. If am having a growth removed, especially from a sensitive area like my face, I am concerned with how it will heal and what it will look like. A physician might reassure me as follows: "The body will begin to develop scar tissue in about 7 days. This process will continue for about 6 months, at which point the body will sense that it has developed too much tissue and it will then begin to dissolve this tissue over the following 6 months." I experience relief at hearing this story. I now know something that reduces anxiety. The scientist/physician here is, as observer, presenting the hypothesis of the healing process as a story of *the body's* intent and recognition of when to start and stop phases of the process of systemic self-organization.

Ethics

From this viewpoint of *systemic self-organization*, it would not be possible to blame the body, tissue or even the physician if the process went wrong in some way. This is because, in describing nature as a system in this way, the physician is doing so from the "as if" perspective, that is, as a hypothesis. If the system does not unfold in the expected way, it would mean only that the hypothesis failed the test and this failure would trigger the formulation of a new hypothesis. In effect the failure of the hypothesis arouses interest in moving on the search for a better hypothesis. Truth here has the pragmatic sense that is found in the long run among the community of scientists. There is no ethical implication in the system's movement. Instead, medical ethics would concentrate on the actions of individuals, for example, the physician's negligence due to insufficient sleep, excessive alcohol consumption or drug abuse. The "both . . . and" way of thinking can be seen in the way the physician thinks about *both* the human body "as if" it were following its own intention *and* himself as exercising freedom in choosing rational human actions "as if" they expressed moral universals for which he will be held accountable. Kant thus extends the regulative idea, the "as if", to his ethical basis of man's freedom, making it the pivotal concept in his thought.

There is no doubt that forming hypotheses and presenting descriptions in this way, using the language of systemic self-organization, is a valuable tool for the natural scientist. However, it is important to remember that Kant maintained an "as if" perspective and did not want to say that nature had a "mind" of its own. The final states which the system arrives at are not set by the system but by the observing scientist, who puts this language of intention, recognition, decision, and so on, "into" the system in the "as if" mode of hypotheses. The scientist is then *both* a free, autonomous individual *and* an observer discovering the laws of nature, understood as self-organizing systems.

Human action

One can immediately sense how easy it would be to adopt this approach when thinking about human groups, organizations and societies. One might describe them as self-organizing systems, which unfold pattern according to some intention of their own that we ascribe to them. However, Kant was unequivocal in stating that human action could never be thought of in this "as if" approach because that would involve ascribing to the human system the exercise of freedom in choosing a goal, which is really a matter for the human individual only (see Stacey, Griffin and Shaw, 2000). Kant defined a self-organizing system as one that unfolds an "as if" idea, or hypothesis, about the natural world. For Kant, humans are autonomous individuals, not systems. They are free and are guided by universal principles in judging the ethics of their actions. These universal principles are another use of the "as if" mode of making judgments: we come to know the ethical universals in our acting "as if" our actions could be so done universally, by everyone.

My argument then is as follows. We have come to think about human action in terms of a Kantian framework, although in an important way we do so contrary to Kant himself. We think of the autonomous individual choosing goals and actions as expressions of ethical universals, just as Kant proposed. For instance, senior management of large organizations know before taking action that what they propose is or is not in accordance with laws. We do not know ethical universals directly; we act as if, in view of their foreseen results, our actions could be made into universal laws for everyone. The laws we have at any given time are the expressions of such universals. And we also think of an autonomous individual taking up the objective observer position of the scientist in relation to humans collectively. Human collectives are then thought of, contrary to Kant, as self-organizing systems with their own goals and intentions. For instance, Sennett describes the action of senior management as directing the actions of thousands of people in large companies. They observe results and make changes in order to attain their goals.

The result is the "both . . . and" thinking about humans as sometimes being autonomous individuals whose actions express ethical universals and at other times being parts of a system and so subjected to its formative process containing goals and intentions. In doing so we lose sight of the "as if" nature of these goals and intentions, and we also lose sight of anything paradoxical about human action. The example of the struggle against the large corporation, with which I began this chapter, clearly expresses this way of thinking. And the consequence of this "both . . . and" *resolution* of paradox is that human rational autonomy is always split off from the self-organizing system applied to human joint action (see Stacey, Griffin and Shaw (2000) for an elaboration of this point).

But why is it that the "both . . . and" way of thinking has become so pervasive and taken-for-granted? One key reason is, of course, that it is the basis for the dominant way of thinking about the modern notion of the scientific method. The advances in science, and especially in medicine, led easily to attempting to use this way of thinking beyond the bounds of the natural sciences, so that we have come today to use it in a taken-for-granted way in reference to the world we live in and the organizations we are part of. We speak in varying ways of the organization, or parts of the organization, as systems acting with intention, and we also think of management as individuals outside the system who freely choose goals, which are then enacted as the implementation of systems. Perhaps this way of thinking has now become a victim of its own success.

In the rest of this book I want to draw attention to another way of thinking about causality and the ethical basis of what emerges in organizations as self-organization. I will argue that the taken-for-granted elimination of paradox has developed into a habit of thinking that reduces ethics to the justification of individual thought apart from action. Ethics then becomes judging an action in terms of the thought or intention that went before it. This has distracted attention away from the meaning that self-organization might have for human interaction, namely, one that no longer has the sense of an "as if" application by an external observer. The alternative way of thinking I am talking about draws attention to what is really going on in organizations, namely, the self-organization of those participating in the organization as the basis for identity and change. This will mean recovering a way of thinking based on living in the movement of paradox rather than eliminating it. It is a way of thinking that no longer involves the simple observation of organizations as systems. I will be arguing that when we think in the way we currently do, we ignore the very nature of ethics. The price we pay is pointed to in the film plot and the points made by Sennett, described earlier in this chapter: *the destruction of the environment* as the basis for life and *the gradual loss of the human communities* in which all our organizations are embedded. This alternative way of thinking does not eliminate paradox but places it at the very core of understanding. I provide a brief indication of this way of thinking in the next section and take it up in Part II of this volume in Chapters 5 and 6.

Participative self-organization: the reappearance of paradox

The resolution of paradox in thought as *both* individuals with freedom *and* self-organizing natural systems has led us to think, in a taken-for-granted way, of human individuals in two ways, which we do not experience as contradictory. We think of individuals collectively as self-organizing systems and so subject to the "system's" unfolding of intention, forgetting the "as if" assumption about that intention. We also think of individuals as being outside such systems so that they are free and ethically responsible for controlling and changing the system. To say the least, this would have been completely unthinkable to Kant. It would have been completely opposed to his purpose in introducing the idea of the autonomous individual into his thought.

The Enlightenment established, for the first time, the idea of the autonomous individual, which was to become one of the principal foundations of modernist thinking. However, Kant's idea of the autonomous individual stood in tension with the overriding worldview of the individual being part of God's creation. For Kant, the problem was how to reconcile individual autonomy with the wider context of which the individual was a part and so determined by. How can an individual be autonomous and yet a part of God's creation, that is, a part of nature understood in terms of deterministic laws? In today's secular world this may not seem to be much of a problem. Overriding importance is simply attributed to the autonomous individual, who tends to be seen more or less as a universe in him- or herself. However, in emphasizing the individual to such an extent, we tend to lose sight of the tension with the context, that of which the individual is a part. In other words, we tend to lose the tension between the autonomous individual and the group (community/society) of which the individual is part. The tension is lost sight of because it is resolved in the now familiar way of "both . . . and" thinking. Individuals form groups and then those groups impact on the individuals or, to put it another way, groups exist before individuals who are born into and shaped by them. In this way, we lose the tension between individuals as the condition for the possibility of the group and the group as the condition for the possibility of individuals, at the same time. (This issue is discussed in Stacey (2001).) Norbert Elias (1989) cogently expressed this tension when he stated that the individual and the group are the singular and the plural of the same phenomenon, namely, human relating. His words clearly express a paradox, which is a way of thinking that is at the periphery of modernist Western thought.

It is understandable that paradox should remain at the periphery of Western thought. After all, the scientific method, which eliminates paradox using Kant's thinking, has led to enormous advances, and this success is the basis of the resistance to accepting any notion of paradox in the natural sciences. However, the problem of paradox did not simply go away. It appeared again and again in the natural sciences of the twentieth century. For example, a central issue in quantum mechanics was that of natural scientists disturbing, that is, participating in, the systems they were trying to observe "objectively". In other words, a paradox was recognized, namely, that of the scientist participating in and observing a system at the same time. Quantum mechanics theorists then sought to resolve this paradox, for example, in the "collapse of the wave function" implying that the quantum micro-world changes in two different ways, one way when it is being observed and another when it is not. Cybernetics theory, the engineer's notion of self-regulating systems, also confronted the paradox of participant/observer when it was applied to human interaction. Cybernetic thinkers proposed to resolve the paradox with "second-order cybernetics" in which the observer was incorporated into the system. The result was a wider system incorporating a narrower one as the system of the system. This inevitably leads to infinite regress: every time a system is described, something outside the system is doing the describing and setting the goals, and this something then has to be incorporated into an even wider system. In *Complexity and Management* (Stacey, Griffin and Shaw, 2000), my co-authors and I described this process of infinite regress, which eventually leads to the conclusion that everything is connected to everything in a transcendental system incorporating everything. Von Foerster (1992), for example, returns to metaphysics and the Kantian notion of ethics as a system of universals. But in doing so he and other second-order cyberneticists reassert the "both . . . and" thinking of systemic self-organization, where the ethics is outside of the system. In the next three chapters, I will explore the implications for ethics of these developments in systems thinking.

However, the resistance to thinking in terms of paradox and the drive to resolve the paradoxes encountered, is now being challenged in the natural sciences. Thinking about emergence and self-organization is being reformulated in the complexity sciences and is undermining some fundamental analogies and inferences taken from the natural sciences into the human social sciences. The Nobel Prize winning chemist, Ilya Prigogine, was the first to formulate this new view of self-organization, one that accepts rather than eliminates paradox, when he talked about order emerging from disorder in far from equilibrium conditions (Prigogine and Stengers, 1984; Nicolis and Prigogine, 1989). The notion of order and disorder present *at the same time*, as a paradox, challenges what has become one of the main pillars of Western scientific thinking concerning causality and time.

We notice this dominant way of thinking about cause and time, with its taken-for-granted elimination of paradox, when we ask questions like:

- How is it that organizations stay the same in order to get work done and also change in order to surprise the competition?
- Are we actively forming the organizations we work in, or are we being formed by these organizations?
- Are organizations simple or are they complex?

What we spontaneously tend to do, is to argue that in each instance organizations are both. They both change and they stay the same. They are both forming us (as cultures) and we are forming them (planned structuring and re-engineering). They are both simple (explicit procedures) and complex (unstructured networks). Notice that in each answer we find the connectives "both . . . and". We have a taken-for-granted ability not to sense that the questions we are asking could be taken as paradoxical. However, in Prigogine's new questioning of self-organization we find the expression "at the same time". What is now being challenged in the natural sciences by thinkers like Prigogine, therefore, is precisely *the validity of the elimination of paradox*. Prigogine draws attention to a notion of self-organization, which is by its very nature paradoxical. He talks about the presence of order and disorder *at the same time* in far from equilibrium conditions. Taking this perspective we would answer the questions posed above in a very different way. We would say that organizations stay the same and change at the same time, that we form them while being formed by them at the same time, that they are simple and complex at the same time. The challenge being presented by thinkers like Prigogine, therefore, is to explore just what paradoxical answers like these might mean when it comes to making sense of our experience of life in organizations. What view would we take of ethics? What would this mean for the way we think about leaders?

Modern scientists insist on eliminating paradox because they hold that paradoxes distort an objective view of the world. Prigogine argues, to the contrary, that in eliminating paradox in thought, scientists do not see what is in front of them, in their experience, namely, the presence of order and disorder at the same time in far from equilibrium conditions. The key phrase is "at the same time". Prigogine is in the position of the external observing scientist, but he is drawing attention to something that does not have the separation of internal and external. This is the paradoxical "at the same time" of order and disorder that he refers to as self-organization. In terms of Kant's thinking the scientist is hypothesizing and imputing the self-organization into a "system", "as if" the system were itself intending its final state. Prigogine's view is very different: nature is to be understood as perpetually constructing a future that is not known before it evolves.

This series, *Complexity and Emergence in Organizations*, seeks to take seriously what this view of self-organization might mean for human interaction. In *Complexity and Management: Fad or Radical Challenge to Systems Thinking* (Stacey, Griffin and Shaw, 2000) my co-authors and I argued for the importance of noticing the difference in causality between systemic self-organization and what I will be referring to in this

Box 1.1 "Both . . . and" as opposed to "at the same time"

Some examples may help to clarify the important distinction I am making here, and to differentiate the further possibility of "either . . . or".

Napoleon gained a reputation as a hero of the French revolution by destroying the old absolutist powers across Europe. He also gained a reputation as a despot and dictator in his internal rule of France. Biographers can choose either perspective and try to make a case that their view is the "real" Napoleon. The views would in this sense be mutually exclusive and contrasted as "either . . . or". *Either* he was a liberating hero *or* he was a despot. The "both . . . and" perspective resolves this by portraying *both* as the *one* Napoleon. This is a dilemma, but it can be resolved by demonstrating, for example, that as a foreign conqueror he was a hero, while as an internal administrator he was a despot. The dilemma is no longer in tension; it is resolved. The third possibility, that of "at the same time", is radically different in that it holds on to what it means that this one man was, in all his actions, driven by the paradox of being both a liberating hero and a dictator at the same time. Holding this sense of *at the same time* is to become aware of key paradoxes and it remains uncomfortable. The very essence of such paradoxes is that they do not settle down to a resolution.

An example of how such paradoxes characterize businesses is The Body Shop. The central paradox of the company is that it is committed to ecological ideals and at the same time to making a profit by competing on the world market. This paradox is never resolved – but it generates problems again and again at all levels and in all the activities of the company, which are analyzed and fixed as dilemmas that are resolved. For instance, take the recent dilemma concerning whether or not to continue supplying cosmetic kits for business class passengers on British Airways. Such kits were excellent commercial advertisements of the Body Shop's unique approach to body care, but were linked to airline travel, in relation to which there is growing evidence of its contribution to the destruction of the ozone layer protecting the earth.

These distinctions between "either . . . or", "both . . . and" and "at the same time" are echoed in the metaphor of evolutionary change as a stream.

* The rationalist position of "either . . . or" is that of the detached observer on the bank looking at the stream as a whole separate from himself and the banks.
* The second viewpoint, that of "both . . . and", is that of a person steering a canoe on the stream. This person is constantly facing the problems that rocks present and resolving the dilemmas of constantly adjusting to retain the balance required to keep the canoe afloat and in the stream between the two banks.
* The third perspective, which is analogous to the sense of "at the same time", is that of being the stream, caught up in the generation of forward movement, with no fixed point from which to settle into the certainty of "being a stream".

volume as *participative self-organization*, by which I mean Prigogine's paradoxical perspective on self-organization. In *Complexity and Management*, we discussed in detail how systemic self-organization combines two forms of the causality of purpose (teleology). It combines *both* the rational teleology of the free choice of individuals *and* the formative teleology (the "as if" purpose of the system imputed by the scientist). In the case of participative self-organization, there is no purpose imputed by the scientist. Instead, the process is seen to have its own cause, or purpose, namely, the process of constructing the as yet unknown future. Such a process is understood as transforming itself from within, that is, as having a transformative teleology. Table 1.1 compares the two notions of self-organization.

Participative self-organization and ethics

I have been arguing that systemic self-organization has been widely applied to human social systems, despite Kant's warnings against doing

Table 1.1 *Comparison of systemic self-organization and participative self-organization as ways of thinking*

Systemic self-organization	Participative self-organization
. . . posits *both* an autonomous individual as external observer (subject) *and* a self-organizing system (object) of which the subject is a participating part	. . . posits a process of interactive participation between self-conscious embodied subjects who are observers and participants, subjects and objects at the same time
. . . describes system evolution as unfolding in accordance with some hypothesis ascribed to it by the observer/scientist. The cause of the movement is this hypothesis	. . . describes the process of evolving interaction as transformation from within, as its own cause
. . . eliminates paradox in order to describe the system as a whole	. . . accepts paradox in order to understand the immediate phenomenon of experience
. . . is viewed as moving toward purpose which has originated externally and been put into the system which is then viewed "as if'" it had the purpose itself	. . . causes itself in moving toward the purpose which is intrinsic to the process
. . . views change in terms of the formulation of a new hypothesis	. . . views change as the perpetual construction of the future (sustaining identity and potentially transforming it)

this. I have also been pointing to the kinds of problems that we encounter in our thinking when we ignore Kant's strictures. The question now is whether the notion of participative self-organization can assist us to understand human social interaction in a more useful way. For instance, consider again the story of the film and Sennett's description of the deterioration of community and identity, with which I started this chapter. The ethical perspectives of both the film plot and Sennett's critique were based on the intentions behind the actions of both the "system" and some autonomous individuals. In other words, ethics was linked to the thought apart from action. If we were to try to understand these two accounts from the perspective of participative self-organization we would immediately be faced with a number of paradoxes. The people involved were all participants as employees (internal) and observers as residents of the community (external), at the same time. The participants were forming the interactions and being formed by the process of interaction at the same time. There is, therefore, no simple possibility of knowing how to judge the outcomes of action before acting, since the future is being constructed in the interaction.

When we locate ethics in the intention, or thought, apart from or before the action, we are assuming that the likely outcome of the action can be known before the action is taken. It is only on this basis that we can allocate praise and blame. However, when the intention arises in the action, as it does in participative self-organization, and when the outcome of the action cannot be known in advance of acting, then a different view of ethics is required. In other words, a different way of thinking about how we morally account to each other for our actions is called for, one that takes account of the paradox of "at the same time". Time is then no longer simply the linear predictability of before and after. Rather, time is circular in the sense that the emerging future is constructed, as is the understanding of the past, in the self-organizing processes of interaction in the living present.

Throughout the following chapters, I will be arguing that the interaction between people in the movement of the living present, in which they create the future on the basis of the past, is the very essence of experience. Our experience is the experience of interaction in the present. However, the linear time of thinking in "both . . . and" terms leads us to take this experience of the living present for granted, as we locate the causes of what we do, not in our participative interaction with each other, but in some "system", which is beneath, above or behind our experience. We do this when we talk about "culture" as a cause of human action, or when we refer to "shared values", or when we claim that we cannot act without a "vision", or when we ascribe the causes of our acting together to a "common pool of meanings", a "group mind", or "simple rules". In all of these cases we are trying to explain our experience of interaction in terms of something that exists before that interaction so that our interaction simply becomes the kind of systemic unfolding Kant held to be applicable only to nature.

The legal systems of the West are built on the notion that people working together in groups to do business with others are in some sense "one". The word "corporation" comes from the Latin "corpus", that is "body", and other designations such as "societé" convey something similar. This is also the sense of "organ" in the word "organization". However, this designation of a "body" to a group of people is purely hypothetical, "as if". Forgetting this "as if" and attributing direct agency to these groups has become a habit of thought leading us to think and talk about groups as objects, as things, which are simply "there". We do this in many theories of communication and meaning. For instance, consciousness in psychological theories is commonly taken to be a thing, a given point of departure on the basis on which various phenomena can be explained. Gestalt theory does this with the concepts of "field" and "ground". Cultural theory suggests that "culture" is something with causal powers over human interaction.

Although explanations along these lines may be useful, they do have a drawback. They encourage us to forget their "as if" sense so that we take them for granted and lose our curiosity about how they emerged and how they change. For example, take the account of scar tissue given above. A surgeon who has reduced his practice to routine operations might well have only one story to tell. "The body will begin building scar tissue in 7 days and will continue to do so for 6 months. It will then recognize that it has built too much tissue and will begin to dissolve tissue for the next 6 months." Such an explanation relieves anxiety, but it also stops further questioning, in that it ignores the "as if" attribution of intention to the body. Another surgeon, aware of the "as if" nature of his description, might develop more plausible hypotheses and make the patient aware of these. When the "one story" explanation of scar tissue healing is taken as a given, the tendency is immediately to think of manipulating the healing process, taking steps to speed it up or slow it down. This can, of course, be beneficial and the pharmaceutical companies place their best bets on product developments to do just that. However, it does close down further thinking about the nature of health and illness.

In organizations we are in danger of remaining at the level of the "one story" and forgetting that theories of culture, leadership and ethics are "as if" stories. In organizations, cultures are audited and compared, and then choices are made for change. Any success in these endeavors tends to reinforce the forgetting of the "as if" and increase the sense that our world is one of objects which we can manipulate. We then lose curiosity about a whole sphere of our experience, which is about the emergence of what we have come to think of as objects, or systems, to be manipulated. And this way of thinking is evident even when we think of ourselves as individuals. We talk about ourselves as having "mental models", or "internal worlds", and we locate our motivation in "the unconscious". In doing this, we are postulating another "system" lying behind or beneath our actions and coming to think of them as causing those actions. The result is the location of explanations for our interactions in individual or collective systems that lie outside the interaction itself and account for it. The explanation of our interactions is then distant from our experiences of those interactions themselves.

The next section briefly examines what participative self-organization might mean in human interaction. This leads to explaining our interactions from within our participation in them. The explanation does not appeal to any level other than the experience of participating in the interaction. I will be arguing that participative self-organization has immediate implications for thinking about the ethical consequences of acting in organizations. As soon as we think differently about ethics, we must think differently about leadership. Leaders would not just be individuals outside the system observing the system, forming visions for its development and making plans for strategy and change, but would paradoxically be participants and observers "at the same time" in the paradoxical processes of perpetually constructing the unknown future. I turn now to a way of understanding how we perpetually construct the future.

Complex responsive processes and the question of ethics

In earlier volumes in this series (Stacey, Griffin and Shaw, 2000; Stacey, 2001) my co-authors and I suggested a theoretical basis for thinking about mind, consciousness, culture and other social phenomena as all emerging in complex responsive processes of human relating. We argue that such a perspective offers a much more immediate reflection of our experience, that is, how we live in local situations in the movement of the present with its paradoxical "at the same time" constraints of the past and on-going construction of an unknown future. This perspective draws attention to processes that are no longer "as if " in that they are about the experience of interactions between us in the present, rather than any system outside of that interaction, such as "culture" or "mental models". I am arguing for the letting go of the "as if ", taken-for-granted world of "both . . . and", in order to think from within interaction in terms of participative self-organization.

For example, consider how one might think about the story with which I began this chapter, that of acids leaking into a community's water supply. Instead of immediately looking for the cause in "the system", "as if " a large corporation and its leaders acted negligently, one would explore how the occurrence of on-going leakages could have emerged in the patterns of interaction between all of those involved. One would start asking how the pattern of relating between people, how the emerging patterns of communicative interaction between them, could be constructing an on-going future of acid leaking into their own water supply. One would wonder what kind of emerging leadership was implicated in that on-going construction of the future and just how people were ethically accounting to each other for actions that polluted their own water supply. All participants in the large corporation's operations were forming what was happening and at the same time they were being formed by it in terms of individual and collective identities. This way of looking at social interaction will be developed in detail in Chapter 5 as a theory of complex responsive processes of relating.

The purpose of sustaining and transforming identity is, therefore, the cause of the movement of human action toward a "known-unknown" future. That movement is the participative self-organizing process of bodily communicative interaction between people, forming and being formed by itself at the same time in a circular, reflexive and self-referential causality. Participative self-organization is thus the patterning of communicative interaction between people in which variations arise based on the diversity of those interacting. The interaction itself amplifies small differences into discontinuous, genuine change and is thus its own cause in transforming, from within, simultaneously sustained identity. In all forms of communication, but primarily in language, meaning emerges in local processes experienced as the movement which is the "living present". This refers to the temporal paradox of experience in which freedom of choice and intention are experienced within the constraints of the past, in the process of movement into an unknown future. Meaning emerges in these complex responsive processes of relating and may take many forms, including the conflicting constraints of power relations characterized by inclusion and exclusion, and the ideologies that sustain and shift these relations.

Complex responsive processes as participative self-organization provide, therefore, an organizational perspective of simultaneously cooperative and competitive interaction, which has direct consequences for ethics. George Herbert Mead, the American pragmatist and social theorist (1862–1931), refers to the fundamental importance of understanding conflict in relation to the overriding importance of purpose:

> The first implication that flows from this position is that the fundamental necessity of moral action is simply the necessity of action at all; or stated in other terms, that the motive does not arise from the relations of antecedently given ends of activities, but rather that the motive is the recognition of the end as it arises in consciousness. The other implication is that the moral interpretation of our experience must be found within the experience itself.
> . . .
> If we were willing to recognize that the environment which surrounds the moral self is but the statement of the conditions under which his different conflicting impulses may get their expression, we would perceive that the recognition must come from a new point of view which comes to consciousness through the conflict. The environment must change *pari passu* with the consciousness. Moral advance consists not in adapting individual natures to the fixed realities of a moral universe, but in constantly reconstructing and recreating the world as the individuals evolve.
> . . .
> There may be, indeed, intellectual processes involved in stating this moral order, but such statement is confined, in the nature of the case, to apologetic and speculative thought, to thought which cannot be a part of the immediate moral consciousness.
>
> (Mead, 1908: 314–17)

From these quotes we can see that Mead is arguing against Kant's notion of ethical universals as in any sense "fixed realities", apart from and before action and against which human conduct is to be judged as ethical or not. This would imply that the meaning of that action could have been known in advance. Instead, he is suggesting that the ethical interpretation of action is to be found in the action itself, in the on-going recognition of the meanings of actions that could not have been known in advance. That continual recognition requires new points of view that emerge in the conflictual interaction in which the future is perpetually being created. In other words, ethical meaning does not reside in external universals to be applied to interaction but, rather, ethical meaning continually emerges in the interaction itself. Ethics are being negotiated in the interaction.

It is important to understand Mead's idea of "arising in consciousness", "immediate consciousness" and "self". Stacey (2001) develops Mead's understanding of the emergence of mind, self and society (Mead, 1934) as a basis for understanding complex responsive processes. Stacey emphasizes that the processes of mind/self are always actions of a body, experienced within a body. He argues that the mind/self is silent conversations/private role plays. These are not stored as representations of a pre-given reality, but are continuous, spontaneous action in which patterns are reproduced in repetitive forms as continuity of identity and, at the same time, as potential transformation of that identity. Interaction between bodies, the social, and interaction of a body with itself, mind, is the experience of both familiar repetition of habit and the potential of spontaneous change.

> The process is not representing or storing but continuously reproducing and creating new meaningful experience. In this way, the fundamental importance of the individual self and identity is retained, along with the fundamental importance of the social. In this way, too, both continuity and potential transformation are always simultaneously present.
>
> (Stacey, 2001: 89)

What he is talking about here is participative self-organization in which both the individual mind and the group/social emerge at the same time.

In this volume, in further developing Mead's insight into the emergence of ethical motivation in the participative self-organization Stacey describes, I will not only be taking the perspective which he takes, that of "self/mind", but also the perspective of "person". All references to "individual self" or "individual mind", as well as to "person", are easily misunderstood in terms of the rationalist notion of the autonomous individual that we have come to take for granted. It is important to define a position that moves beyond this and to this end I will be exploring the long tradition behind the concept of "person", which draws attention to the process of recognition in interaction. In Chapter 5, I will develop the concept of person on the basis of this tradition of thought that has always differentiated it from the concept of the autonomous individual. This concept of person provides a unique basis for developing the idea of emerging ethical motivation within the emergence of sustained identity and possible transformation.

When ethics is understood from the perspective of participative self-organization/complex responsive processes, that understanding immediately challenges the notion of leadership as a simple distinction between the leader and the followers. The view of ethics I am referring to is clearly not based on the notion of "antecedently given ends", that is, simple thought before action. The idea that leaders form strategies and plans for change before action, and then persuade others to follow them, is clearly based on the notion of thought before action. A different notion of leadership is required when one moves to thinking in terms of participative self-organization.

The sense of sustaining our identity – an identity far more complex than simply that of "victim" or "follower"

If one shifts perspective on ethics in the sense that Mead suggests, then one must also shift perspectives on the nature of leadership. In Part I of this book, I will be drawing attention to the way in which systemic self-organization as a way of thinking alienates questions of ethics from everyday social interaction by locating leadership in *both* autonomous individuals *and* in an all encompassing "whole". Such a view, however, perpetuates simplistic fantasies that the roles of leader and follower are a "given", a fact of human nature. In Part II, I will work out a basis for understanding that we as groups of persons, in the on-going sustaining of our identity, together create a great variety of leadership roles for as well as the roles of those who have their identity in relation to this leadership *at the same time*. A great number of leadership "themes of identity" are available to us in all situations we find ourselves in. Because of the anxiety around the unknown and the uncertain we often choose themes that protect us and provide escape from this anxiety. Identity as persons in a group is always embodied, that is, in human bodies, and in a complex local context of which identity is the unique expression. In sustaining our identity as persons in a group we perpetually create our future and make spontaneous and intentional choices for which we are ethically responsible. We deal with the known, but also the unknown; the certain, but also the uncertain; the predictable, but also the unpredictable, in a radical and paradoxical sense at the same time. Together we create CEOs, COOs, and CFOs, along with general managers, department heads and supervisors. We create those who serve as models and examples, representatives and strategists. We create priests, bishops, rabbis, employees, bosses, bullies, monarchs, generals, ruthless princes, presidents, mayors, prophets and physicians. We create lackeys, sycophants, volunteers, soldiers, citizens, patients, the faithful, servants, members, people of virtue, criminals, terrorists, monks and conspirators. All of these roles emphasize that, while we make choices in sustaining our identity, which we somehow justify as "good" in making them our purpose, they are by no means always made in terms of a broader common good.

It is only in understanding this sustaining of identity as a more complex process than systemic self-organization that we can remain alert to our responsibility to articulate the purposes of the broader contexts. We create in participative self-organization the meaning of the identities we have as persons in human bodies in numerous and varied groups and with each other in local situations in the movement of the living present.

Outline of the book

Part I of the book explores the scientific legitimization of leadership theory and argues that it is based on a systemic view of self-organization, which has important implications for ethics. The underlying model is that of the leader as detached, scientific observer of the organization, which eliminates the paradox of being both observer and participant in the organization at the same time.

Chapter 2 reviews the basis of modern systems thinking about organizations in the philosophy of Immanuel Kant. He developed the "both . . . and" way of thinking to eliminate the paradox of humans being part of nature and yet autonomous. I will argue that this is the basis of modern thinking about the learning organization, most notably in the work of Peter Senge. Although Kant argued that humans are autonomous and so cannot be understood as parts of a whole, or system, this is just what the theory of the learning organization does. Senge's framework provides a way of thinking about *both* participation in a self-organizing whole (systems thinking, shared visions and teams), ultimately of a nature harking back to the wisdom of the ancients, *and* the autonomous individual (personal mastery, mental models and visions). This thinking results in a split, as a kind of figure-ground resolution of paradox, with regard to ethics, where there is *both* the Kantian ethics of the autonomous individual applied to the actions of leaders in designing the system *and* the identification of the vision and the ethics of the harmonious whole to which individuals freely consent to conform. This thinking also results in a split with regard to leadership, where there is *both* the leader as autonomous individual *and* leadership emerging in the systemic self-organization of the whole as shared values and common purpose. Participation is defined as individuals participating in a whole that is larger than them, rather than as ordinary everyday interaction between them.

In Chapter 3, I explore the work of those who argue that organizations should be thought of as living systems. Many of those taking this perspective appeal to the complexity sciences to support their argument. However, I will suggest that despite the move to complexity they continue to employ the same Kantian notion of systemic self-organization as Senge does in relation to the learning organization. They frequently make an emotive appeal for a return to ancient wisdom, supposedly now made scientific by the complexity sciences. This advocates complexity theory as a basis for leaders to build more caring communities. The suggestion that an organization is a living system reflects a holistic philosophy, which sets up a whole outside of the experience of interaction between people, a whole to which they are required to submit if their behaviour is to be judged ethical. This distances people from their actual experience and makes it feel natural to blame something outside of their actual interaction for what happens to them. It encourages the belief that they are victims of a system, on the one hand, and allows them to escape feeling responsible for their own actions, on the other.

Chapter 4 describes how organizational culture has come to be thought of as an autonomous system of values and norms, and more recently as the simple rules of some complexity theories, which individuals internalize and to which they conform. Leaders come to be conceived of as autonomous individuals who can manipulate and control the autonomous system of culture. This constitutes Kantian "both . . . and" thinking in which there is no sense of any paradox in thinking that a system that is supposed to be autonomous is nevertheless thought to be controlled by an individual who is autonomous. This theory of culture and leadership has ethical implications that are not usually made explicit. I will explore these in Chapter 4. Ethical behaviour is understood to be determined by the reasoning individual, on the one hand, but because organizations are thought of as autonomous cultural systems, like individuals, the need for ethical choice of action is also applied to such reified organizations. This dominating view of ethics removes the consideration of ethics from the ordinary everyday interactions of people constituting an organization. *Ordinary, feeling individuals relating to each other disappear from the sphere of ethics.* Participation becomes participation in an idealized systemic whole, often linked to such systemic wholes as the forces of nature or some kind of mystical union. The ethical and moral responsibility of individuals is related to this mystical whole rather than to the everyday contingencies of ordinary life in organizations. Culture comes to be thought of as an overriding, autonomous, harmonious whole to which "good" people freely choose to conform. The notion of participation as ordinary interaction between people and the notion of ethical and moral behaviour as our accounting to each other tends to be lost.

The chapter will also examine the thinking of Mead who talks about this kind of approach as a feeling of enlarged personality. He pointed to the way in which this kind of thinking constitutes *cult values* that divert attention from what people are actually doing, focusing instead on some idealization. The psychological technique of simply maintaining a cult is to present to the imagination a situation free from the ordinary obstacles of social life or nature. Cult values set up idealized ends that are considered to be inviolable, a harmonious whole which everyone is forbidden to argue with. If anyone does, they are immediately accused of selfishly introducing conflict. When we talk about organizational culture as harmonious wholes and leaders with visions, we are talking about organizations as cults. While we are not able to live without cult values, such as democracy, justice and love of neighbour for example, we need to be aware of the dangers of thinking that we can achieve *conflict-free* ethical behaviour through *direct conformity* to cult values.

Part II of the book argues that it is necessary to let go of the modernist concept of the autonomous individual and Kant's systemic self-organization to develop a theory of participative self-organization. Instead of understanding individuals as participating *in self-organization,* where it is some whole that is self organizing, the perspective I will be developing is one in which participation *is self-organization*. Here, there is no self-organizing whole outside of immediate, ordinary daily interaction between living bodies. The task in Part II is to work out a basis for understanding participative self-organization as the process sustaining and potentially transforming identity. This requires developing a concept of participation that includes the embodied human being but is not limited to the modernist concept of the autonomous individual.

From the perspective of participative self-organization, Chapter 5 explores an understanding of selves as emergent persons in social interaction, as an alternative to the modernist understanding of the individual as autonomous. This interaction is understood, in turn, as complex processes of relating. This perspective immediately focuses attention on the importance of local communicative interaction in the living present, particularly its thematic patterning, its gesture-response structure and its reflection in ideologies and power relations.

In Chapter 6, I draw together the central argument of this book and explore its implications. I argue that theories of ethics are also theories of leadership. In the dominant view, ethical universals are thought of as "fixed realities" against which human conduct is to be judged, apart from and before action with meaning known in advance. Ethical leaders are those who are able to understand the consequences of their actions better than others, or have proven themselves worthy of imitation because of the way they keep to the contract. Others, therefore, voluntarily agree to follow them and tend to be lumped together as followers. I propose, on the basis of Mead's thought, an alternative view of ethics and leadership. The ethical interpretation of our experience is found within the experience itself as new points of view that emerge in the conflictual interaction in which the future is perpetually being created. This view of ethics avoids simply idealizing in a cult manner; it focuses on how idealizations are functionalized in the everyday conflicts in which we are always negotiating the future on the basis of the past. As groups evolve and develop a past they begin to recognize various members in roles, one of which is leader. The role of leader emerges in the interaction and those participating are continuously creating and recreating the meaning of the leadership themes in the local interaction in which they are involved. Groups tend to recognize the leader role in those who have acquired a greater spontaneity, a greater ability to deal with the unknown as it emerges from the known context.

Chapter 7 provides a summary of the central arguments developed in previous chapters. My central argument is that there is a very widespread tendency in organizational and management theory, including most of the developments influenced by the natural complexity sciences, to adopt a perspective that I have called systemic self-organization. This involves positing a dualism. On one side of this dualism there are leaders, understood as autonomous individuals, who formulate visions, values, and so on that are to be directly applied to a system, such as the organization or the culture, which constitutes the second side of the dualism. Such a system is understood in terms of some transcendent or idealized whole, which provides leadership, and participation is taken to be the participation of individuals in this whole. In other words the whole system is reified and ascribed intentions or qualities such as "harmonious", "caring" or "soul". Individuals so participating are "good" or compassionate, while those who do not are characterized as "bad" or "selfish". In other words, leadership and ethics become matters of explicating the rules or qualities of the harmonious whole and of individuals conforming to it. I described this as the direct application of cult values. The result, I argue, is a large number of dualistic splits, for example, between the autonomous leader and the abstract leadership provided by the harmonious whole, and the split between the good and the bad individuals. Thinking in this dualistic way eliminates paradox and mystifies leadership. The ethical is abstracted from direct experience and located in some kind of idealized universal whole outside of direct experience. The result, I suggest, is the kind of experience with which I started this chapter in which we experience ourselves as the victims of the very systems that we think of ourselves as having created. As an alternative way of thinking I propose a participative self-organization perspective in which organizations are understood as complex responsive process of relating in the ordinary social interaction of people in their local situations in the movement of the living present. This perspective is essentially paradoxical in that persons form social interaction while being formed by it at the same time in a process characterized by the known and the unknown. Here participation is the direct interaction of persons with each other.

Part I
Leadership and systemic self-organization: participation in systems

Once upon a time there was a man who sought escape from the prattle of his neighbours and went to live alone in a hut he had found in the forest. At first he was content, but a bitter winter led him to cut down the trees around his hut for firewood. The next summer he was hot and uncomfortable because his hut had no shade, and he complained bitterly of the harshness of the elements.

He made a little garden and kept some chickens, but rabbits were attracted by the food in the garden and ate much of it. The man went into the forest and trapped a fox, which he tamed and taught to catch rabbits. But the fox ate up the man's chickens as well. The man shot the fox and cursed the perfidy of the creatures of the wild.

The man always threw his refuse on the floor of his hut and soon it swarmed with vermin. He then built an ingenious system of hooks and pulleys so that everything in the hut could be suspended from the ceiling. But the strain was too much for the flimsy hut and it soon collapsed. The man grumbled about the inferior construction of the hut and built himself a new one.

One day he boasted to a relative in his old village about the peaceful beauty and plentiful game surrounding his forest home. The relative was impressed and reported back to his neighbours, who began to use the area for picnics and hunting excursions. The man was upset by this and cursed the intrusiveness of human beings. He began posting signs, setting traps, and shooting at those who came near his dwelling. In revenge groups of boys would come at night from time to time to frighten him and steal things. The man took to sleeping every night in a chair by the window with a loaded shotgun across his knees. One night he turned in his sleep and shot off his foot. The villagers were saddened by this misfortune and thereafter stayed away from his part of the forest. The man became lonely and cursed the unfriendliness of his former neighbours. And all these troubles the man saw as coming from outside himself . . .

(From Philip Slater, 1970)

The last century witnessed the growth of the most complex global organizations humankind has ever known. As these organizations grew, theories of management emerged which spoke to the concerns and anxieties around their size and power. It is not surprising that again and again such theories sought a basis in the natural sciences on which to found their legitimacy. The reason for this can easily be seen in the status that the scientist has acquired in modernist society. The early scientific management theories of Taylor and Fayol were the first to apply principles of the natural sciences to the management of organizations and in doing so set powerful precedents, which are influential to this day. The organization was split into a number of activities and management was defined as the activities of forecasting, planning, organizing, coordinating and controlling through setting rules that others were to follow. In the hierarchy, rational thought and justification were at the head of the pyramid, just as thinking powers were located in the individual brain by rationalist thinkers.

Leadership is the role of sustaining the on-going identity and purpose of any group or organization. It would be hard to overestimate its importance in this sense. Certainly over the course of the last century the leaders of organizations were seen to be exercising enormous power and producing results contributing to the on-going improvement of society and the lives of its citizens. Thousands of books and articles on the subject of leadership are testimony to this perceived importance. We have become aware of the greatly increased power and responsibility of the leaders of large organizations and the importance of their acting ethically to construct a future in which we continue to survive. Leadership theory has also continued to seek legitimization in the natural sciences.

In the chapters in this Part, I will examine various aspects of this scientific legitimization of leadership theory and argue that it is based on the systemic view of self-organization, described in Chapter 1. I will explore the implications this has for ethics and leadership. My purpose will be to lay the ground for exploring in Part II what it would mean to move away from the model of the leader as detached, "scientific" observer of the organization. This will address the way in which current leadership theories eliminate the paradox of being both observer and participant in the organization at the same time. In doing this I will be challenging dominant thinking around leading and following.

2 Leadership: two questions seven years apart

- Ron's question: linking leadership, communication and teams
- Alberto's question: the emergence of leaders

During the 1990s, while working in Germany, I became aware of the spreading influence of two waves of management theory flowing, 7 years apart, from reformulations in the natural sciences. These management theories originated in the United States and following their impact in that country, they later spread to organizations in Europe. The first of these waves took the form of various strands of thinking based on cybernetics and systems dynamics, perhaps the most influential example being Peter Senge's framework set out in *The Fifth Discipline* (1990). Senge drew directly on systems dynamics, whereas earlier systems thinkers, who developed the version of cultural theory now taken for granted in management thinking, had relied primarily on cybernetics and general systems theory. The particular version of cultural theory referred to was first developed in general by Talcott Parsons (1951) in his theory of social systems and in particular with regard to management theory by Edgar Schein (1992) and Charles Hampden-Turner (1994). In this chapter, I will be focusing attention on Senge's thought, leaving the impact of cultural theory for discussion in Chapter 4. The second wave of influence from the natural sciences on management theory, referred to above, was that of chaos and complexity theory. This also reached European organizations somewhat after its initial impact in the United States and I will be discussing it in the next chapter. Looking back, I remember now how two questions, one posed by a manager at the start of the 1990s and the other raised at the end of that decade, brought home to me the influence of these two waves of thinking on management practice at the grass roots level.

Ron's question: linking leadership, communication and teams

There were a number of reasons for being optimistic about Europe's economic future at the beginning of the 1990s. The timetable for establishing a single market and a single currency was in place. There was a widespread belief that this new single Europe was going to become an economic sphere in which companies would benefit from the greater size of the market, the increased transparency of taxation and other regulations and the opportunity to reduce bureaucratic restrictions. It was believed that cost savings flowing from these changes would be greatly enhanced by downsizing, restructuring and the re-engineering of business processes, all measures that had already proved both controversial and successful in the United States. Managers were facing these prospects in a context of the enormous increase in the power and influence of financial markets and institutions that had taken place in the 1980s. This shift in power, sparked by figures such as Michael Milken and his junk bonds, had resulted in transforming the power base and the self-image of the leaders of business organizations, who now found their options for action significantly more limited by powerful financial markets. It is into and out of this climate that those at the head of organizations began to develop an interest in systems thinking, and the new scientific legitimacy and importance that management theorists using it were giving to the role of leadership.

In the early 1990s, I was working in Germany for a globally operating US company. The name of the department I worked in had been changed from "Human Resource Development" to "Strategic Personnel Development" shortly after my joining the company – the first of three name changes to come over the next 4 years. The thinking behind this first change was to signal a renewed focus on leadership development at all levels. The senior executives of the company in the USA had followed the advice of major consulting organizations in a "me too", "best practice" strategy of radically flattening the hierarchy of its businesses and restructuring them in what amounted to a far-reaching decentralization. The role of the renamed department was typical of such departments in large organizations undergoing structural change: we offered help to managers in changing their behaviour and developing the skills necessary to do their work in the new situation, in the belief that problems in social interaction were located in the individual. Soon after the implementation of the restructuring we received a number of requests from high-level managers which were markedly different from those we had regularly heard before. The requests all had to do, in some way, with the theme of "listening". There seemed no obvious reason why these requests should be appearing virtually "out of the blue". I had the opportunity to work with one of these managers; in the sessions with him and his team I began to understand the enormous attraction of systems thinking for making sense of experience in organizations.

The strength of systems thinking

One of the calls we had about listening was from Ron, the American head of manufacturing in one of the major divisions and as such responsible for three plants around Europe. On the phone he mentioned that he had been very perplexed in recent exchanges with some of those reporting directly to him. They had all indicated in differing ways that he "was not listening". Ron had raised this in a meeting with his whole team and felt he was still confused by what it was they were trying to say to him. He was especially puzzled by why this was happening now; in previous years he had never heard any comments about "listening". This is what led him to make the call to our department. He was looking for some perspective on what it might be about.

In our initial meeting he spoke of different possible explanations, such as his difficulty in learning foreign languages and other possible gaps in his communication skills. Ron was typical of high-level managers in this particular organization: he had risen very quickly in the hierarchy because of his exceptional analytical skills coupled with very firm but pleasant social skills. I was initially as perplexed as Ron was about the suggestion that he was "deficient" in listening skills. To the contrary he seemed to listen with well above average concentration. We, of course, eventually came to discuss the restructuring of the organization and its impact on his work. He emphasized that he felt very positive about the changes, but began to describe how routines in the office were changing in completely unexpected ways. The office space had been reduced in accordance with the flattened hierarchy and some of his subordinates were taking advantage of this to speak more readily with Ron's boss. He felt irritated at first, then began to sense that there was really no problem and it often saved time. Other aspects of the changes meant that his team had much greater leeway in making decisions concerning key areas of their business.

After only a few conversations, Ron himself came to the insight that what had been the key to his success in the past, his analytical powers, was now standing in the way of the shift he needed to make if he was to function effectively in the kind of meetings and conversations with his team brought about by the restructuring of the organization. He needed to allow others more leeway in influencing decisions. This would mean, on the one hand, slowing the speed of his analytical move to closure on decisions in some instances and, on the other hand, developing the habit of exploring alternatives with the members of his team. A "happy ending" was evident when I attended one of their meetings a few months later, where the main discussion centred on plant closure. It had become clear that one of the three plants would have to close, although which it was to be was yet to be decided. Ron fought an intense battle to keep all of his team involved in the decision-making process, despite the loud rumblings and a threatened ultimatum from the US executives of dire consequences if a decision was not made soon. Ron had gained a widespread reputation for listening beyond limits that were comfortable for many senior managers!

This story might be taken as a good example of understanding experience and change in organizations from the perspective of the behaviourist model. From this perspective change is a matter of developing specific skills in individuals based on the belief that it is behaviour that changes behaviour. Alternatively, this story could be understood in a radically different way. I read Senge's *Fifth Discipline* shortly before meeting Ron and was very enthused by what I immediately perceived, agreeing with Senge, as a far better way of understanding organizations than the simpler behaviourist models, which "human resource" development programmes were based on at that time. At the same time, I was surprised at the lack of interest in Senge's book in Germany, even in the US companies located there. In the initial conversations with Ron, I began to understand that it was the earlier changes in organizations in the USA that had paved the way for the acceptance of systems thinking and that this scale of restructuring change was now beginning to affect companies in Germany. From the point in our conversation when Ron began speaking of the impact of the restructuring, I thought of Senge's central tenet that one should not think of changing behaviour with behaviour. From the systemic perspective he makes the point that it is changing the structures that changes behaviour. He is referring here to what he terms "systemic structure", which is concerned with the key interrelationships that influence behaviour over time.

The changes in organizations in the USA, which I am referring to, were based on such systemic thinking and the implementation in turn created a climate in which now someone like Ron, upon hearing these ideas, immediately found that they made good sense of his experience. He read the book and in a few meetings with him and his team we discussed the ideas. Ron sensed that ideas in the book made him better able to make the shift from the successful highly analytical thinking which had been the basis of his rapid moves up the ladder of the organization. His focus shifted from the simple cause/effect thinking of behaviourism to systemic self-organization and the search for systemic leverage points that leaders can use to achieve large-scale changes. The "listening" behaviour shifted from being only about a skill located in the individual to being indicative of large-scale changes in patterns of behaviour resulting from the restructuring. Instead of just taking, as given, the need to change from one behaviour to another, as one would in a purely behaviourist model, he could now understand how the need for a behavioural change had come about and what that change might mean. This kind of change seemed to fulfill the belief that planned changes should affect the whole organization in a way that was foreseen by those arguing for the restructuring. It seemed that, as a matter of fact, when senior executives in the USA designed a new system with a much flatter hierarchical structure, its implications would emerge in the systemic self-organization of the new system, thousands of miles away in Germany. Managers in the new system would find the need to interact with each other in different ways and they could understand more of this if they thought in systems terms and of themselves as members of a learning organization. Two years later the name of our department was changed to "Organizational Learning Services", a decision made in the United States rather than in Germany.

The learning organization: the argument against Kant

The above story points, I think, to the central argument and the main strength of systems thinking. Again and again, throughout Senge's work and that of other systems theorists, the manager is put into the role of the scientist in Kant's approach, as described in Chapter 1. The scientist attempts to understand nature by testing hypotheses, or regulative ideas, which impute a purpose-seeking mind to nature. They do this "as if" nature had such a mind of its own, although the purpose is their own, as stated in their hypothesis. The scientist, as observer external to the system, forms a theory and then puts it into the system to test it. Systemic self-organization *only makes sense* when coupled with the detached observer.

In Senge's framework, this is exactly the position that the leader is required to take up in relation to the organization. The focus of this book is to examine how management theorists have repeatedly taken this modernist idea of science as the basis for a hard science of social interaction with important ethical implications. At this point I am focusing on Senge's work as a well developed example of an approach common to systems thinking. Readers interested in comparing the differing approaches, variations and refinements of systems thinking can find a critique of this in *Complexity and Management* (Stacey, Griffin and Shaw, 2000).

Of course it was not Ron in the above story who was initially in this position of the scientist. It was the executives and consultants in the USA who imposed new rules and structures onto the system. At that point, Ron and others in the system discovered themselves playing out in a self-organizing way what the new rules and structures would come to mean in terms of behaviour. As free human beings, they were compelled to participate in a system not of their own choosing and so discover how they needed to function to fulfill the unfolding dynamics of the system.

Surprisingly, however, when people read a book like that of Senge's after such an experience, they do not feel that they have been unjustly manipulated or inhumanly treated. There is something taken-for-granted about how this type of intended change of behavioural patterns affecting tens of thousands of people can be undertaken on the assumption that there is tacit consent and no one will find that their sense of freedom or choice has been violated. Perhaps they accept, without question, what has happened to them because they too can take a role external to the system and test changes to it. Ron, as a part of this new system, was doing just that in relation to his team. This raises a question. Was Kant wrong in thinking that systemic self-organization could not be applied to human social interaction? Senge's argument for the learning organization represents a very broadly based example of precisely such an application and there is no doubt that this approach did help Ron to make more sense of his experience. Kant's argument against applying systems thinking to human action has to do with concerns about human freedom and ethics. In the following sections, therefore, I want to look at the question of whether Kant was wrong from the point of view of:

- leadership;
- participation;
- communication;
- social interaction;
- issues concerning ethics.

The learning organization as a theory of leadership

Senge unequivocally believes that leaders are not made to order but, rather, make themselves. "Systems thinking, personal mastery, mental models, building a shared vision and team learning – these might just as well be called the *leadership* disciplines as the learning disciplines" (Senge, 1990: 359). I think it is important to take Senge seriously here and regard the learning organization as primarily a leadership theory rather than just a theory of systemic change. Then, what becomes immediately apparent is that systems thinking, personal mastery, mental models and building a shared vision together amount to an inspirational call for the freedom and responsibility of leaders in *making themselves*. What Senge is doing here is emphatically reaffirming the Kantian notion of the freedom of the autonomous individual. He refers a great deal to Eastern thought in explaining the discipline of personal mastery, but I argue that he presents a view that is completely consistent with the Western ethical tradition of focusing on the individual as the centre of choice in shaping the future.

However, Senge also makes an extremely important shift from Kant's thinking in one respect. The world that Kant lived in, two centuries ago, was still dominated by the metaphysics of the Middle Ages and belief in a world ordered by universal ethical principles founded in the end on philosophy and theology. Kant's rational individual followed the categorical imperative of acting in such a way that his or her actions could become universal laws for everyone to follow. This was his "as if" thinking, the regulative principle in testing action. It is hypothetical because only the results of action would reveal whether that action was in accordance with the universal principles or not. But it is also a regulative idea because it can serve as a universal norm before the action is taken. In today's secularized world, Senge speaks of "vision" as central to the concept of personal mastery, where that individual vision is not concerned with self interest.

> The sense of connectedness and compassion characteristic of individuals with high levels of personal mastery naturally leads to a broader vision. . . . Individuals committed to a vision beyond their self-interest find they have energy not available when pursuing narrower goals, as will organizations that tap this level of commitment.
>
> (Senge, 1990: 171)

In taking the perspective of systemic thinking, Senge views the rationality of the autonomous individual as a "synergy of reason and intuition" on the basis of which that individual should understand "connectedness to the world" and "commitment to the whole" (ibid.: 171).

Here, Senge departs from Kant in applying Kant's notion of a whole as a self-organizing system to human interaction. For Kant, any sense of the "whole", as a basis for an ethics, could only have been the metaphysics of God-given universal principles guiding human action, which he called a not-to-be-defined whole. He did this because to define the whole would be to remove human freedom. For him, human freedom meant that in their actions humans were discovering the ethics of those actions, just as the scientist discovers the laws of nature. However, in a nebulous way, supported by ideas in Eastern thought about the harmony of the world, Senge is suggesting that it is the role of leaders to define the "whole" for their organization in terms of visions and values, which are to be applied to individual actions. Senge then goes further and creates a "both . . . and" ethical position whereby the individual is committed both to the modernist idea of centred autonomy and to the whole of the organization as a system with its visions and values. This is the core of Kant's objection to using systemic self-organization in reference to human interaction. It necessarily entails determining a content for the whole, the on-going purpose and survival of the organization, and this would, for Kant, eliminate the true nature of human freedom. This is because individuals would then be making choices on the basis of a given system and not on the basis of universal principles, taking all of the community and society into consideration, as revealed in their actions. So, Senge subtly reaffirms Kant's "both . . . and" thinking in speaking of connectedness to the world, "the whole", on the one hand, and commitment to the organization as "a specific systemic whole", on the other. The "both . . . and" mode of thought is also evident in talking about both the masterful autonomous individual and participation in systemic wholes. But in doing so, he applies systemic wholes to human action, contrary to Kant's intention, and talks about commitment to these systemic wholes. Senge's considerable emphasis on the autonomous individual, however, provides enough scope to retain the Kantian ethics, which are the basis of traditional business ethics. Traditional business ethics are very much focused on individual choice in accordance with timeless universal principles. This perspective will be examined further in Chapter 4.

However, as a leadership theory built on the nature of somewhat nebulous systemic wholes (visions and values), Senge's learning disciplines do go beyond the limitations of traditional business ethics, in that they are concerned with on-going actions in organizations that sustain its identity and purpose while making constant changes. This is where Senge's leadership theory departs significantly from the traditional idea of leaders isolated at the top of hierarchies. He develops systems thinking as a basis for an ethics, that is, a basis for understanding the work that the leader does. This is broadly developed as a multifaceted role of designer, steward and teacher. Taking an ocean liner as a metaphor for the organization, Senge points out that most executives make the mistake of seeing their leadership role as that of captain or navigator. From the viewpoint of the learning organization, Senge sees executives as the designers of the ship. To the traditional leadership role of designing policies, strategies and systems, he adds the *on-going design over time of the system*. This concept of time, one in which the design of the system is changing, is very important for Senge. It is one of the main insights he wants to draw attention to in having people play and reflect on the "Beer Game", in which players act out over time amplifying changes in the chain of production, distribution and sales. He claims that without the discipline of systems thinking those acting in organizations forget this time factor, forget that the system itself is changing, and take action based on simple cause and effect thinking. The designer is constantly striving to understand the system as a whole, which includes this notion of time, and makes necessary design adjustments. The same is true for the leader as steward in terms of the on-going development of the purpose of the organization. As teacher, the leader fosters the learning of everyone in the organization, searching for leverage points whereby this learning can be exponentially increased. The leader is, thus, both outside and inside the organization, which is thought of as a system. He or she is outside in the sense of setting strategies and plans which are *to be accomplished* over time, so defining the systemic whole, and inside in the sense of participating in the movement toward these objectives over time.

Although Senge violates Kant's injunction regarding human interaction in terms of systemic self-organization, he clearly appeals, in a taken-for-granted way, to the Kantian thinking that eliminates paradox. This is very important in developing the notion of the leader as being *both* outside of the organization as a system as a designer *and* being inside the system as a participant. It is the "both . . . and" habit of thought which allows us to take this for granted. There is no paradox here because first you think about the leader in one way and then you think about the leader in another way, in a figure-ground manner. Senge does not sense that human freedom is being violated since everyone in the organization is seen to be a free autonomous individual who has committed both to his or her own personal vision and to the organization as a whole. The evolving whole is the vision (strategies, goals and purposes) of the leaders. For Kant, it is this whole that reduces human freedom to consenting to the whole. Senge, therefore, has to develop a new ethics concerning the on-going work toward the survival of the whole because traditional business ethics is based only on the perspective of the leader being outside the system as an autonomous individual. To develop an ethics related to participation in the "whole", Senge speaks of mission, shared vision and commitment to the whole. This is a worldview that he finds in various Eastern thinkers and earlier cultures such as that of the Native Americans. It is not surprising that this is then developed as a working ethics of continuously seeking consensus and harmony in the expression of difference, elaborated in a theory of communication and social interaction.

Participation in the learning organization: communication

I want to return to Ron's question about listening in order to illustrate the theory of communication supporting Senge's view of systems thinking. As I mentioned above, a number of managers requested help from our department around this question at the time of the implementation of new organizational structures. Using Senge's leadership theory, it was possible to understand Ron's experience of the changes from a different perspective. In his discomfort with those reporting to him talking more frequently to his boss and with their complaining that he was not listening, Ron was experiencing the shift in power in the organization. He had definitely lost some sense of his own power and had no simple way, in the behaviourist sense, to begin acting less in one way and more in another. In this regard, Ron's experience was comparable to that of the senior executives of the corporation in the USA. As power shifted to the financial markets in the 1980s, these executives had also found themselves in a new situation, which they did not understand. The attraction of systems thinking, as put forward in Senge's five disciplines, is that it draws attention to precisely the kind of power shifts and changes in interaction that managers at all levels of the organization were experiencing, and offers a theory that provides some sense of recovering power – necessarily an ethical issue because it is about how people in organizations relate to one another. Managers could think of themselves as designers of the system, stewards of its functioning and teachers of the members of their teams. This implies a theory of communication and interaction which replaces that of the simple hierarchy and behaviourist interaction.

What makes Senge's thinking on communication readily accessible is that he begins with the individual, as does behaviourist thinking. This means that the taken-for-granted thinking of communication in terms of the sender-receiver model is, at an important level, not challenged because communication continues to be understood in terms of movement of signals from one individual to another individual. In this theory of communication, an individual's mind is thought of as a system of mental models, an inner world, inside that individual's head. Mental models constitute a key discipline of the learning organization and with them come the whole cognitivist theory of human psychology. These mental models are understood to have been structured in past experience into personal values and beliefs, as well as assumptions about, and expectations of, others and the world in which people are interacting together. It is on this basis that one individual chooses an action in relation to another individual. (For a detailed treatment of this, see Chapters 2 and 9 of Stacey, 2001.) This theory provides a powerful way of explaining Ron's experience of the actions of those around him. The important difference from a simple behaviourist explanation – that Ron was still acting as an analytical thinker and should change his behaviour with behaviour – is the perspective of a system of interrelated mental models and the importance of the factor "over time". These two factors represent the deeper insight to be gained from playing the "Beer Game". As the game is played "over time" the players develop mental models of what is going on. These form the basis of the actions they take. As the game continues, players who change their models based on an increasing understanding of the system as a whole will be those most likely to contribute to the survival of the system. Senge's metaphor for those who are unresponsive and do not change their mental models is that of the frog in water who does not notice the small increments in temperature until it is too late and the water begins to boil the frog.

In participating in the learning organization, therefore, people are communicating with each other by transmitting signals and interpreting them on the basis of mental models; when they are effective, their mental models change over time. (See Part I and the Appendix on autopoiesis in

Stacey, 2001.) Again, I argue that this theory represents a clear example of the taken-for-granted "both . . . and" way of thinking with its elimination of paradox. Those communicating are understood *both* to be individuals, and as such have mental systems for which they are responsible, *and* to be participants in a system for which they are also responsible. This is clearly an appeal to an ethical responsibility, in which individuals are sometimes thought of as autonomous and sometimes thought of as participants in a system, in a kind of figure-ground movement of thought. Senge sees this. In fact he must deal with it in order to maintain the "both . . . and" position and not to have to face the contradiction of having a group of autonomous individuals and a system at the same time. And he deals with it in his overriding thinking concerning the nature of the whole system and his ethics of commitment to that whole. Commitment to the whole provides a theory of social interaction that is the "glue" of the five disciplines of the learning organization.

Participation in the learning organization: social interaction

It is important to remind ourselves at this point about Kant's thinking about "wholes". According to Kant, the idea of systemically self-organizing wholes provides the scientist with a way of making testable hypotheses about nature. Systemic wholes are a way of thinking about nature. But according to Kant, systemic wholes cannot provide a way of thinking about human interaction. This is because doing so would define in a real sense what cannot be defined in any limiting manner, namely, the nature of the whole as the basis on which individual humans exercise their freedom in choosing their actions. This not-to-be-defined whole was for him a metaphysics of universal principles about the nature of human freedom. It is only in interacting that we implicitly reveal what we believe these principles to be. For this reason, Kant suggested that it would be better not to maintain that humans *are* free, but rather in all our actions to bear witness to our belief that humans *should* be free. This is an important element in the synthesis of thought by which Kant attempted to free his thinking from the dogmatism of the Middle Ages, with its clearly defined universal laws, but at the same time found an ethics on universal laws. He did this by suggesting that the ethical universals were to be discovered in action, not defined before action. In affirming the thinking which was at that time just beginning to understand humans as individuals, Kant maintained that one example of such a universal principle, to be discovered in action, was that the individual should never be considered simply as a means to an end, but rather always as an end in him/herself. The thinking in the monastic tradition of the Middle Ages was of course based on the concept of taking vows, for instance as a ritual expression of free consent. Conformity was viewed as a goal to be achieved through discipline.

Despite the move to a secular world, allowing for a plurality of beliefs or lack of belief as to any metaphysical foundation for ethical action, Kant's thinking on ethics has remained the basis for the mainstream worldview of natural scientists and of "business ethics", including all the social interaction comprising organizing and doing business. It is understandable that the taken-for-granted way in which scientists think of themselves as both private, ethically responsible individuals and as detached observers of systemic wholes makes it less likely for them to challenge the basis of Kant's thinking. However, there is perhaps a growing realization that the Kantian model is inadequate for understanding human participation in the processes of change in organizations. I think that the move that Senge is making in trying to think of ethical motivation in terms of social interaction reflects this growing dissatisfaction, and to this extent I agree with him. However, I question his particular theory of social interaction as participation in systemic wholes and I argue that in the "both . . . and" basis of his leadership theory, he does after all remain within the Kantian worldview. Insofar as Senge maintains a focus on the individual, he simply reaffirms the traditional Kantian basis. He seems to enter new territory in his theory of social interaction, namely, building shared visions, team learning and dialogue, all as participation in the whole. Thus the question becomes: has Senge moved beyond Kant's thinking to a new ethics in understanding the motivation of social interaction in organizations? As I have already said, I argue that he has not.

Senge is convinced that systems can contribute to the understanding of change, motivation and creativity in organizations and he recognizes the need to underpin this belief with a theory of social interaction. The five disciplines are as a leadership theory also necessarily a theory of social interaction. All the individuals in the organization are to work toward personal mastery and their own vision, but this alone could be explained in terms of the ethics of the autonomous individual. Because the discipline of systems thinking is in a real sense already presumed in the explication of the four other disciplines, Senge repeatedly refers to the importance not only of commitment to one's person, but also to the organization. Personal vision becomes shared vision and the learning of personal mastery becomes team learning. What is constantly emphasized is that individuals must also get beyond themselves to a higher motivation and commitment to the whole. This gets to the key difference between Kant's worldview and ours today. Kant's world was still influenced by thought that represented a unity of philosophy and theology. Remember that Christianity was a dominant belief system in the West, which made it feel quite natural to think of a common metaphysical basis for ethical interaction, a not-to-be-defined whole. In the organizations we work in today, however, we find a great diversity in the personal beliefs of individuals, based on their past and their experience, concerning these questions. Is it possible to appeal to something comparable to the universal principles Kant appealed to that would be *binding for all individuals in terms of an organization as a whole*?

Without doubt Senge believes that this is possible. If the individuals commit to the organization, they are committing to something that will enable them to be more than they could ever think of being as individuals. In teams they can become creative through dialogue. One would think that most leaders would be shocked in reading: "If any one idea about leadership has inspired organizations for thousands of years, it's the capacity to hold a shared vision of the future we seek to create." (Senge, 1990: 9) One might immediately think that this downgrades the importance of the leader. However, perhaps it does not shock because it can be read from either side, if you will, of the "both . . . and" way of thinking. One can understand it as meaning that the shared vision is that of the leaders, or one can understand it, from the other side, to mean that the leadership is in the all encompassing whole which also holds in a real sense the vision. This second side of the "both . . . and" is what Senge is developing in the disciplines of mental models and building a shared vision.

When individuals commit to this "genuine vision", that is, shared vision, they learn. "What has been lacking is a discipline for translating individual vision into shared vision – not a 'cookbook' but a set of principles and guiding practices. . . . In mastering this discipline, leaders learn the counter productiveness of trying to dictate a vision, no matter how heartfelt" (Senge, 1990: 9). Again, this can be read from either side of the "both . . . and" way of thinking. Do they want the vision to be the one they develop, communicated in a new way, or do they want to learn that it is counterproductive to work against the shared vision – that vision which is held in a real sense in a whole in which they are participating? If they get it wrong, it means that they are not genuinely committed, and that means that they are not participating, but rather letting selfish interests prevent them from sharing the vision.

This is in turn dealt with in the discipline of team learning and its central concept of dialogue, in which Senge develops the thinking of the physicist David Bohm (1965, 1983; Bohm and Peat, 1989). Today, more than a decade after the publication of Senge's work, this concept of dialogue has become, for many, the key to understanding and improving communication and social interaction in organizations. Senge and Bohm claim that dialogue is a form of communication that the Greeks (hence the use of the Greek word dialogue) and many primitive cultures understood but that we have lost. Senge (1990: 9) sees it as the "capacity of members of a team to suspend assumptions and enter into a genuine 'thinking together' . . . a free-flowing of meaning through a group, allowing the group to discover insight not attainable individually". Dialogue occurs when a group of people access a common pool of meaning that flows through them. Here again there is a notion of some whole, this time a transcendent whole of meaning, in which members of a group participate. Such participation is not possible for individuals on their own so it is teams, not individuals, which are the fundamental learning units in the organization. Increasingly it becomes clear that what Senge is referring to is an intelligence that is beyond the individual. Senge compares organizational learning to what has been referred to in other cultures as transcendence, shared and direct intuition, and knowing of the highest, of God. It is in participation in such transcendental wholes that an organization is capable of "generative learning". (For a critique of Bohm's concept of dialogue see also Chapter 9 of Stacey, 2001). In a sense we are back to Kant's notion of a metaphysical level, a not-to-be-defined whole, as the basis of ethical interaction. Only now, the whole is to be defined in terms of shared visions and values. Notice the very specific meaning of participation in Senge's thinking. It is participation in a transcendent whole, not simply interaction between people.

The question now is this: why does Senge end up with having to pose a transcendental whole as the basis of the learning organization and, therefore, as the basis of leadership and ethics? Or to put it differently, why does Senge need a metaphysical basis for his theory of leadership and ethics? The answer, I suggest, lies in the very nature of systems thinking.

Participation and second-order cybernetics

It is very important to understand clearly what participation means in referring to systemic self-organization. It is, therefore, helpful at this point to look at the thought of Gregory Bateson (1973; Bateson and Bateson, 1987), who provides the basis for the concepts of mental models and double-loop learning developed by Chris Argyris and Donald Schon (1978). Their work, in turn, is the foundation upon which Senge builds his theory. As mentioned in Chapter 1, second-order cybernetics seeks to resolve the problem of the reappearance of a paradox – the problem of being participant and observer at the same time – by introducing the observer into the system that is being observed. Bateson defines the nature of this participation. He differentiates new levels of learning as the boundary of the system is widened to include the observer, where the observer is also understood as a system standing outside a lower-order system and designing or identifying it. Second-order cybernetics is essentially about the recognition of systems which are determining lower-order systems and thereby resolving the apparent paradox into a "both . . . and" formulation. Bateson starts with the classic example of a cybernetic system, that of central heating. The resident of a room sets the desired temperature at the system's regulator located at the boundary between the system and its environment, which is the temperature in the room. The system then regulates itself through the feedback of information about the gap, or error, between desired and actual room temperatures. The system cannot change its own setting and so it cannot learn or evolve. It simply repeats its error-activated behaviour.

Bateson then introduces the resident into the system. Now the system consists of the resident and the central heating system. The environment is still, of course, the temperature in the room. However, the boundary of the system has now been extended to include the skin of the resident, who changes the temperature setting. When the skin of the resident registers an uncomfortably low temperature for a while, he turns the regulator setting up and the boiler is turned on. Later the resident may feel too warm and turn the setting down. In this way, the brain of the resident is seen to be a cybernetic device in much the same way as the heating system, and together they constitute the expanded system. The structure of this larger system has changed in an important way because now the number of states it can move through is much larger. The change in the total system is not due to responses to one specific error as it was before, but to a range of errors that do not fit the resident's requirements.

From the perspective of the logically lower system, the heating system, the addition of the resident amounts to the inclusion of the observer who can control it and this has implications for learning:

- The resident/heating system displays what Bateson calls Learning Level 1 in that the resident changes the lower level system by changing the setting, so increasing the number of alternatives open to the whole system. This learning is error-activated in that it is triggered by a gap between the resident's habitual comfort levels and his current experience. Later, Argyris and Schon (1978) used this idea to talk about single-loop learning, which occurs when people alter their behaviour without changing their mental models, that is, habits.
- If the resident were to change his habits of altering the setting, then the system would display Learning Level 2 because there is once more a widening of the range of alternatives open to the system. This level of learning is of a higher logical category in that it expands the range of Level 1 alternatives. Once again it is error-activated in that the resident will change his habits because the old ones do not meet some new or higher required standard. Argyris and Schon (1978) called this double-loop learning and it too features as a central concept in the learning organization as a change in mental models (Senge, 1990).
- The system could potentially display Learning Level 3, which expands the range of Level 2 alternatives. Bateson thought that humans very rarely achieved this level of learning and the examples he gave of it were religious conversion and personal change through psychotherapy.

Human beings are regarded, in this development of systems thinking, as living cybernetic systems that can understand and control lower-level cybernetic systems, which include themselves. Note what is happening here. First, there is a self-regulating system that works automatically to remove an error, a gap, where the action is triggered by the detection of the error. This applies to the central heating system but the notion of error-triggered action is then used to form a theory of human learning, which becomes a cybernetic, error detecting process.

This happens when the perspective is widened to take in the human observer, designer or controller of the system. It is the human who sets goals for the system. In other words, the human specifies what an error would be and he/she does this according to some mental framework in his/her mind, a mental model. The system now includes the person who makes a choice and he/she can detect an error, a gap, between what he/she experiences and what he/she wants as determined by his/her habits, or mental model. He/she can respond to this error and set a new goal for the system without in any way changing habits, mental model, or understanding of the world. In other words the mental model, which remains the same, is now part of the higher-order system and this higher-order system can learn. This learning is itself a cybernetic process in that experience of an error triggers a change in the goal set for the lower-order system. Mental models, then, are higher-order cybernetic devices that change the goals for the lower-order cybernetic system. This is Learning Level 1, or single-loop learning, made possible by including the objective observer's fixed mental model in a widened system. Note that the process of changing mental models remains outside the definition of the Learning Level 1 system.

However, the system can now be widened to include this observer's observing of him/herself performing the single-loop learning. He/she may find that as he/she changes the temperature setting according to habit, or mental model, this does not yield the satisfaction sought. This error could trigger a change in habits, that is, mental models. The process for changing the mental model is now part of an even higher-order system and the mental model can also change as a result of the choice of the human. When it does so Learning Level 2, or double-loop learning, is achieved. The system is now widened to include the process of changing mental models and this too is thought of as a cybernetic system. However, the process that triggers the process of changing the mental model, something to do with satisfaction and dissatisfaction, or preference, is still outside the definition of the Learning Level 2 system.

The system can now be widened even further to include this observer observing him/herself changing the preferences that trigger the choice to change the mental model. He/she becomes aware of him/herself learning in a double-loop way and this is presumably made possible by a mental model of the process of changing the mental model. This process of changing preferences is now included in an even wider system. However, once again, there is now the problem of defining the process by which he/she becomes aware of the need to change preferences. Bateson found he could not identify what this would be and fell back on mysticism or deep personal change that nobody finds easy to explain.

This kind of wider system is where Senge locates the learning organization, which is understood to be participation in the third level of a second-order cybernetic system. Just as Bateson pointed to, the move to incorporate the observer, the autonomous individual, into the system leads to an infinite regress which can only stop when some kind of transcendent whole, some kind of mystical conversion process is stipulated. I argue that it is an inevitable consequence of thinking in systems terms that one ends up having to postulate participation in some mystical, transcendent whole. Going back to the question at the end of the last section as to why Senge posits participation in a systemic whole of a transcendent or metaphysical kind, the answer is that it is because he employs systems thinking.

It is important to remember, at this point, that the five disciplines are a theory of leadership. Senge is broadening the traditional idea of leader to one that includes a theory of participation in systemic wholes. The *leaders* have the power to determine what is put into the system in terms of the goals, plans and strategies, but they also then participate in the *leadership* of the learning organization so that leaders and leadership become somewhat different ideas. The first, that of the leader, is located in the autonomous individual and the second, that of leadership, emerges in the systemic self-organization of the whole. In the move from the discipline of mental models and personal mastery to those of shared vision and team learning participation in this whole is defined. The teams and their shared vision are the systems of participation in what becomes a wider system. But of course such leadership is invested in certain people who determine the content of what becomes the "sets of principles and guiding practices" that are the wider system. As such only the leaders also stand outside the system and exercise human freedom in its full sense. In attempting to work out a leadership theory based on social interaction in systemic self-organization, Senge has put forward a theory that reduces ethical choice for those participating in the learning organization to a constant search for a freely chosen submission to a larger transcendent whole. Thus the creativity he speaks of is not in the system. Any genuine change or novelty would have to come from outside the system in the form of new goals, strategies or plans of the leaders for whom ethics is that of the Kantian autonomous individual. The chosen goals, strategies and plans would be played out in the system and result in changes in the sets of principles and guiding practices.

Issues concerning ethics

Senge maintains a "both . . . and" distinction between, on the one hand, the leader as an individual acting to form the purpose of the organization and, on the other hand, leadership as participation in the organization as a systemic whole. In doing this, he remains within the limitations of traditional business ethics based, on the one hand, on the autonomy of the individual and, on the other hand, on a metaphysical self-organizing whole, namely, the common pool of meaning of the whole organization that is the basis of dialogue. I will be returning to this distinction in Chapter 4, but here I want to emphasize the ethical issues of this kind of participation in a self-organizing system.

A distinction is made between those who foster the learning organization and those who do not. Team learning occurs when those on the team give up their individuality and focus on the larger perspective that lies beyond the individual. "At the heart of a learning organization is a shift of mind – from seeing ourselves as separate from the world to connected to the world . . ." (Senge, 1990: 9). I argue that what Senge is developing here is an ethics of harmony which speaks eloquently to the large number of people in today's society who have an enormous longing to belong and find identity in some kind of group. However, this harmony is achieved at the price of conformity – based on a clear "ethical imperative" that one must give up one's individuality in order to participate in a "a set of principles and practices". Bateson was reluctant to define what third-level learning might be, hinting only that it involved something mystical. What Senge has done is to define this third level as a whole, the content of which is the strategies, plans and goals that the leaders have the power to determine and others are to conform to. This power relation remains hidden behind a language about commitment and empowerment on the basis of participation in the system.

In the end Senge does not go beyond Kant, but rather repeats his "both . . . and" way of thinking, while ignoring Kant's achievement in moving out of the Middle Ages and into the age of Enlightenment. While Senge's work represents an attempt to move to an ethics of social interaction, he unwittingly falls into descriptions of that interaction that strongly echo the moral stance of the institutions of the Middle Ages, which demanded the discipline of obedience to sets of principles and practices that led to a recognition of identity. The Enlightenment affirmed the individual, which led to democracy and the concept of citizenship; today we have gone to the extreme of individualism whereby the single individual is regarded as an isolated cell, a matter that will be taken up in Chapters 4 and 5.

Summary of the argument so far

So far in this chapter, I have been exploring notions of leadership and ethics in organizations from the historical perspective of the development of Western thought. Starting with the Middle Ages, thinking was based on the notion that nature, of which humans were unquestionably a part, was revealing the laws of God's creation. Nature was thought to move according to universal, unchanging laws and humans came to know something of these laws through authoritative revelation. Humans were a part of nature but they differ from other creatures in having souls, making them free to choose whether or not to act according to the universal ethical principles (laws) that were revealed as dogmas. Humans were rewarded when they acted according to these principles and punished when they did not.

The scientific method represented a major departure from this way of thinking in that the universal, timeless laws governing nature were thought to be discovered by the scientist who objectively observes nature, formulates hypotheses about the laws and then tests them, so progressively moving toward a fuller and more accurate understanding of the laws. These laws were understood to take the form of linear "if–then" causal links, and for the first time humans began to experience themselves as having reason and judgement which they could act on as individuals. In other words, the empirical approach began to question the dogmatic one. However, these developments in thought led to the view that nature had laws of its own, no longer necessarily a reflection of God's order, and it looked like humans were also subject to these laws, creating a problem for the notion of human freedom. In addition to this, another key question arose. How it is that reasoning individuals are able to formulate hypotheses? In other words, the question is how humans are able to categorize phenomena in nature and identify relationships between them.

In the tradition of Plato, Kant argued that humans are able to categorize phenomena and identify relationships between them because they possess an innate capacity to categorize and relate. This is expressed in his notion of the categories as innate ideas of time, space and cause–effect. He added to this his notion that we also have the innate capacity to formulate regulative ideas. By this he meant that we can observe nature and formulate hypotheses about the purposive movement of nature where those hypotheses take the form of "as if" intention. We are able to understand nature "as if" it were moving toward some end and he suggested that this end would be a mature state of itself. However, this purpose is not in nature itself but, rather, it is we, as objectively observing scientists, who can understand nature "as if" it were moving towards the end that we have postulated. Kant incorporated this notion of "regulative ideas" into a systemic approach in which organisms in nature are understood as wholes consisting of parts and in the interaction of the parts, both those parts and the whole emerge. So, we can understand nature in terms of hypotheses we formulate in which organisms are thought of as systemically self organizing wholes to which we ascribe a purposive movement toward end states which are mature forms of themselves, all as a way of more deeply understanding nature. The hypotheses we formulate could well be wrong and then we would have to formulate others, so gradually improving our knowledge.

Turning to humans, Kant argued that although they are part of nature, they are different and cannot be understood as parts of a whole, or system. They cannot be understood in this way because then they would be subject to the whole and as such not free. Instead, he argued that we have to think of ourselves as autonomous individuals. This means that each individual, having a soul, is free to choose how to act. In arguing in this way, he was picking up on the rationalist view of reasoning human individuals, for example, the work of Locke, that was emerging at that time. He was bringing a teleological perspective to human action and arguing that individuals could set their own goals and strategies using their powers of reason. The question then became how an autonomous individual could know which acts to choose so that autonomous individuals could live together. In other words, the question was how autonomous individuals could know what ethical choices were. For mediaeval thinkers the answer was to follow the revealed dogma. In Kant's time dogmatic rationalists presented a new alternative to revealed dogma, arguing that the dogma, the ethical principles, could also be identified by human reason on its own. Kant wanted to bring this rationalist perspective into tension with the arguments of the empiricists, that is, those employing the scientific method. To do this, he argued that the notion of the "regulative idea" could be applied to human conduct just as it could to nature.

In the case of human conduct, the regulative idea was Kant's categorical imperative, that is, his notion of ethics. This meant that in matters of ethics, just as in relation to nature, autonomous individuals as scientists could objectively observe their own conduct. Ethical actions could be understood "as if" they were actions that could be performed by everyone because then the principle behind the action would reflect a universal law. This is the categorical imperative. So an individual could formulate hypotheses about an ethical action, testing them against the regulative idea or categorical imperative "as if they could be performed by everyone". As people proceed in this way, different formulations of the categorical imperative emerge, for example, "treat others as you want them to treat you" and "do not treat other people as means to an end since all people are ends in themselves". These imperatives have the character of universals but they do not dictate what to do in any specific situation. In specific situations people have to choose what to do, testing their actions against the categorical imperatives and using them to justify what they have done. In this way, just as we can progressively build up a body of knowledge about the timeless universal natural laws governing nature, so we can progressively build up a body of knowledge on timeless, ethical imperatives for human conduct. Ethics is firmly based on the reasoning capacity of the autonomous individual who can discover the universal principles of good conduct through what amounts to the scientific method.

Precisely because individuals are autonomous, are ends in themselves, are free to choose their actions, Kant held that they could not be thought of as parts of a whole, as a system, as other organisms in nature are. However, in a metaphysical way he did hold that the ethical imperatives reflected a not-to-be-defined whole to do with God. Kant, then, presented a notion of ethics as a body of universal imperatives that already exist, just as natural laws do, to be discovered by autonomous individuals, just as natural laws are, and expressed in a body of timeless ethical imperatives, just as natural laws are timeless and universal. It is this notion of ethics that forms the basis of traditional business ethics today – a notion of universal codes of conduct discovered or formulated by autonomous rational individuals as the basis upon which they are to judge their own and each others' conduct. In this way of thinking, the leader is an autonomous individual, as is everyone else, charged with developing ethical behaviour.

I have also been arguing that it is very important to note what Kant accomplished in his thinking. He developed a "both . . . and" way of thinking that resolves paradox in that there is both natural law and autonomous individuals without any sense of this presenting a paradox. Essentially the same way of thinking applies to both nature and human action in that both are to be rationally understood through the scientific method of testing hypotheses as regulative ideas. These regulative ideas are applied to systemic wholes, in the case of nature, and they are to be understood as ethical imperatives reflecting a metaphysics of a not-to-be-defined whole in the case of human action.

The next step of my argument has been to show how present day systems thinking proceeds within a Kantian framework, with one important exception. Systems thinkers today do apply the notion of systemic wholes and systemic self-organization to human interaction. Or to put it another way, they hold that some autonomous individuals can define Kant's metaphysical not-to-be-defined whole, which is then to be applied to other humans. They do this in the form of defining visions and values for human interaction. Here the "both . . . and" way of thinking is quite clear. On the one hand, there are autonomous individuals, the leaders, who define vision and values and Kantian ethics applies to them. On the other hand, there is the system of humans, including the leaders once the whole has been defined, to whom the visions and values are to be applied. This leads to an ethics that is quite contrary to Kant, in that now autonomous individuals are required to participate in, submit themselves to, some larger whole or greater good. No longer are the autonomous individuals trying to discover in their actions what the ethical imperatives reflecting the not-to-be-defined whole are. Instead they are required to submit themselves to the visions and values revealed to them by their leaders. In doing so they lose their autonomy and we are back to medieval thinking in terms of revelation. The move to participation, understood as submission to a harmonious whole, means that humans are either not autonomous individuals, that is, they are not free, or that they are autonomous and free to choose but the ethical choice is that of submission to a larger harmonious whole in which they lose their autonomy. Again we have "both . . . and" thinking in that the individual is sequentially free and then not free. For Kant, individuals were always free because they were always choosing their actions, as individuals, and discovering their ethical nature. Kant did think within the overriding teleology of God's creation and so did think of individuals participating in God's creation, but as free autonomous individuals choosing and testing their actions. This is very different to the systemic wholes of systems thinking variously described as shared values, common purpose, common pool of meaning, transpersonal processes, group mind, collective intelligence, simple rules, and so on. These terms all reflect the notion of some transcendental whole, a move to metaphysics as the basis of ethics, but this time a metaphysics of revelation rather than discovery in action.

Senge's framework, then, provides a way of thinking that understands organizational life as *both* participation in a self organizing whole (systems thinking, shared visions and teams), ultimately of a transcendental nature harking back to the wisdom of the ancients, *and* the autonomous individual (personal mastery, mental models and visions). This thinking results in a split, as a kind of figure-ground resolution of paradox, with regard to:

- *Ethics*. There is *both* the Kantian ethics of the autonomous individual applied to the actions of leaders in designing the system *and* identifying the vision and the ethics of the harmonious whole to which individuals must conform.
- *Leadership*. There is *both* the leader as autonomous individual *and* leadership emerging in the systemic self-organization of the whole as shared values and common purpose.

Notice also how participation is defined in a very specific way. It means individuals participating in a whole that is larger than the individuals participating.

The problem with the learning organization as a theory of leadership and ethics

The framework I have been exploring in this chapter creates a number of problems. First, there is the problem to do with freedom. The freedom to choose actions and explore their ethical implications is located primarily in the leader, when in the role of system designer, while the other members of an organization are required to conform to the emerging leadership of the whole, as indeed must the leader in the role of steward and teacher. This is not understood in any way as paradoxical. Any inherent contradiction is simply not noticed. Second, and closely linked to the first, there is the problem to do with novelty. There is no explanation of how the leader comes to design the system or form the vision imposed on the system. This is taken as given in some unexplained way. Furthermore, this means that the systemic whole is simply unfolding the given vision as regulations and practices. In this process of systemic self-organization there can be no novelty because the system is unfolding what is already enfolded in it.

This immediately points to the third problem, namely, to do with the complete removal of diversity and hence, conflict. In Chapter 5, I will be taking up the matter of diversity and presenting reasons for claiming that the emergence of novelty necessarily requires interaction among diverse persons. Diverse persons, by definition, are not submitting to the whole and so losing their individuality. Furthermore, diverse persons are bound to conflict so that conflict is an essential characteristic of evolving novelty in human interaction. The theory of the learning organization completely ignores conflict and its role. The learning organization presents a utopian view of human beings harmoniously consenting to the greater good of the larger whole. This is a theory of what ought to be, but certainly not of what actually is. For thousands of years humans have called for harmonious conflict-free living together. This has never happened and there is no sign that it is about to. Focusing on what ought to be rather than what actually happens can be seen as a defence against having to face and try to understand the destructive processes that we all engage in on an ordinary everyday basis. The theory covers up the greed, envy, jealousy, hate and aggression that are as much a part of human life as caring, loving and giving. Finally, and closely linked to the covering up of conflict and destructive human action, is the complete covering over of power and ideology in human relationships. Although systems thinking and the theory of the learning organization certainly provides us with more assistance than the behaviourist models they superseded, their usefulness is highly limited by the way in which they ignore matters that are so pervasively a part of everyday life in organizations.

I want to return now to the discussion in Chapter 1 about the film of a factory polluting the ground water causing surrounding residents to develop cancer. I pointed there to the curious way in which local residents experienced themselves as victims of a system without recognizing that they were also employees of the factory and so contributing in some way to what had happened to them. I think they were experiencing themselves in just the kind of split way I have been showing that systems thinking about organization leads to. The split is, therefore, not simply a matter of philosophical interest but one of tremendous practical importance. The way we are currently thinking may actually be contributing to our seeming inability to halt the way we are destroying our environment. This is a powerful motive to look for alternative ways of thinking.

The problems I have been outlining seem to me to call for very different ways of thinking and it is for these reasons that I have been attracted to insights emerging from the new sciences of complexity. The potential they might provide is pointed to in the second question I mentioned at the beginning of this chapter.

Alberto's question: the emergence of leaders

The last two decades have witnessed a growing awareness of the work of scientists doing research based on the mathematics of chaos theory and fractal geometry (Stewart, 1989) and what were coming to be called complex systems (for example, Gell-Mann, 1995; Kauffman, 1995). Books such as *Chaos* by James Gleick (1988) and *Complexity* by Mitchell Waldrop (1992), along with articles in journals and newspapers, reached a wide readership and helped to spread knowledge about the work being done at the Santa Fe Institute in the United States and at institutes in Brussels and Austin, Texas headed by Ilya Prigogine (Prigogine and Stengers, 1984). These books and articles not only spread awareness of the research but generated a great deal of enthusiasm. Some of the key concepts became buzzwords, for example, non-linearity, self-organization and emergence, unpredictability, sensitivity to initial conditions and attractors, among many others. The work of many of these scientists clearly focused on what I have been referring to as systemic self-organization. Kauffman (1995), for instance, refers to "those wonderful Kantian wholes". But there was also a general sense that the thinking was going beyond science "as usual" and entering a new frontier. There was an emphasis on self-organization and emergence, which for some developed further the work of second-order cybernetics and for others pointed toward a new science.

A number of management theorists saw the complexity sciences as a new basis for understanding the stability and change experienced in organizations (for example, Stacey, 1991; Wheatley, 1992). They pointed to the scientific thought applied in previous management thinking and argued that the insights coming from research in the complexity sciences completely undermined traditional scientific thinking. The management theories they referred to were almost exclusively derived from the mechanistic thinking of scientific management, which was the basis of the first attempts to provide management theory with a hard foundation in the natural sciences. The main argument was that there was a new mathematics and science of which managers must become aware if they wanted to maintain competitive advantage. This of course generated immediate interest on the part of many of those responsible for leadership development in large corporations.

One such was Alberto who was head of leadership development department in an organization providing development assistance to countries around the globe. Alberto had kept abreast of the growing corpus of complexity-oriented books on management theory, coming to this with a good knowledge of systems thinking and associated theories, such as the learning organization. It was in a discussion with him during the formative period of this book, that Alberto posed a question which I thought represented a significant shift. He said that when those in his organization went into countries seeking development assistance, they had, of course, to work with the leaders. They were in the position of having to ask who the leaders were and then work with those that were identified. This often proved to be a problem, since the key issue on many projects turned out to be about breaking through the protected interests of those in power – but they were the ones who had been identified as the leaders. In going into other situations the problem was often the lack of any identifiable leaders for the projects they wanted to initiate. Alberto was familiar with the emphasis on self-organization and emergence in the management literature on complexity theory; he asked, how then, if one is coming from complexity theory, would one think about the emergence of leaders and what influences would be important in such a process. There is an important element in this question that makes it improbable that it would have been asked many years earlier.

Scientific management, the first attempt to base management theory on science, located the skills necessary for management in the individual and thought about change in terms of behaviourism; hence terminology such as "young high potential". The potential of the organization was thought to be located in the individuals as individuals. As a consequence, organizations canvassed schools and colleges, headhunting those who seemed to "have" what was needed. The concern here is with potential leaders as individuals with the required competences. Systems thinking represented the next major attempt to base management theory on science. In this chapter, I have been drawing attention to how systems thinking about organizations is based on "both . . . and" ways of thinking. On the one hand, the individual possesses skills and strives for personal mastery as leader and, on the other, there is a basis for emergence but it is the emergence of *leadership* in the system. Individuality must be given up to participate as a team in the learning of the learning organization. There is nothing to prevent both retaining the notion of the potential of the organization being in the individual *leader* and the notion that *leadership* emerges in social interaction. But the two are never brought together. Alberto's question could be understood as asking whether organizational theory based on the complexity sciences has something new to say about this. Can we ask not simply how leadership emerges but how a leader emerges in social interaction? How would this be self-organizing? How would it take place and what could be done to recognize or even to influence it?

In Chapters 5 and 6, I will be developing a way of answering these questions. The perspective I will be taking is one that colleagues and I, at the Complexity and Management Centre, have been developing over the past few years. We call this the theory of complex responsive processes of relating (for a detailed account, see Stacey, 2001). The implications of this perspective for ethics and leadership are briefly set out in the following paragraphs and then developed in detail in Chapter 5. The purpose of providing this brief outline here is to enable the reader to make an initial comparison of the theory of the learning organization discussed in this chapter and the complexity-based perspective of organizations as living systems to be discussed in the next chapter, with the theory I will be developing in Chapter 5.

The theory of complex responsive processes holds that in their communicative interaction with each other, persons form and are formed by groups (organizations and societies), *at the same time*, as continuity and potential transformation. The experience of being together patterns, and is patterned by, communicative themes of a narrative-like nature, largely in conversational interaction. From this perspective, ethical conduct requires individuals to participate in continuous interaction with each other, in which they create the meaning of their interaction. All conduct is on-going processes of communicative interaction in which individuals perpetually negotiate with each other what *"ethical"* means in the living present of their local interaction. Individuals are then not autonomous. Persons are not *simply* free because they continuously constrain and enable each other's actions. Freedom is to be understood as the jointly created enabling constraints that emerge in the interaction between persons and the spontaneous novelty emerging in the person, which has the potential of transforming the identity of the group. It is paradoxical in that interaction simultaneously enables and constrains. And it is paradoxical in that the actions of a person are simultaneously both selected in terms of that person's history and called forth by the actions of others. From the point of view of ethics, good actions are emerging with bad ones, at the same time, and the distinction is being perpetually negotiated between persons. These judgments/distinctions between good and bad are themes patterning and being patterned by the interaction and many of these themes become habits. In other words, they are perpetually reproduced with little variation but there is always the potential for transformation.

This perspective, partly drawn from analogies with the complexity sciences, presents a very different kind of participation to that of the learning organization. It is not participation in a whole but the participation of persons as communicative interaction with each other. The ethics are not given in any kind of whole or autonomously discovered by an individual, but continually negotiated in the interaction between persons, around the habits of ethical precepts formed by others interacting before them. This raises question about how we should think about leaders and leadership, to which I will turn in Chapter 5. Before, that, however, in Chapter 3, I will explore how some of the most popular writers on complexity and organizations deal with the question of leaders and leadership, and the ethical implications of their treatment, asking whether they have any new answers to questions about leadership and ethics. In doing this I will be laying the ground to identify the differences between the complex responsive process perspective and others also based on the complexity sciences.

3 Complexity: are organizations really living systems?

- *Leadership and the New Science*
- *The theory of complex adaptive systems*
- *The Soul at Work*
- *Surfing the Edge of Chaos*
- *The problem with "living systems" as a theory of leadership and ethics*

In this chapter, I review the work of some of the writers who argue that chaos and complexity theories provide a way of understanding organizations as living systems. Those adopting this approach claim that a combination of systems thinking with the complexity sciences yields a theory of living systems that makes a significant difference in understanding emergence in organizations. I will be reviewing three examples of this approach, namely, Margaret Wheatley, Roger Lewin and Birute Regine, and Richard Pascale. All of these writers develop ideas around the points examined in the theory of the learning organization in the last chapter to do with:

- leadership;
- participation;
- issues concerning ethics.

Examining their work under the above headings will facilitate comparison with Senge's theory of the learning organization. Senge's theory was developed within the framework of second-order cybernetics and it essentially avoided paradox. The three writers examined in this chapter, however, refer to the reappearance of paradox in complexity theory. They all see paradox playing a role in social interaction in organizations but they have different views on its definition and implications.

Leadership and the New Science

As the title of her book indicates, Margaret Wheatley views leadership as the key implication of chaos and complexity theories for organizations. Her view of this is very close to that of Peter Senge. It is by recognizing and working with, not against, the processes in systems that leaders can achieve a more human and a more creative organization. She stresses the need for leaders to understand the simplicity of living systems in nature, so coming to the full realization that there is a much simpler way to organize, namely, nature's way. For her, just as for Senge, leadership is participation in a higher-level system. She also attaches much the same importance to the notion of vision, which is not to be understood as the traditional "evocative message about some desired future state delivered by a charismatic leader" but, rather, as a field, "unseen but real forces that influence people's behavior" (Wheatley, 1999: 15). But for Wheatley, recognizing that organizations are whole systems is only a beginning. The first step is

> construing them as "learning organizations" or as "organic" and noticing that people exhibit a self-organizing capacity. . . . My own experience suggests that we can forego the despair created by such common organizational events as change, chaos, information overload, and entrenched behaviours if we recognize that organizations are living systems, possessing the same capacity to adapt and grow that is common to all life.
>
> (ibid.)

Wheatley is suggesting here that the new sciences imply that organizations are not just systems but living systems. They are quite literally alive and need to be thought about as one thinks about organisms in nature from the perspective of the new sciences.

It is important to note the significance she attaches to understanding that organizations are living systems. For her, the essence of living systems, which she understands from complexity theory, are the simple rules of nature according to which living organisms function. She believes that this has direct implications for the leaders of organizations, namely, to lead in a simpler way, and that the new knowledge enabling them to do this is to be found in the rediscovery of ancient wisdom by complexity science. Content with understanding organizations as living systems, she does not develop as broad a theory of communication and learning as Senge does. Furthermore, while Senge draws on systems dynamics to understand organizations in terms of the tension between positive and negative feedback mechanisms, Wheatley calls on a number of different sources. She takes account of open systems theory (von Bertalanffy, 1968) and bases her "new science" on Fritjof Capra's *Turning Point* (1983) and Ernst Jantsch's *The Self-organizing Universe* (1980). Both of the last-named view the world as a web of living systems. She also incorporates the theory of autopoiesis (Maturana and Varela, 1987), which posits that the distinctive characteristic of all life is self-creating systems. She links all of these sources to the Gaia theory proposed by James Lovelock (1988), the grandest scale system of all, which understands the earth as a whole to be "a self-regulating system, a planetary community of interdependent systems that together create the conditions which make life possible" (Wheatley, 1999: 12). While Wheatley states that these sciences may only provide metaphors for human behaviour, it is clear that she has a sense of a general theory applying to all of nature including human social interaction. The self in "self-reference" applies, for her, to both natural systems and the self of human psychology.

Another important source of Wheatley's thinking is to be found in Ilya Prigogine's theory of systems that move from disorder to order in far from equilibrium conditions. However, she has a rather different understanding of Prigogine's work to mine. In Chapter 1, I introduced his work as an example of the reappearance of paradox in current thinking, in contrast to Kant's elimination of paradox. Kant's theory of systemic self-organization involves the scientist putting a determined end state into the system. This makes it look as if the system has a mind of its own, so eliminating paradox by having a mind for a system and a mind for a scientist without explaining how this is possible. The example I gave of this was the doctor's account of the healing of scar tissue, in which it sounded as if the scar tissue and the body were intentionally recognizing and making decisions: "The body will recognize that it has built up too much scar tissue and will begin to dissolve it." It is exactly this kind of description that Wheatley brings into her discussion of Prigogine's theory of self-organization.

> But Prigogine's work offered a new and more promising future. He demonstrated that any open system has the capacity to respond to change and disorder by reorganizing itself at a higher level of organization. Disorder becomes a critical player, an ally that can provoke a system to self-organize into new forms of being. As we leave behind the machine model of life and look more deeply into the

dynamics of living systems, we begin to glimpse an entirely new way of understanding fluctuations, disorder, and change. . . . A system can descend into chaos and unpredictability, yet within that state of chaos the system is held within boundaries that are well-ordered and predictable. . . . This revelation has been known throughout time to most human cultures; we just needed the science to help us remember it.

(Wheatley, 1999: 12–13)

The forms change, but the mission remains clear. Structures emerge, but only as temporary solutions that facilitate rather than interfere. There is none of the rigid reliance that I have learned in organizations on single forms, on true answers, on past practices. Streams have more than one response to rocks; otherwise there'd be no Grand Canyon. Or Grand Canyons everywhere. The Colorado river realized there were many ways to find ocean other than by staying broad and expansive.

(ibid.: 18)

In the end, then, Wheatley comes to a "both . . . and" position, much as Senge did, with a system having purpose and an autonomous individual also having purpose. For her, it is once again an overriding system that assures the emergence of order. She often refers to this in mythological terms, for example, as the order of Gaia emerging from Chaos. Prigogine's understanding of paradox, in which we are perpetually constructing an unknown future, disappears completely. Although Wheatley often speaks of paradox, it is obvious that she understands it as the "both . . . and" position which resolves paradox. She does not sense Prigogine's meaning of order and disorder "at the same time". For her the system "responds" to change by "reorganizing itself" at a "higher level of organization" and the river "realizes" a way to find the ocean. The two levels are the basis of the "both . . . and" so that there is no real sense of the unknown. She understands participation in organizations in the same way as Senge: both the level of the individual and the level of the organization, with an ethics of the individual and an ethic of the whole.

Participation in organizations

Wheatley says that we must look for the "*invisible processes rather than the things that they engender*" (Wheatley, 1999: 153, her italics). She maintains that when scientists look behind phenomena, they see the processes that give rise to the forms. For her, participation means to learn to live in this process world. "It is an entirely new way to be. Life demands that I participate with things as they unfold, to expect to be surprised, to honor the mystery of it, and to see what emerges" (ibid.: 153–4). It is clear that for her these processes are a higher level of system and the individual must learn to allow themselves to be formed by them. This is very similar to Bateson's description of third-level learning and Senge's learning organization. Bateson said that third-level learning had to be some mystical process about which he could say nothing, and both Senge and Wheatley affirm the mysterious nature of this level of system. For both of them, being a part of such a system is what participation is about. Although Wheatley, like many others basing their thinking in chaos and complexity theories, emphasizes the relational nature of participation, like Senge she speaks of finding the self in participation in higher wholes. Not to participate, she says, leaves one isolated as an individual.

> All living beings create themselves and use that "self" to filter new information and co-create their worlds. We refer to this self to determine what's important for us to notice. Through the self, we bring form and meaning to the infinite cacophony of data that always surrounds us. Yet it is very important to note that in all life, the self is not a selfish individual. "Self" includes awareness of those others it must relate to as part of its system.
>
> (Wheatley, 1999: 167)

There is then a relationship between individual activity and the whole. In participation the self-reference is the "source of growth" and describes "systems of relationships where both interdependence and individual autonomy are necessary conditions" (ibid.: 168). The precondition for "embracing" this participation is gaining the insight that we "live in an orderly universe" (ibid.) The relationships of those who participate in this sense are then seen to be "healthy", so that Wheatley's descriptions of communication is similar to dialogue, as described by Senge and Bohm, with an emphasis on harmony and consensus.

Issues concerning ethics

Using the term "healthy" immediately implies its opposite, namely, "unhealthy". Implicitly, individuals then have to consider whether they are contributing to healthy or unhealthy relationships. Individuals are engaged in healthy relationships, on Wheatley's criterion, only when they are in relationship to, participating in the "processes", that is, the higher-level system of the organizational whole and the even higher-level system of the orderly self-organizing universe. For the individual self to participate, that individual self must have a genuine identity as opposed to being a selfish individual and that genuine identity is derived from participation in not just one but in two higher wholes. Consider what this equation of identity and ethical action means. On the one hand, there is an individual who is free to choose between healthy and unhealthy relating so that ethics is an individual matter and, on the other hand, there are two higher wholes in which this individual must participate in order to have a genuine identity rather than a selfish self, that is, in order to act ethically. This is the same as Senge's "both ... and" thinking, only this time there are two, rather than just one, higher wholes. The first whole is the same as Senge's whole, namely, the organization and implicitly, therefore, its current management and power structure. The participation that yields genuine identity is thus conformity to the current power structure of the organization. However, the constraints and questions of power relations in human interaction cannot be bounded as a system. To do so would always mean to freeze the current ideology and power structure as a system. The ethical imperative around healthy relations and not being a selfish individual in Wheatley's thinking can only serve such interests, similar to the sets of principles and guiding practices Senge mentioned. The second whole is the orderly self-organizing universe; participation in this, to acquire a genuine identity, means harmony with, connection and submission to, nature and its simpler way. Ethical action is equated with conforming and submission to harmonious wholes. To reiterate, this is "both ... and" thinking that eliminates paradox. Certainly, leaders of organizations would not find conformity to the organizational whole at all paradoxical because organizations are systems unfolding the visions, strategies, plans and goals that they have determined.

However, Wheatley claims that her perspective is one that does deal with paradoxes, which she sometimes refers to as puzzles. She refers to spirit, meaning, purpose and consciousness as paradoxes. Although, of course, the social sciences have dealt with these topics, she claims that they have not seen them as paradoxes, maintaining that the traditional social sciences refuse to have anything to do with paradoxes. To deal with paradoxes from the standpoint of the new sciences means, for her, dealing with them more playfully. She quotes the Nobel Prize laureate

Sir Peter Medawar (in Judson, 1987: 3) who said that scientists build "explanatory structures, telling stories which are scrupulously tested to see if they are stories about real life" (Wheatley, 1999: 161). Wheatley expresses her enthusiasm for the idea of telling stories, speaking of wonderful experiences of weaving tales around campfires and playing with imagination. She suggests that we must look at ourselves "truthfully in the light of this fire and stop being so serious about getting things 'right' – as if there were still an objective reality out there . . ." (ibid.: 161).

Wheatley does not see the importance of the "as if" which she herself uses in this statement. Medawar is simply stating that the method of scientific inquiry, as suggested by Kant, is one of forming hypotheses about nature *as if* the hypotheses, for as long as they prove to work as a systemic whole, were reality. When further tests prove the opposite, another hypothesis is formulated and tested. This was referred to above in the story of the healing of scar tissue. Wheatley is suggesting that a more playful way of telling stories would recover the important paradoxes of spirit, identity and so on. This is especially curious since she has explicitly affirmed the "both . . . and" position eliminating paradox in stating that relationships are about both the autonomous individual and interdependence as participation in the wholes, as described above.

However, the meaning Wheatley ascribes to paradox is not the paradox Kant eliminated in developing the "both . . . and" way of thinking. He eliminated the paradox of humans being part of nature and yet free by postulating a way of understanding nature as system and human action in terms of the autonomous individual. Wheatley is postulating nature as a system and human action in terms of both the autonomous individual who forms visions and a system of human interaction in which the individual participates. We then have a "both . . . and" applied to human action in which there is the individual and two systems. However, what is quite forgotten is the hypothetical and regulative "as if" nature of what the scientist is doing. Nature as system and the organization as system are treated as having intention and purpose to which the individual must submit in order to act ethically. Chaos and complexity theories applied to human social interaction as systems in this way lose the meaning of paradox. With regard to the organizational whole in Wheatley's thinking, there is the same problem found in second-order cybernetics, namely, that the system is determined by something outside of it which has to become a system. This could go on infinitely so it has to be made mysterious and Wheatley does this by posing an even higher-level system, nature itself, even Gaia herself.

To posit two wholes as "both . . . and" is not to eliminate paradox, as Kant did, but to avoid and deny it completely. The paradox disappears. This is not the case for Kant whose regulative idea "as if" does not posit a whole, neither nature as a given reality nor the universal laws guiding human ethical choice. The hypothetical nature of the regulative idea means that we discover in an on-going way that which can never be determined as a given real whole. This provides the legitimacy for science and ethics but it is lost when such wholes are posited and the ethical imperative described in Kantian ethics is used to refer to participation in the whole. Wheatley is right in maintaining that story telling is an age-old way of playing with genuine paradox, but when the context within which the stories are being told has been defined in such a way as to deny paradox, the stories can only be tales of the legitimacy of the current constraints and power structures and the need to pull together to achieve their ends. Wheatley's concept of freedom is derived from the need for information to be free, "freely generated, freely communicated, and freely interpreted . . . our only hope for self-organized order in a world that no longer waits for us to respond" (Wheatley, 1999: 166). This necessity for freedom is another prevailing message in much of the new science. And what emerges from this freedom is "a globally stable system" (ibid.: 167). This is no basis for stories of a paradoxical nature that play with existential questions about our lives.

Returning to Alberto's question

Is there then something significant being said about leadership and leaders in chaos and complexity theories as Wheatley presents them? Despite the apparent differences in the science they refer to, Senge and Wheatley seem to have very similar ideas about leadership. There is more focus on self-organization in complexity theory, but Wheatley deals with it at a macro level with an appeal, even an ethical imperative, to participate at this level. One can only deduce that the people who should become leaders are those who participate better. In reply to Alberto's question as to what complexity sciences would have to say about who emerge as leaders, Wheatley would seem to say "those who participate better". What then would be the criteria for better participation? This could only be more harmony with the processes underlying the current status quo in both the organization and in nature. This is not much different from Senge, apart from the additional requirement of participating in nature, and it could hardly be a recipe for the changes necessary at all levels of leadership to ensure the on-going change required for the survival of the organization. It is implied that the leaders are dealing with this on the basis of their autonomy while all of the organization, including the leaders themselves when they participate, is participating in the processes of a higher level of organization.

I would like now to turn to other authors who have attempted to apply complexity theory to organizations using another source, namely, the theory of complex adaptive systems developed at the Santa Fe Institute in New Mexico. The Santa Fe institute is often spoken of as if it were a group of scholars working on a common project with a great deal of consensus around central issues on complexity. But as a matter of fact there is a deep divide among those at the Institute concerning core issues. I will not take this up here because it is dealt with in Stacey, Griffin and Shaw (2000). Instead I will give a short account of the views of three members of the Institute, relied on by the management writers I will review in later sections.

The theory of complex adaptive systems

Stuart Kauffman (1995) focuses on the process of self-organization. He sees a complex system as one consisting of autonomous individual agents who predict as they interact. However, the order that emerges from agent interaction is a *potential* before it emerges as an actual pattern – it is not something hidden, waiting to be disclosed but something that is co-created by the agents. The individual agents are predicting and then acting, but the overall pattern their interaction produces is emergent in an unpredictable sense. In his view, however, there is still an inevitability about what the system produces – he talks about life as a phenomenon to be expected, not just a chance cobbling together through selection. However, the expectation is not an already existing reality, rather it is a potential unfolded by experience – a movement into the space of the adjacent possible.

> The problem, I believe, is that Hoyle, Wickramasinghe, and many others have failed to appreciate the power of self-organization. It is not necessary that a specific set of 2,000 enzymes be assembled, one by one, to carry out a specific set of reactions . . . there are compelling

reasons to believe that whenever a collection of chemicals contains enough different kinds of molecules, a metabolism will crystallize from the broth. If this argument is correct, metabolic networks need not be built one component at a time; they can spring full-grown from a primordial soup. Order for free, I call it. If I am right, the motto of life is not We the improbable, but We the expected.

(Kauffman, 1995: 45)

He is searching for "the laws of complexity" and identifies self-organization as a second principle of order. He is arguing here against Gell-Mann's conviction that complexity arises from the simple and that the beginning of life can only be explained by chance. But curiously Kauffman remains within the Kantian perspective on modern science. He achieves this by taking a "both . . . and" position on the two principles of order:

The network within each cell of any contemporary organism is the result of at least 1 billion years of evolution. Most biologists, heritors of the Darwinian tradition, suppose that the order of ontogeny is due to the grinding away of a molecular Rube Goldberg machine, slapped together piece by piece by evolution. I present a countering thesis: most of the beautiful order seen in ontogeny is spontaneous, a natural expression of the stunning self-organization that abounds in very complex regulatory networks. We appear to have been profoundly wrong. Order, vast and generative, arises naturally . . . the sources of order in the biosphere . . . now include *both* selection *and* self-organization.

(ibid.: 29)

He avoids speaking of a paradox of these two principles being in a simultaneous relationship by seeing natural selection no longer as the author of evolution, but as the "editor". They are seen as two separate acts of causality. Kauffman understands his work within the Kantian paradigm of science.

Immanuel Kant, writing more than two hundred years ago, saw organisms as wholes. The whole existed by means of the parts; the parts existed both because of and in order to sustain the whole. This holism has been stripped of a natural role in biology, replaced with the image of the genome as the central directing agency that commands the molecular dance. Yet an autocatalytic set of molecules is perhaps the simplest image one can have of Kant's holism.

(ibid.: 69)

> There is a collective molecular autopoetic system that Kant might
> have been heartened to behold. The parts exist for and by means of
> the whole; the whole exists for and by means of the parts.
>
> (ibid.: 275)

Kauffman does not move to a more radical notion of the process of
evolution here but rather remains in a "both . . . and" perspective which
describes process as what is really two separate acts. Furthermore, when
he discusses the nature of the agents in a complex adaptive system, he
refers to agents acting in their own interest and says that only the winners
survive. So, in addition to the self-organizing whole he has autonomous
agents.

Ethical issues concerning Kauffman's thinking

Kauffman's concept of wholes becomes the basis of an ethical position.
Nature is in the end, despite his denials, mystified as the source of these
wholes. For Kauffman being "at home" in nature, in the universe, is our
only consolation as humans:

> Aquinas attempted to find a self-consistent moral code. Kant sought
> the same in his brilliant maxim . . . Nevertheless these hopes for
> consistency stumble in the real world. No one guarantees that the set
> of goals held as "good" will be mutually consistent. Or constant in
> time. We necessarily live in and make conflict-laden worlds.
> Therefore, our political machinery must evolve toward procedures
> that find good compromises. Patches and receiver-based optimization
> have a ring of reality and natural plausibility about them.
>
> (ibid.: 270)

Kauffman is arguing that since a universally consistent ethics,
comparable to the absolute ethics of metaphysics, is not possible, we
must in the end resign ourselves to natural processes. He does not
consider the possibility of the emergence of a self, which attains
self-consciousness and becomes ethically responsive in an evolving
environment. Kauffman's sense of universals is that of Kant: they are
unchanging universal laws. He does not understand these as evolving
also. He maintains that we are part of a process that we are creating and
that is creating us, but we do not become subjects.

> We stand on the verge of creating a vaster diversity of molecular
> forms in one place and time than ever before, we may assume, in the

history of the earth, perhaps in the history of the universe. A vast
wealth of new useful molecules. An unknown peril of fearful new
molecules. Will we do this? Yes, of course we will. We always pursue
the technologically feasible. We are, after all, both *Homo ludens* and
Homo habilis. But can we, *Homo sapiens*, calculate the
consequences? No. Never could, never will. Like the grains in the
self-organized sandpile, we are carried willy-nilly by our own
inventions.

(ibid.: 148)

In the end Kauffman escapes to a macrocosmic perspective and finds
"spirituality, awe, and reverence" at the level of the unfolding universe.
He also posits autonomous agents, which can then easily be understood,
in relation to human interaction, as Kant's autonomous individual. The
resonance with the approach of Wheatley discussed above is too strong to
miss. After discussing the views of Gell-Mann and Holland I will go on
to explore how the implicit ethics of Lewin and Regine follows much the
same train. I will also review Pascale's work, which is firmly based on
the autonomous agent acting in its own interest with only the winners
surviving.

Gell-Mann/Holland

Prigogine argues for what the astrophysicist Arthur Eddington first
referred to in 1927 as the "arrow of time", in which the past changes in
evolution, as opposed to the deterministic time of Newtonian mechanics
and Kant's phenomenal reality. Time is thus irreversible, an argument
which Gell-Mann vehemently refuses to accept. For him

> ... the time asymmetry of signals and records is part of physical
> causality, the principle that effects follow their causes. Physical
> causality can be traced directly to the existence of a simple initial
> condition of the universe. ... From the basic quantum-mechanical
> formula for the probabilities of histories, with a suitable initial
> condition, it is possible to deduce all the familiar aspects of causality,
> such as signals and records pointing from the past to the future. All
> the arrows of time correspond to various features of coarse-grained
> histories of the universe.

(Gell-Mann, 1994: 216–17)

Gell-Mann's term "coarse graining" is a key argument for understanding
science in terms of Kantian deterministic time. The analogy is to the

graininess of photographic reproduction. What is complexity at one level of graininess can be revealed as simple at another, as science discovers more and more about reality. Reality is then a hidden order of universal laws, which are being discovered piece by piece. Evolutionary theory is also bound to these laws.

> Biological evolution, in humans and in other organisms, has no chance of keeping up. Our own genetic schemata reflect in great part the world of fifty thousand years ago and cannot, through the normal mechanisms of biological evolution, undergo important changes in just a few centuries. Likewise, other organisms and whole ecological communities cannot evolve quickly enough to cope with the changes wrought by human culture.
>
> (ibid.: 304)

Gell-Mann's understanding of evolution is the basis of his theory of complex adaptive systems. The emergence of complex adaptive systems is associated with the process of biological evolution. He describes the adaptation as learning and, consistent with his views on science and time, this learning is described very much in the terminology of Watson's behaviourism.

> Although our examination of complex adaptive systems began with the example of learning in a human child, it is not necessary to invoke anything so sophisticated to illustrate the concept. . . . The dog learns, by means of rewards and/or punishments, the schema for the command to stay. Alternative schemata, for example, one that makes an exception for chasing cats, are (at least in theory) rejected as training proceeds. But even if the dog adopts a schema with the exception, a complex adaptive system is still at work. A schema other than the one the trainer intended has survived as a result of competing pressures from the training and the instinct to chase cats. . . . In the sequence of less and less sophisticated organisms, say a dog, a goldfish, a worm, and an amoeba, individual learning plays a smaller and smaller role compared to that played by the instincts stored up through biological evolution.
>
> (ibid.: 60–1)

Evolution as a process is contained in the complex adaptive system as a mechanical process and the result is the action of the agents as described by the observer. Since this concept of time only recognizes regularities, this theory of complex adaptive systems sees the process as acquiring

> . . . information about its environment and its own interaction with
> that environment, identifying regularities in that information,
> condensing those regularities into a kind of 'schema' or model, and
> acting in the real world on the basis of that schema.
>
> (ibid.: 17)

Murray Gell-Mann and John Holland view their research as remaining
within the paradigm of modernist science. In essence they have no
problem with the Kantian distinction of phenomenal and noumenal
realities. They would view ethical and religious convictions as part of the
noumenal sphere and as distinct from their research as scientists. John
Holland's views concerning complex adaptive systems are virtually the
same as those of Gell-Mann. Holland has concentrated his work on the
development of the theory and mathematics of algorithms. This represents
the most detached view of complex adaptive systems and the most centred
view of agency. Holland speaks of the agents as autonomous, which is in
fact how they appear to the observer in a simulation.

Holland cites as an example of a complex adaptive system the central
nervous system (CNS).

> Though the activity of an individual neuron can be complex, it is clear
> that the behaviour of the CNS aggregate identity is much more
> complex than the sum of these individual parts. The behaviour of the
> central nervous system depends on the *interactions* much more than
> the actions.
>
> (Holland, 1995: 3)

He develops his notion of interaction as follows:

> In complex adaptive systems a major part of the environment of any
> given adaptive agent consists of other adaptive agents, so that a
> portion of any agent's efforts at adaptation is spent adapting to other
> adaptive agents. This one feature is a major source of the complex
> temporal patterns that complex adaptive systems generate.
>
> (ibid.: 10)

Next he understands this mutual interaction from the perspective of
individual agents: each agent has a "mechanism for anticipation" that
drives its behaviour. This mechanism is an internal model, or set of rules
according to which the agent acts on the basis of its predictions of the
responses of other agents. He speaks of agents with the capacity for
"lookahead" and "strategy" and holds that:

> The use of models for anticipation and prediction is a topic that, in its
> broadest sense, encompasses much of science. It is a difficult topic,
> but not impenetrable.
>
> (ibid.: 31)

Holland's views on lookahead and strategy are completely at odds with
the concept of an evolutionary theory of action. There is no description of
a process of change but rather a unit of adaptive action similar to
Watson's behaviourism. It is only described as centred prediction and
result. In presenting his argument in this way Holland is defining the
nature of interaction and the nature of the agents who are interacting in a
particular way. He is assuming that each individual agent has what others
have referred to as a "homunculus", an internal model taking the form of
if–then rules, that is, regularities extracted from previous experience of
interaction. These have the time structure of Kant's deterministic time
whereby the future is the repetition of the past. He is assuming that these
rules are then used (by the homunculus, the centred "little man" inside) to
select a response to other agents on the basis of the predicted outcome of
that response. In other words, each individual agent acts in a centred
sense on the expectation of particular responses to that action on the part
of other agents – predicted outcome is the criterion for selecting an
action. Discovery of accuracy or inaccuracy of prediction leads to further
evolution in the agents' internal models. In this way the pattern of agent
identity emerges and such emergence is primarily driven by the ordering
principle of selection, as accuracy of prediction makes survival more
likely.

Holland implies that individual agents (who make predictions and
develop individual strategies) reveal, through their interaction, an order, a
true reality, that was merely hidden before the interaction and is revealed
by it – the "hidden order" in the title of his book. He focuses on the
possibility of predicting that order rather than on the potential for the
emergence of unique, and thus unpredictable, patterns and forms in
specific contexts. With this view of the nature of action and interaction
Holland is then able to focus on the objective, scientific modelling of
complex adaptive systems in order to find the levers that will enable one
outside the system to change it in intentional ways. He cites the immune
system as an example and sees vaccines as the levers that can restore the
efficacy of the immune system in the case of AIDS. The resonance with
currently dominant theory of action in the management literature is clear.
There is the emphasis on centred intentional action and, much as in the
dominant paradigm of management theory, he sees individual agents

observing, predicting and then changing their internal models and so leveraging the whole.

Ethical issues concerning the thinking of Gell-Mann and Holland

Both Gell-Mann and Holland focus attention on the autonomous agents of a complex adaptive system. They extract regularities from their environment and form schemata as the basis upon which they act in their own interest. In addition, they talk about the hidden order of universal laws. Again, we have the "both . . . and" position with autonomous agents, on the one hand, and the whole of hidden order, on the other. There is no sense of paradox in the way they talk about this and clearly the scientist is outside of the system in every sense. In other words, when they come to talk about human interaction, they adopt the position of first-order cybernetics without any sense of the difficulties of participation raised by second-order cybernetics.

Given this approach it is easy to see how, when their thinking is taken up in relation to human interaction, it is implicitly interpreted as a form of Kantian ethics: sometimes the ethics is that of the autonomous individual and at other times it is the ethic based on the hidden order.

Against this background I now want to review first the work of Roger Lewin and Birute Regine and then that of Richard Pascale. The first two authors focus attention on the whole of hidden order but also implicitly assume the importance of the autonomous individual as well. Pascale's implicit ethics is based squarely on the autonomous, selfish, competitive individual subject to selection pressures.

The Soul at Work

Lewin and Regine (2000) unequivocally state that organizations are living systems, which they understand as complex adaptive systems, drawing on the work of Stuart Kauffman. The title of their book is to be understood in both senses of the double entendre: "it is at once the individual's soul being allowed to be present in the workplace; and it is the emergence of the collective soul of the organization" (Lewin and Regine, 2000: 26). From the very start, therefore, they make it clear that they are taking for granted the "both . . . and" position. Individuals are taken to be *both* the agents in complex adaptive systems, where the simple rules governing their interactions have to do with ensuring *caring* relationships, *and* they have souls, that is, they are reflective, autonomous individuals responsible for their actions in a way that is independent of the self-organization of the complex adaptive system. Here again, in the manner of an ethical imperative, there is a distinction between individuals as agents in the system making choices that are caring and participative, so contributing to the health of the system (organization), and other choices which are selfish and make the system (organization) an unhealthy place to work in. There are a number of important points to note about this position.

Lewin and Regine have no difficulty with the individual observing the system and making decisions based on this observation. They take the position of first-order cybernetics without in any way seeing its difficulties or making any attempt to move to second-order cybernetics. The individual is autonomous and also an agent in the system, so that he or she can be either outside or inside the system. Outside the organizational system the agent can also observe the patterns emerging on a more global level, such as cultural patterns, and he or she can make decisions to change these. "In complex adaptive systems, how we interact and the kinds of relationships we form has everything to do with what kind of culture emerges. . . . Many see themselves in a system in which they have little or no influence" (ibid.: 26). As was the case with Senge and Wheatley we find the ethical responsibility for the "health" or good of the system focused on the commitment and caring of the individual. This is even clearer in the theory of complex adaptive systems because of its focus on the agents. If the individual is considered to be the agent, this agent is also considered to have rational powers of thought and freedom of choice. It is because of this that Lewin and Regine introduce the "simple rule" of caring. This simple rule can be taken as Kant's categorical imperative, which can be formulated as the "golden rule": do unto others as you would have them do unto you. Caring includes other examples of Kant's universal laws of ethics, for example, never treat other human beings as a means to an end but only as ends in themselves. What is being reaffirmed is rationalist Kantian ethics based on the autonomy of the individual, which is the basis of traditional business ethics. I will be taking this up in detail in the next chapter.

It is only possible to have the individual inside and outside the system in first-order cybernetics, which takes for granted the elimination of paradox in the "both . . . and" way of thinking. What is then being taken for granted by Lewin and Regine is that the observer is observing the complex adaptive systems from the standpoint of first-order cybernetics. The observing scientist remains detached from the system and can test hypotheses by manipulating the system. In human social interaction, the paradox of being participant and observer at the same time means that there is no experience of being outside the interaction. As we have seen in Senge's and Wheatley's thought, and now again in Lewin and Regine, this paradox is eliminated by the "both . . . and" way of thinking by which the individual, in a serial manner over time, can be either outside the system or inside. Again in Lewin and Regine it is precisely this avoidance of paradox that is identified *as paradox*. The word soul is used, then, to refer to wholeness as a centre of action, that is, "work". "When more interactions are care-full rather than care-less in an organization, a community of care and connection develops, creating a space for the soul at work to emerge" (ibid.: 26). In that the individual is seen as an autonomous whole and the organization also an emerging whole, there is no paradox.

Leadership

Lewin and Regine's concept of leadership is built, however, on what they are referring to as paradox. They state for instance that the leaders must come to a new understanding of themselves.

> It entails a reflection on yourself; placing aside ego-driven needs and instead finding gratification and satisfaction in cultivating others; it's embracing the leader as servant. It's turning to the organization in a personal way as a way of changing the culture to one that accepts change.
>
> (ibid.: 264)

A few lines down the same page they write: "It begins . . . with nothing short of a personal conversion, that is, a difficult and often painful process of learning to let go of the illusion of control." The leader is, on the one hand, capable of changing the culture and, on the one hand, must give up the illusion of control. To reiterate, this represents the taken-for-granted elimination of paradox in the "both . . . and" way of thinking. The individuals see themselves as forming the organization and being formed by the organization but in a serial manner, now doing one and then the other.

This immediately poses the problem of how to get it right, that is, knowing when to do one and when to do the other. The onus of this choice is located in the individual leaders who must learn new skills. Lewin and Regine also refer to these skills as practices: leaders should be "allowing" – the "paradox" of freedom with guidance; they should be "accessible" – the "paradox" of being visible, that is, available when needed, and invisible when not needed; they should be "attuned" – the "paradox" of knowing through hunches, intuition and senses, and not knowing all the facts. This is summed up in statements like: "What organizations need are leaders who can see the complexity of their organization, a clarity at both the macro and micro levels that informs their choices about direction" (ibid.: 270). There is here a remarkable similarity to Senge's discipline of personal mastery and it is not surprising that Lewin and Regine go on to speak of the importance of teams or groups in a similar manner to that of Senge and Wheatley.

Participation

Again the unit of participation in the organization is the team.

> The intent behind emergent teams is to cultivate people's competencies so they can be as good as they can be, and to create diverse opportunities for them to participate in and contribute to organizational goals. People in emergent teams . . . actively participate in shaping the task that might impact the entire organization. The belief here is that when people are connected to their work and to the organization, people flourish . . .
>
> (ibid.: 284)

Lewin and Regine distinguish between these non-linear emergent teams and linear routine teams, for example, a surgical team performing a routine operation. Here again we have a "both . . . and" way of thinking, implying the standpoint of first-order cybernetics where the leader as external observer decides which would be appropriate for any given situation. Lewin and Regine find that the paradox of emergent teams "which is characteristic of the creative zone, is potential contained within parameters. . . . From a few simple guidelines, complex behavior, rich with adaptation and creativity, can arise" (ibid.: 295–6).

There are two important points here. First, the quotes above provide examples of another meaning Lewin and Regine give to what they are calling paradoxes. The fact that complexity would emerge from a few simple rules is counterintuitive, but not paradoxical, if it can be scientifically demonstrated. They cite the demonstration of the Boids computer simulation, which reproduces flocking patterns on the basis of only three simple rules of interaction among individual agents. This is counterintuitive since "there was long the belief in science that complex order in the world was generated by complex processes" (ibid.: 38), but there is nothing paradoxical about it. The second point, which is more important, is that they appeal to the insight concerning simple rules as a basis for releasing human creativity. As a matter of fact, running simulations based on a few given rules produces no creativity whatsoever. They see the Boids in the simulation wheeling and turning in pattern and avoiding obstacles in their path, but what is unfolding is merely that behaviour which was enfolded in the system in the rules. What the simple rules thinking represents is, then, a new form of control. (See Chapter 7 of Stacey, Griffin and Shaw, 2000.)

Ethical issues concerning Lewin and Regine's thinking

Like Senge, Lewin and Regine move to thinking of ethics in terms of social interaction as systemic self-organization. Their particular version of this, because of their use of the term "soul" and the imperative concerning caring in relationships, becomes much more a presentation of traditional business ethics focused on autonomous individuals whose thinking is apart from action. The agents in the kind of complex adaptive systems Lewin and Regine propose are, as humans, capable of thought apart from action. In such deliberation before action possible outcomes are considered in terms of the good of the whole organization, that is, what they refer to as the soul of the organization. Here, as was the case with the learning organization and with Wheatley's concept of participation in an orderly universe, Lewin and Regine express the source of commitment and ethical action in terms of idealized wholes. Individuals must give up themselves in order for this whole to emerge, which then becomes the basis for the action already taken. This means that the participants are not focused on the everyday potential emerging from conflict and difference, but rather on an idealized and harmonious whole.

Next, I turn to the work of Richard Pascale who also writes from the premise that organizations are complex adaptive systems but does precisely the opposite to Lewin and Regine. Pascale sees conflict, not caring, as the essential quality of relationship in human social complex adaptive systems.

Surfing the Edge of Chaos

Pascale (Pascale *et al.*, 2000) also claims that organizations are living organisms, and that as such they are complex adaptive systems. It is not just a metaphor for organizations. Nevertheless, he uses the terminology in both metaphorical and literal senses. For example, he views the mathematical term "attractor" as a key concept in understanding complex adaptive systems, but also uses it in the metaphorical sense in speaking of managing from the future, which is his term for "vision", as being an attractor, drawing the organization forward. Also speaking of managing from the future, he claims that

> the force that draws the performer (trapeze artist) forward on the high wire is analogous to a strange attractor. What the trapeze artist "controls" is the psychological context for the undertaking. As this image suggests, three elements – (1) past and future fitness peaks, (2) strange attractors, and (3) a mental map for the journey – are the keys to managing the future.
>
> (Pascale *et al.*, 2000: 244–5)

It can suffice here, without going into the details of his understanding of these concepts from complex adaptive system theory, to see how Pascale sees them as tools to be used by the manager as an observer of the system.

Leadership

In a manner which is very similar to that of Lewin and Regine, Pascale describes the leader as being in a "both . . . and" position. He bases his distinction on Ronald Heifetz's distinction between "technical (i.e. operational) leadership" and "adaptive leadership" (Pascale *et al.*, 2000: 37). Operational leadership is to be applied in conditions of relative equilibrium, the routine surgery Lewin and Regine mentioned. "If a company is in a crisis; if downsizing, restructuring, or reducing costs is called for, if sharpened execution is the key to success, then operational leadership is the best bet" (ibid.: 38). Adaptive leadership, on the other hand, makes happen what would not otherwise have happened. It responds to an "adaptive problem" whereby the current repertoire of solutions is inadequate or "just plain wrong" (ibid.: 39). Here again it is the individual leader who must choose. "The point is: Over time (and even concurrently) organizations need evolution *and* revolution. . . . The trick is to clearly identify the nature of the challenge and then use the right tool for the right task" (ibid. 38). It is taken for granted that the leader can observe the system from outside and choose among possible alternatives to apply to the system. This is again the position of first-order cybernetics and the elimination of the paradox because it is thought to be possible to be inside or outside of the system. Pascale also uses the learning concepts of Argyris, as developed in Senge's disciplines of the learning organization, but he makes no attempt to develop a theory of a third level of learning in organizations, as Senge does.

Social interaction

Pascale differs significantly from the other authors reviewed in this chapter in that he focuses on conflict as the most important quality of relationship in looking at the organization as a complex adaptive system. The leader, again from a position external to the system, judges when adaptive leadership is necessary and then considers how much the system needs to be disturbed. "Leaders are to the social system what a properly shaped lens is to light. They focus intention and do so for better or worse. If adaptive intention is required, the social system must be disturbed in a profound and prolonged fashion" (ibid.: 40). Pascale says that this is achieved by

> (1) communicating the urgency of the adaptive challenge (i.e. the threat of death), (2) establishing a broad understanding of the circumstances creating the problem, to clarify why traditional solutions won't work (i.e. sustaining disequilibrium), and (3) holding the stress in play until guerrilla leaders come forward with solutions (i.e. making room for genetic diversity). This sequence generates anxiety and tension.
>
> (ibid.)

The leaders are "behind the lens" taking action to disturb the "system" of the team. But there is no discussion of how this intention to act into this particular group emerged.

The references to this kind of external manipulation of complex adaptive systems in order to "force" self-organization as "revolution" in an organization can also be found in Nonaka (1988). Like Pascale he separates intention from the relational context of self-organization and espouses a concept of leadership directly at odds with any possibility of self-organization – that of "leading the masses".

> The methodology of revolution is to make the present regime become unstable while a determined group of revolutionaries lead the masses to a new direction. Similarly in the development of a strategy or a new business, the most typical process of creating information, is also a process of creating a self-organizing team within an organization with the ability to form its own order and making it grow into an organized body which would transform the whole organization. Because the manner in which the initial conditions to self-organizing is determined greatly affects the subsequent formation of order, top management must give sensitive consideration not only on how to set the stage in general, but also on how to select the leader and members of the group and how to support the subsequent processes of group activities.
>
> (Nonaka, 1988: 37)

Social interaction is driven by conflict but the leaders introduce the source of the conflict into the team. This puts Pascale's emphasis on conflict into a new perspective. It is also linked to his understanding of paradox. What he is interested in is the dynamics of the power law at the edge of chaos. It is a property of the edge of chaos that many small perturbations will cascade through the network but only a few large ones will. In other words, there will be large numbers of small extinction events but only small numbers of large ones. It is this property that imparts control, or stability, to the process of change at the edge of chaos.

Although he is aware of both the destructive as well as the creative potential of the dynamics, it is the leaders who are to get it right and the individuals on the team who are to be productive. Should they fail to do so it is their "fault" in falling into the destructive dynamics at the edge of chaos. It is the leaders who then imagine themselves "surfing" the edge of chaos, enjoying the "release" of new creative potential in their organizations. To understand Pascale's thought on productive teamwork it is necessary to look briefly at his concepts of socialization and paradox.

In 1985 Pascale published an article entitled "The paradox of corporate culture: reconciling ourselves to socialization". He expresses in the article an unreserved enthusiasm for socialization and defines the paradox as the dilemma that

> we are intellectually and culturally opposed to the manipulation of individuals for organizational purposes. At the same time, a certain degree of social uniformity enables organizations to work better. . . .

U.S. firms that have perfected and systematized their processes of
socialization tend to be a disproportionate majority of the great self-
sustaining firms which survive from one generation to the next. . . . It
is time to take socialization out of the closet. . . . the challenge for
managers is to reconcile this with the American insistence upon
retaining the latitude for independent action. It is neither necessary
nor desirable to oscillate from extreme individualism to extreme
conformity. We can learn from those who have mastered the process.

(Pascale, 1985: 28–9)

In his book *Managing on the Edge* (1990) Pascale develops further what
he means by paradox. Like the edge of chaos, it is understood as
something to be used for the purposes of leaders. It is a "launching pad"
(Pascale, 1990: 110) for blasting beyond the confines in which the
organization finds itself. "No longer held captive by the old way of
thinking, we are liberated to see things we have known all along, but
couldn't assemble into a useful model for action" (ibid.). The
exploitation of paradox means that if one side of the paradox blinds you,
you move to the other. This way of using conflicting models means that
you can simply see and think more. Pascale has probably the most naïve
and straightforward formulation of the "both . . . and" elimination of
paradox. Both sides are affirmed. The only challenge is to get it right.

What then is the context of getting it right? What is the context of the
"paradox"? The overriding organization as system, for Pascale, is culture.
When the individual is properly socialized in the culture, he or she enters
into "productive conflict" in teams and "self-organizes" at the edge of
chaos to produce creative results that the leaders have "programmed"
into the social interaction, the culture, to ensure the survival of the
organization. In another article (December 1997) Pascale, Millemann,
and Gioja write of dealing with culture, the system of the organization.
Inspired by medical science, they have developed four vital signs to be
measured, similar to the measurement of pulse, blood pressure and so on
in medicine. "The four vital signs we identified . . . give us a working
definition of culture and tell us most of what we need to know about the
operating state of any company" (ibid.: 129). These vital signs are:

- *Power*. Do employees believe they can affect organizational
  performance? Do they believe they have the power to make things
  happen?
- *Identity*. Do individuals identify rather narrowly with their
  professions, working teams, or functional units, or do they identify
  with the organization as a whole?

- *Conflict*. How do members of the organization handle conflict? Do they smooth over, or do they confront and resolve it?
- *Learning*. How does the organization learn? How does it deal with new ideas?

Again we find the focus on the identity of the organization, the whole of the organization, as a key factor in the survival of the system. The "both ... and" elimination of paradox occurs in having both the leader steering the system and the survival of the system in the identification of individuals with the whole. This in effect eliminates genuinely dealing with the destructive potential in human relating and posits a reality in which everything can be "got right". It plays the emergence in complex adaptive system theory off the destructive elements. And it does the same in ethics.

Issues concerning ethics

It would be hard to imagine a position more adverse to the core intentions of Kant's thought than that of Pascale. Kant developed the "both ... and" way of thinking and that of the regulative idea, the "as ... if ", in order to be able to establish a basis for human freedom in the autonomous individual who was not bound to natural law. The essence of the regulative idea guiding human freedom is the categorical imperative, which states in one formulation: you may never use another human being as a means to an end, but only as end in him- or herself. Pascale and his co-authors, and also Nonaka (1988), express most explicitly that the role of leadership is to do exactly the unethical in Kant's sense: to induce crisis into human teams in order to take advantage of "productive" self-organization for the survival of the whole. But they develop no theory of ethics for this new sense of the whole, but rather "play" Kant's ideas "off " one another. The culture, the whole of the organization, can be diagnosed as being ill, like human individuals, and the course of possible cures prescribed in the same way. Decisions are then taken on this basis, but it is the members of the team who act under a Kantian imperative to be productive as a self-organizing team. The judges of this are the leaders who will use results as a means to further the survival of the organization, but these of course are again seen in terms of their own strategies and goals, the instruments of their power. Power is a necessary reality of organizations. But there is no standpoint from which it is understood as self-organizing in Pascale's approach.

The problem with "living systems" as a theory of leadership and ethics

In my view, there are questionable aspects of thinking about organizations as living systems.

First, those proposing this view frequently make emotive appeals for a return to ancient wisdom, supposedly now made scientific by the complexity sciences. This is advocated as a basis for leaders to build more caring communities and also as the basis for countering the global exploitation of the planet. A frequent example used of ancient people who possessed this wisdom is the Indians of North America. The argument about ancient wisdom is also often supported with references to Buddhist philosophy and to ancient mythology. It is said that ancient people had a much stronger, wiser sense of community and that they were closely in touch with nature, respecting nature in a way that secured a sustainable environment. It is claimed that we have lost all of this. But is it true that ancient peoples were so wise? It could be that they had a different sense of community because they lived in smaller groups and were more bound together because of their experience of being more subject to the whims of the natural environment over which they felt they had very little control. It may be that there is no direct causal relationship between not "destroying" their environment and the fact that their numbers were small. So, what happened when ancient people did live together in large numbers in relatively small areas? We can get some idea of what happened through the archaeological information provided by those who have studied, for example, the ancient Mayan civilizations. Take the great city of Teotihuacan:

> This city was founded at about the time of Christ in a small but fertile valley. . . . On the eve of its destruction at the hands of unknown peoples, at the end of the sixth or the beginning of the seventh century AD, it covered an area of over 6 square miles (20 square km) and it may have had a population of between 100,000 and 200,000 people, living in 2,000 apartment compounds. To fill it, Teotihuacan's ruthless early rulers virtually depopulated smaller towns and villages in the Valley of Mexico.
>
> (Coe, 1999: 83)

Over the next centuries a number of cities at least as large as this rose and fell, sometimes as the result of conquest but often for reasons now difficult to identify. Eventually, all the great Mayan cities were abandoned:

One can only conclude that by the end of the eighth century, the Classic Maya population of the southern lowlands had probably increased beyond the carrying capacity of the land, no matter what the systems of agriculture in use. There is persuasive evidence for massive deforestation [the Maya used slash and burn methods] and erosion throughout the central area. . . . In short, overpopulation and environmental degradation had advanced to a degree only matched by what is happening in many of the poorest tropical countries today. The Maya apocalypse, for such it was, surely had ecological roots.

(ibid.: 152–3)

The development and fall of the Mayan civilization does not suggest that the ancients had some form of wisdom that we have lost. On the contrary, there are some striking similarities with modern civilization. For me, the appeal to ancient wisdom harks back to Rousseau, with the modification of substituting the "ancient savant" for his "noble savage", neither of which actually existed. The appeal to Buddhism is also, in my view, misplaced. It takes a number of deep insights completely out of their cultural context and easily assumes that they can somehow be transplanted into a completely different culture. Trying to base a theory of leadership and ethics in mythology is also a way of moving away from our direct current experience.

The second difficulty I have with basing ideas of leadership and ethics on the notion of the living organization is one I have been stressing throughout this chapter. The suggestion that an organization is a living system reflects a holistic philosophy. It sets up a whole outside of the experience of interaction between people, a whole to which they are required to submit if their behaviour is to be judged ethical. This distances us from our actual experience and makes it feel natural to blame something outside of our actual interaction for what happens to us. It encourages the belief that we are victims of a system, on the one hand, and allows us to escape feeling responsible for our own actions, on the other. Or, it alienates people. They come to feel that they are insignificant parts of some greater whole and that there is nothing much they can do about it. So, if the environment is being degraded people feel that it is hopeless and there is nothing they can do: the change has to come at the level of the whole system. Another response to this is to adopt a revolutionary stance and work for the overthrow of the system, perhaps even by violent methods. The problem with the call to submit to a higher system is that instead of promoting love and caring, it may actually generate feelings of alienation and even acts of violence.

The third difficulty is this. Organizations are not things at all, let alone living things. They are processes of communication and joint action. Communication and joint action as such are not alive. It is the bodies communicating and interacting that are alive.

The appeal to ancient wisdom, the reification of organizations as living organisms and the belief in a whole outside the experience of local interaction in the living present, taken together, reflect an underlying ideology that underpins particular challenges to current power relations. This is an ideology that makes it feel natural to simply denigrate large corporations and business activities in general and oppose what feel like uncontrollable forces called, for example, globalization, and to do this even employing violence.

At the end of the last chapter I indicated the general outlines of the approach to ethics that I will be developing in Chapter 5. This is an approach that stays with our experience of interaction and regards the ethics of action as a process of perpetual negotiation. This process of communicative interaction is one in which we together create what happens to us and it is one in which small differences can be amplified. What each of us does matters even though we cannot know what the outcome of our actions will be. It is possible that small actions can escalate to transform global situations. For me, this is an empowering perspective and also one that makes it impossible for me to escape the responsibility I have for my own actions. I argue that unlike the perspective that moves off to some whole outside our experience, and so leads us to feel hopeless, victimized or rebellious, this perceptive encourages us to pay attention to what we are doing and encourages us to believe that this is effective in some way, even though we cannot know how.

Returning to Alberto's question

I would argue that the authors reviewed in this chapter, all of whom implicitly rely on the systemic form of self-organization, have not offered any theory of the emergence of leaders or leadership. They are in fact reaffirming elements of the traditional theory of business ethics based on Kant's thinking and that of utilitarianism. They are all developing, in very similar ways, theories of an organizational whole, which is a "living system" with a life of its own. And all appeal in varying ways to ethical principles, implicit in such concepts as "caring", being "productive", shedding the "egoistic" individual for the sake of this greater "reality", in order that it might be "healthy". What is emerging from this is a leadership theory based on conformity.

What has come to dominate management and organization theory in the last decades is a theory of organizations as living systems, which has important roots in Maturana and Varela's (1987) theory of autopoiesis. They developed the theory as one of biological systems reproducing themselves. The systems are self referential and thus self-producing, hence the Greek term for such a process, autopoiesis. I mention this here, because Maturana and Varela conflicted when Maturana proposed applying the theory to human systems in a way that was based on very similar principles to those of Kant. Varela insisted that the theory could only be applied to natural systems and not to organizations of human beings (see Bednarz, 1995). In spite of this, the theory has been taken up and cited as support for systemic self-organization by the rapidly growing number of authors developing what many refer to as revolutionary insights into the nature of stability and change in organizations. What I am questioning in this book is the basis of an ethics of human action and human freedom that could support such a theory. All of them speak of "whole" systems, the learning organization, the soul at work, culture, and so on, which form individuals in the organization, but only if they act "ethically" in giving up their independence, egos and so on, in order that the whole be "healthy", "productive", "caring".

Returning to the film plot involving the contamination of ground water by a large utility mentioned in Chapter 1, as well as Richard Sennett's accusation that large corporations are corroding the character of individuals, it is interesting to note how the tables have been turned using the same idea that large organizations are individuals and can be referred to as good or evil on the basis of their "actions". This is the crux of the argument in linking systemic self-organization and ethics. It is done to justify broadly very black and white arguments – depending on the perspective taken. Those criticizing from a larger context have no basis to take this "individual" to court. They can only take individual leaders to court, based on the principle of premeditated intent, that is, thought apart from action. Those in the company leave these broader contexts behind, that of mother, father, home owner, citizen, church member, and are expected to split themselves in the "both . . . and" manner, deciding ethically when, one after the other, they find themselves in each of the varying groups. They form and are formed by the identity of these groups but this paradox of forming and being formed "at the same time", being all of these identities in the one identity we are co-creating in any given action, is eliminated in that it is silenced. This silence allows the contamination of the ground water and the corrosion of character to continue. We are the people doing this and the second part of this book will deal with the alternative way of looking at self-organization, participative self-organization, which keeps this truth in mind.

The question is then whether systems thinking really moves beyond what might also be considered to be the strength and convincing power of behaviourism. Senge is correct in pointing out that simple cause and effect disappear in taking the perspective of systemic self-organization, but that, as argued in Chapter 1, was exactly what Kant had in mind in developing his theory to provide further support for the scientific method. One can also view the stimulus and response of behaviourism as a simplified system. In fact in doing so one can move towards understanding what G.H. Mead meant in saying that the stimulus and response idea is correct, but then again wrong because they are seen as two different acts. Mead argued that it is simply necessary to view stimulus–response as phases of one act. This would mean that the detached observer would disappear.

But before turning to these questions in the second part of the book, in the next chapter I want to look more carefully at some of the important theories which are used in varying ways by those developing human organizational theory on the basis of systemic self-organization. These include:

● culture;
● the importance of Kant's thinking in traditional business ethics.

4 Social interaction: viewing our selves as autonomous individuals

Chapter 2 pointed to how systems theory, as developed by Kant in his *Critique of Judgement* (1790), is a method of understanding nature as organism rather than simply mechanism. According to Kant, we cannot know reality itself, only the appearance of reality. It follows that he was not claiming that nature *was* a system, only that the scientist could think about it *as if* it were one. In other words, for him, systems thinking consisted of regulative ideas, or hypotheses, about the development of a system, which is the appearance of nature, not its reality. This method of looking at nature "as if" it were following the laws of a given hypothesis was taken up by mathematicians and became a theory of modelling at an abstract level. The success of such modelling led to the reification of the systems models, that is, to the taken-for-granted understanding that they were things. They came to be thought of as reality itself and eventually these models were applied to human interaction. Chapter 3 went on to show how more recent thinking has moved a step further to a theory of living systems in biology, particularly in the theory of autopoiesis (self-producing systems). These theories of living systems in the natural sciences have also been taken over into the social sciences so that human social systems are now often treated as self-reproducing autonomous unities. Francisco Varela, who along with Umberto Maturana developed the theory of autopoiesis, himself warned against such a move from the physical domain of biology to the social domain because of the ethical implications (Bednarz, 1988: 60). This was precisely the objection of Kant.

As I have already stated in previous chapters, Kant resolved and "eliminated" the paradox of determinism and autonomy by creating the "both . . . and" way of thinking which is at the very core of systems thinking. Kant's resolution provided a basis *both* for the autonomy of nature regarded as systems *and* also the autonomy of individuals who, with their "mere" reason, could know the appearance of nature and also the actions they themselves should take. This way of thinking, therefore, is concerned, above all, with autonomy. Autonomy is, if you will, writ large on the banner of the modernist revolt against the Middle Ages and the hierarchical, classifying systems of metaphysical thought which were the basis for feudal social reality. Systems in medieval thinking were the ordered presentation of the reality of God's creation in thought. Theology was the highest of the "sciences" since it was concerned with God's revelation about the created world. Starting with Kant, however, the concept of "system" took on a new meaning as autonomous self-organizing wholes. This meaning has been retained up to the present time. Indeed, the current move to thinking about living systems is a reaffirmation of Kant's concern for the autonomy of systems, that is, their unity and wholeness, which can supposedly be uncovered by science as it learns the universal laws of nature. The notion of organizations as living systems imports this concept of autonomous wholes into thinking about human interaction.

In this chapter, I will examine this issue of autonomy and argue that it is the key concern of current mainstream theories of organization, culture and leadership. I will argue that these theories reify the system of culture as a thing, an organic whole, which leaders are supposed to be able to manipulate and change according to their own goals and purposes. Kant made a clear distinction between the autonomy of the system in nature and the autonomy of the individual, and he thought about both in terms of regulative ideas, the hypothesis or "as if", because we do not directly know the reality of nature or ethical human action as things, but rather the universal laws governing them, which we discover by testing in action. For Kant, there is *both* autonomy in the manner in which humans know and act in the natural world and in reason-based freedom *and* there is also a reality in itself and universals laws of morality that we cannot know directly. Kant establishes an autonomy for *both* the natural sciences as systems *and* an autonomy for the individual in a way of thinking which resolves paradox into a "both . . . and".

It is important to recall from Chapter 3 that many authors writing about organizations from a complexity perspective use the concept "paradox" in a way that is synonymous with Kant's "both ... and" position. Leaders are regarded as being in a paradoxical position because they must "get it right" in terms of steering the autonomy of the system to a balanced position between two opposing extremes – it is these extremes that are said to be paradoxical. The leader is autonomous as an individual observing the system and the system is autonomous as a self-organizing whole, but this is not seen as paradoxical at all. While Kant would not have taken this position because he would never have regarded humans as systems, the potential for taking such a position is certainly to be found in his thought. In the following section, I will consider how theories of culture are founded on the notion of autonomy and then I will turn to Kant's concept of the autonomous individual. The latter concept, with its emphasis on thought apart from action, remains the cornerstone of business ethics and leadership in our world today. Later on in this chapter, I will examine the implications for using the dual concept of autonomous cultures and autonomous leaders in the theories of living systems to be found in current management and organization theory. This will provide a basis to move on in the next chapter to the implications of the reappearance in the natural sciences of paradox in its genuine meaning as opposed to the "both ... and" position. I will be arguing for an alternative to basing social interaction on the concept of the autonomous individual.

Culture: developing leadership theory on the basis of cybernetic theory

The main theories of culture in the literature on organizations have all been influenced by the thought of Talcott Parsons. In the late 1940s he introduced the cultural theory developed by anthropologists into sociology. However, in doing so, he made an important shift. He framed the concept of culture in terms of the new systems thinking being developed at that time by Ludwig von Bertalanffy and others. Introducing a theory of culture into social theory in this way brought with it the early cybernetic paradigm of system-environment and it is in this form that culture has been developed in management theory. Niklas Luhmann, who studied under Parsons, credits Bertalanffy's theory of systems with providing the basis for a shift to this new way of thinking because it "enabled one to interrelate the theories of the organism, thermodynamics, and evolutionary theory" (Luhmann, 1995: 6–7).

Together with Edward Shils (Parsons and Shils, 1951), Parsons developed a general theory of action based on his understanding of culture in systems terms. This is an evolutionary theory of action in the tradition of Aristotle's theory of evolution, according to which phenomena can be observed to develop from one form to another. In other words there are fixed points of reference in the evolution of forms of action just as there are in cybernetic systems. For Parsons, the important regularities of form are those of function. "This organization of action elements is, for purposes of the theory of action, above all a function of the relation of the actor to his situation . . ." (Parsons, 1951: 5).

Parsons' theory of social systems remains in the scientific paradigm of modernism in that the social scientist objectively observes and describes cultural systems as the regularity of functions. The subject is treated in terms of a role, which is the "the primary point of direct articulation between the personality of the individual and the structure of the social system" (ibid.: 26). Culture then becomes a system of functional roles through which individuals become socialized. The action is centred in the system and individuals passively learn their roles in the system. Parsons emphasizes:

> First, that culture is transmitted, it constitutes a heritage or a social tradition; secondly, that it is learned, it is not a manifestation, in particular content, of man's genetic constitution; and third, that it is shared.
>
> (ibid.: 15)

Roles as the basic elements of social/cultural systems are thus linked to normative consensus, which means that values and norms become the overriding concern. "Identification . . . means taking over, i.e. internalizing, the *values* of the model" (ibid.: 221).

> A value pattern in this sense is always institutionalized in an *inter*action context. Therefore there is always a double aspect of the expectation system which is integrated in relation to it. On the one hand there are the expectations which concern and in part set standards for the behavior of the actor, ego, who is taken as the point of reference; these are his "role-expectations". On the other hand, from his point of view there is a set of expectations relative to the contingently probable *re*actions of others (alters) – these will be called "sanctions". . . . The relation between role-expectations and sanctions then is clearly reciprocal. What are sanctions to ego are role-expectations to alter and vice versa.
>
> (ibid.: 38)

The "passivity" of the individual in this theory of action results from relating activity to a system, detached from the objectively observing scientist, in which there are fixed points of reference as in early cybernetic thought. It is "as a point of reference, as he who holds a status or performs a role" (ibid.: 25) that the individual actor is a unit in the social system. Parsons developed a leadership theory based on roles as "points of reference" in a social system.

An example of a fixed point of reference in a cybernetic system is the thermostat in a heating system, described in Chapter 2. This is a first-order cybernetic system rather than a second-order system that incorporates the observer (see the discussion on Bateson in Chapter 2). In a first-order cybernetic system there is a circular feedback, essentially a serial "loop" of actions connected by cause–effect links in deterministic time. At each point, the system refers back to a goal and makes a choice between a limited number of possible, predictable outcomes; it is this choice of predictable outcome related to a goal that constitutes the controlled behaviour of the system. *In this sense, the points of reference become points of control. It was the retention of this kind of control that made the introduction of the new paradigm of culture into the dominant theory of management action possible.* The "loops" in first-order cybernetic systems are closed input–output circuits, making it possible to focus on these "joints" in the "loops", each of which affects the others, so constituting points of leverage by means of which managers can change the whole system. The dynamics of the system are thought of in terms of equilibrium, balance and leverage. What happens then in management theory is that the new paradigm of culture is taken over and in a real sense subordinated to the dominant concern for control.

In later developments of theories of social action, Parsons (1966), and also the important theorist, Luhmann (see Bednarz, 1988), moved away from thinking of the individual as the unit of the social system. Instead they saw individual body and individual mind as other systems. Parsons saw that the concept of the individual included many aspects which he groups in differing systems. He viewed these as concentric circles (systems of systems). In the centre is the body as a system surrounded by personality as a system that is in turn surrounded by culture as a system. The surrounding systems exercise, in each instance, more and more influence on the circles they contain. Parsons compared the greater influence of culture, for instance, to the small dial of a washing machine, which brings a much larger mechanism into action. Luhmann went further and addressed the problems of participation. For him, the subject is a psychic system and participates as such in the social system in which meaning is self-referential and self-organizing. This is, of course, less static than the image of circles that Parsons presents, but Luhmann implies the technological approach suggested by the analogy with the washing machine. Luhmann views decision-making processes as self-organizing in social systems in which subjects are viewed as separate. This remains in the end the spirit of Kant's *Critique of Pure Reason* in which he defines the categories that form reality.

However, the most popular systemic theories of leadership today naively continue to view the individual as the unit of the social/cultural system, which continues to be understood as controllable in the way just described. I would now like to turn to two examples of cultural theory, based on Parsons' early theory of action, which have gained wide acceptance among management theorists and have become the basis for the everyday way in which culture is now referred to in offices around the globe.

Two examples of cultural theory

Despite differences in their view of culture, Edgar Schein and Charles Hampden-Turner assume the same basis of action in asserting the validity of *both* the rationalist theory of intentional action *and* the evolutionary theory of action developed by Talcott Parsons in his theory of social systems. Consider how the two authors just referred to develop their theories of culture in organizations.

Edgar Schein

Schein adds elements from gestalt theory to describe the emergence of cultural values and artifacts from basic assumptions that ground the culture.

> If one asks oneself why one needs the word *culture* at all when we have so many other words such as *norms, values, behaviour patterns, rituals, traditions*, and so on, one recognizes that the word culture adds two other critical elements to the concept of sharing. One of these elements is that culture implies some level of *structural stability* in the group. When we say that something is "cultural", we imply that it is not only shared but deep and stable. By deep I mean less

> conscious and therefore less tangible and less visible. The other element that lends stability is *patterning or integration* of the elements into a larger paradigm or gestalt that ties together the various elements and that lie at a deeper level. Culture somehow implies that rituals, climate, values, and behaviors bind together into a coherent whole. This patterning or integration is the *essence* of what we mean by "culture".
>
> (Schein, 1992: 10)

Schein, therefore, firmly places his theory of culture in the service of the dominant concern for stability and control, particularly by linking culture to leadership. Although changes in culture are described in the emergent process terminology of gestalt theory, it is the leaders who play the key role in embedding and transmitting the culture. It is here, at the level of the theory of action, that Schein's work reveals its dependency on the fixed points of reference of cybernetic theory, and this is the basis of the "both . . . and" character of his thought. Schein's work combines the process theory of action of gestalt theory with the control points of reference of cybernetic theory. The evolutionary adaptation between the system and its environment is functionalized in Parsons' sense of role and the emergence of gestalt theory is instrumentalized in reaching the goals of the leaders.

Parsons had the fixed points of reference of the cybernetic system in mind when he formulated his early concept of leadership as the role of an individual (later he no longer believed the individual to be the unit of a system): "The focus on relational context, as distinguished from technical goal, is the essential criterion of a leadership or executive role" (Parsons, 1951: 100). This is the point of reference for the adaptation of the system to the environment in the evolutionary formulation of first-order cybernetic theory. As Schein expresses it:

> We need to understand along what dimensions leaders think in creating and managing groups. The issues or problems of external adaptation and survival basically specify the coping cycle that any system must be able to maintain in relation to its changing environment.
>
> (Schein, 1992: 52)

He then identifies the cycle as

- mission and strategy;
- goals;

- means;
- measurement;
- correction.

The leader exercises leadership at the points of reference, that is, reference to the context of the system as Parsons expressed it. The leader is thus the self-contained (autonomous) individual planning action for the organization as system according to predictable outcomes. In this sense the overriding theory of intentional action fully subsumes the evolutionary theory of action in cybernetic theory. When Schein moves to a definition of culture, on the other hand, it is described in terms of the evolutionary theory of cybernetics:

> A pattern of shared basic assumptions that the group learned as it
> solved its problems of external adaptation and internal integration,
> that has worked well enough to be considered valid and, therefore, to
> be taught to new members as the correct way to perceive, think, and
> feel in relation to those problems.
>
> (ibid.: 12)

So, on the one hand there is the leader as an autonomous individual standing outside the system and making choices for it and, on the other hand, there is the self-regulating system in which individuals are merely units.

Charles Hampden-Turner

Hampden-Turner's theory of culture develops, to a much greater extent, the dynamics of cybernetic systems underpinning Parsons' theory of social systems. He focuses on the feedback concept and the dynamics of equilibrium and balance developed in early cybernetic research. For Hampden-Turner culture "is no particular thing or object, but a pattern which appears both through time and across the organizations . . . The most fundamental characteristic of culture is dilemma itself" (Hampden-Turner 1994: 24). Hampden-Turner moves on from this statement of the "essence" of culture to a definition of culture:

> A corporate culture is a cybernetic system . . . culture is in a state of
> balance between reciprocal values. Culture gives continuity and
> identity to the group. It balances contrasting contributions, and
> operates as a self-steering system which learns from feedback. It

> works as a pattern of information and can greatly facilitate the
> exchange of understanding. The values within a culture are more or
> less harmonious.
>
> (ibid.: 21)

> All cybernetic systems process feedback about changes in the
> environment and make appropriate course corrections. . . . To call a
> culture cybernetic is to imply that it steers itself and perseveres in the
> direction it has set itself despite obstacles and interruptions.
>
> (ibid.: 25)

Hampden-Turner's leadership concept reduces paradox to "balancing
between" and has the same "both . . . and" characteristic as that of
Schein: the system steers itself, on the one hand, and leaders steer it, on
the other.

> Indeed, the successful leaders described in this book exert their most
> direct influence upon their companies by using the corporate culture.
> The leaders help to shape the culture. The culture helps to shape its
> members.
>
> (ibid.: 17)

Leaders external to the system form that system and then they are formed
by the system because they are members of it. This is not seen as a
paradox, but rather as a dilemma to be resolved into balance – "getting it
right".

Developing the theory of culture

Schein and Hampden-Turner share the learning concept derived from
early cybernetic research, which views systems as inherently striving for
balance that is achieved by the system "learning" from negative and
positive feedback in exchange with its environment. Hampden-Turner's
concept of dilemma takes this further by means of the concept of balance
inherent in Parsons' concept of pattern variables in social systems. This
theory of pattern variables is in turn based on the concept of fixed points
of reference, which Parsons took from cybernetic theory.

> The next step is to begin to lay the groundwork for dealing
> systematically with the differentiation of roles. This involves careful
> analysis of the points of reference with respect to which they become

differentiated. For only with a systematic analysis of these points of reference is any orderly derivation of the bases and ranges of such differentiation possible.

(Parsons, 1951: 46)

Parsons then lists such variables as opposing "forces" in a tension that achieves balance: universalistic patterns versus particularistic patterns; diffuseness versus specificity; neutrality versus affectivity. Hampden-Turner develops these variables as dilemmas that each culture brings into balance in a unique way and he applies this theory of dilemmas to organizational culture in general. It is the leader's task to control the feedback and turn "vicious cycles" into "virtuous cycles" to resolve dilemmas by bringing them into balance. This compounding of the exercise of control derived from the theory of points of reference in cybernetic systems has found very broad acceptance in management theory today and is a taken-for-granted element of the thinking of the authors discussed in Chapters 2 and 3. It is the role of leaders to take advantage of systemic self-organization in the course of the evolution of their companies. In this theory, culture change and evolution are subsumed by the dominant concern for stability and control resulting in a claim of validity for *both* the rational theory of action based on the autonomous individual *and* the evolutionary theory of action in cybernetic theory.

Culture is viewed as an external force that influences the interaction of groups. This means in essence that culture is a first-order cybernetic system, where the problem of the external observer is ignored. However, Schein and Hampden-Turner then argue that leaders can stand outside of the culture and react when it becomes "dysfunctional". When they do this they are taking the perspective of a second-order cybernetic system, where the observer becomes part of the system. The paradox is resolved in a serial manner over time, "first . . . then" which represents the typical argument of "both . . . and":

> Culture and leadership are two sides of the same coin in that leaders first create cultures when they create groups and organizations. Once cultures exist, they determine the criteria for leadership and thus determine who will or will not be a leader. But if cultures become dysfunctional, it is the unique function of leadership to perceive the functional and dysfunctional elements of the existing culture and to manage cultural evolution and change in such a way that the group can survive in a changing environment. The bottom line for leaders is

> that if they do not become conscious of the cultures in which they are
> embedded, those cultures will manage them. Cultural understanding is
> desirable for all of us, but it is essential to leaders if they are to lead.
>
> (Schein, 1992: 15)

This "both . . . and" perspective is what many organization and
management theorists are referring to today as paradox (see Chapter 3). It
is claimed that culture is paradoxical because culture acts on individuals,
on the one hand, and the control theory of centred action is also valid, on
the other hand. However, what they are calling paradox is simply stated
as "both . . . and" so that the paradox is not held. In such statements of
"both . . . and", the evolutionary theory of action is in fact denied as a
fundamental theory of action. As a theory of change, it is therefore
rendered hollow and counterfeit. *It is the task of the individual to see to it
that evolutionary change, in this instance cultural change, serves their
personal goals and the goals of the organization.* Any sense that action
means acting into the unknown is not recognized. The responsibility is
centred in the individual based on the corresponding thinking of the
individual as autonomous. Culture as such is reduced to an instrument in
the service of the goals and strategies of the current leaders. Such a view
of systems as reified objects is very different from the further step to
considering systems as living that was first taken by Maturana and Varela
who emphasized the autonomy of the biological system (see Bednarz,
1988 and Mingers, 1995). I will return to this matter in the third part of
this chapter, but first I want to explore the ethical implications of the
theories of culture so far discussed.

Modernist ethics: individual thought apart from action

As Peter Gay writes in his book *The Enlightenment*, "Intellectual
revolutions rarely proceed by enormous leaps; certainly in the German
states the Enlightenment emerged not through sudden mutations but
through gradual, minute variations" (Gay, 1970: 329). Kant brings
together in a transforming synthesis the key "mutations" of his times:

- a new theory of the nature of reality and the natural sciences;
- a new theory of a causality of freedom and the autonomy of rational
  man;
- a new theory of ethics based on the regulative, "as if" idea of the
  categorical imperative.

It was 1784 when Kant published his famous essay "In answer to the question: What is enlightenment?" He defined it as the emergence of man from his self-imposed tutelage, suggesting as its motto "Sapere aude" (Dare to know). Peter Gay interprets this as daring to "take the risk of discovery, exercise the right of unfettered criticism, accept the loneliness of autonomy" (Gay, 1970: 3). The task that Kant faced was overwhelming: on the one hand, to reconcile the claims of science to certain and genuine knowledge of the world with the claim of philosophy that experience could never give rise to such knowledge; on the other hand, to reconcile the claim of religion that man was morally free with the claim of science that nature was entirely determined by necessary laws.

But Kant was also awakened from his "dogmatic slumbers" by Hume's skepticism and denial of the existence of causality or a self. Hume's thought undercut the claims of the natural sciences to necessary general truths about the world with his assertion that the principle of causality was an illusion of the existence of a relation between events which could just as well be explained as associations *in the mind of the observer*. If all human knowledge necessarily came from *observation* of particular instances, these could never be legitimately generalized into certain laws, since only discrete events were perceived, never their causal connection.

This threatened the basis of Newtonian science, which was based on such a causal principle. Thus the problem of understanding the observer and the phenomenon became the core of what was to become the modernist synthesis. Kant's first step in establishing the autonomy of reason was to argue that reality itself, that is, the objective thing in itself as the object of knowledge, cannot be known directly in itself. To attempt to do so entraps us in "antinomies", that is, paradoxes. What we can know is *how* we know things in themselves, that is, the forms of our knowing. Kant then turned his attention to the rigorous study of these forms, one of which is causality. He clarified the legitimate sphere of this study by arguing for the distinction between what he referred to as a causality based on the deterministic succession of time and a causality of freedom, that is, man's exercise of his autonomy in setting for himself categorical imperatives based on "pure practical reason". His *Critique of Pure Reason* examines the first of these causalities and his *Critique of Practical Reason* examines the second. The first causality is that of deterministic time, the basis of mechanistic science. Kant focused our attention on knowing only what can be known, but in doing so he split off the unknown as such, in the sense that its existence is posited but it remains hidden and we can only gradually discover its laws.

> Now and again we hear complaints about the shallowness of the mentality of our age and the decline of solid science. I do not see that those sciences whose foundations are secure, like mathematics, physics etc., deserve this reproach; on the contrary, they retain their former repute for solidity, and as far as physics is concerned, they even surpass it.
>
> (Kant, *Critique of Pure Reason*, quoted in Gay, 1970: 132)

Kant's ethics is based on his concept of autonomy, the idea that universal moral principles are the object of rational choice, that is a causality based on freedom, which is the sphere of pure practical reason. As the American social theorist John Rawls argues in his book *A Theory of Justice*: "The principles of their actions do not depend upon social or natural contingencies, nor do they reflect the bias of the particulars of their plan of life or the aspirations that motivate them" (Rawls, 1971: 252). The essence is the categorical imperative: acting on the principles that would be chosen if they were to become universally binding for all people. Kant understood categorical imperatives as principles of individual action. They apply to the individual in virtue of his nature as a free and equal rational being. These principles are therefore universal and are not affected by any particular desire or aim of the individual. Their universality is always expressed in the "as if" of regulative ideas.

Concerning practical aims and desires Kant introduces what he refers to as hypothetical imperatives. We form these hypothetical imperatives with specific ends in mind, including definite steps as the effective means to achieving these ends. But when we do so we are subject to the laws of nature and its deterministic causality. At this point Kant in effect splits ethics as it was known in ancient Greece into the deterministic timeframe of science and the goals man sets for himself in a causality of freedom. Aristotle had maintained that all actions are to have as their "final" end the ultimate good. His *Nichomachean Ethics* is a formalization of what began as teachings on moral customs and developed into practical institutions teaching people how to live, including politics and economics. (Aristotle's theory of causality is treated in another volume in this series: *Complexity and Management*, Stacey, Griffin and Shaw, 2000). Kant in his *Critique of Judgement* used Aristotle's idea of teleology for the first time in a very different way, namely, as a basis for formulating a new regulative idea of making hypotheses and understanding nature as self-organizing systems. As a result of this Kant then became concerned with only an "ideal" sphere of universal laws when he turned to ethics. As Henry Sidgwick formulates in an influential interpretation of Kant's ethics in 1888: ". . . nothing in Kant's ethics is more striking than the idea that a man realizes his true self when he acts from the moral law, whereas if he permits his actions to be determined by sensuous desires or contingent aims, he becomes subject to the law of nature" (Sidgwick, 1888: 516. See also Rawls, 1971: 254). It is precisely this split in Kant's thinking into a "both . . . and" position on ethics that provided the basis for the kind of thinking we find today in organization and management theory. On the one hand, ethics is idealized to *thought apart from action* and, on the other, the *everyday living experience of the present* in social interaction is no longer regarded as a topic of ethics. Ethics can be "mechanized" in deterministic systemic self-organization.

The key to such an idealized view of ethics as thought apart from action is the concept of the autonomous individual. Acting on the basis of categorical imperatives as an autonomous individual is to act according to universal principles as a free and equal rational being. As John Rawls expresses it:

> Our nature as such beings is displayed when we act from the principles we would choose when this nature is reflected in the conditions determining the choice. Thus men exercise their freedom, their independence from the contingencies of nature and society, by acting in ways they would in the original position [the categorical imperative]. Properly understood, then, the desire to act justly derives in part from the desire to express most fully what we are or can be.
>
> (Rawls, 1971: 256)

If we take the example of suicide, it was immoral in terms of medieval metaphysics because it was against the natural law, a system of universals to which the actions of men must conform. Kant argued differently in a famous essay on this question. His argument was that the individual in doing so would be using life to end life. As a rational person he/she could not make a universal principle out of this "as if" it were valid for all, so he/she recognizes in their freedom that it is universally wrong. This ethical sphere of causality of freedom is detached from the hypothetical imperatives of everyday life where people are going about the achievement of their aims and desires in the context of deterministic causality. The essence of rationalism is this *separation of the question of freedom from the context of nature and society* in the "both . . . and" way of thinking.

The autonomous leader: a Kantian perspective on leadership

When Rawls speaks above of Kant's imperatives as "the desire to express most fully what we are or can be" we can "hear" in this language of categorical imperatives the unmistakable "ring" of what we know today as vision statements. It is likewise the theoretical basis of the earlier formulations of corporate principles; but the term vision statements which is being used today makes it much clearer that the action, even in its appeal to universal principles, is located in the individual. This provides justification for the role of top management. The complementary theory of hypothetical imperatives forms the basis for management's role in formulating strategies. It is important to note that if such a justification is put forth for the role of top management in formulating company vision statements, they alone are, in Kant's sense acting as autonomous, free and rational persons. *But they exercise this freedom in independence from the contingencies of nature and society.* Management would then be formulating the visions for their company in independence from nature and the society in which the company is embedded. In the Kantian sense of autonomy, the endorsement of the vision statements of top management by others is in effect the surrender of their autonomy.

How is it possible that Kant's thought, which is based on the egalitarian respect of persons, has come to be the basis for organizations acting blindly in their own interests and ignoring those of the society and nature in which they are embedded? Is it possible to build an egalitarian leadership theory on such principles? As a matter of fact Kant himself considered this problem in his essay "Founding a metaphysics of morals" (1786). Here Kant deals with what we today would call organizations; he refers to them as a "realm of ends" (I am translating the German word "Reich" as realm, avoiding the connotations of "kingdom"). To reassert autonomy, Kant formulated a categorical imperative for this realm of ends: each reasoning being is to act at all times in such a way "as if " it were establishing laws for this "realm of ends". To underpin his argument, Kant at this point reiterated his elimination of paradox and his definition of freedom as autonomy, that is, the property of the human will to establish itself as a law. This would be a paradox had Kant not eliminated paradox in his *Critique of Judgement* by splitting the laws of nature from the laws of reason by means of the "as if " regulative ideas. Thus the individual in establishing laws does so on the basis of reason alone. He establishes these "as if " laws for an ideal "realm of ends" independent of the "as if" laws that govern nature, including those of the human passions of the body which are governed by the laws of nature.

In his essay "A Kantian theory of leadership" (2000), Bowie presents the implications of Kant's thinking based on this passage in "Founding a metaphysics of morals". For him such a "realm of ends" provides the basis for understanding leadership as egalitarian.

> The implementation of such a view requires that the leader turn followers into leaders. In other words the leader transforms the relationships in an organization so that those who had been followers could now be considered leaders.
>
> (Bowie, 2000: 189)

> What I am really arguing is that the basis of a Kantian theory of leadership is autonomy. What should the relation of a Kantian leader to his or her followers be? The leader should enhance the autonomy of his or her followers. At the extreme the leader transforms followers into leaders. The leader drives leadership down through the organization by making people at lower levels in the hierarchy decision-maker leaders themselves rather than mere followers.
>
> (ibid.: 191)

Bowie then goes on to describe such CEOs as Percy Barnevik of ABB and Jan Carlzon of SAS as examples of such Kantian leaders in a manner typical of recent management literature.

This underlines the point made above that in organizational theory of this kind it is only senior managers who are leaders in the Kantian sense of being fully autonomous individuals. They allow others to share in this autonomy. Participation becomes participating in the leadership of the leaders. Kant himself, in his discussion of a "realm of ends", which was for him an ideal world of reasoning individuals, provides the basis for a theory which then, contrary to his own view, understands an organization as a systemic whole. The organization as such could not, according to Kant, be considered a systemic whole and the thought that it could "ruled" by the "reason" of such a whole would have been absurd, to say the least. Kant developed systemic thinking in order to support the scientific method in its understanding of nature's laws. To do this he split nature as system and reason, where the autonomy of nature was purely hypothetical.

The authors treated in the last chapter, however, have taken the further step of arguing that natural systems actually are living "wholes" and now attribute the reasoning characteristics of the autonomous individual to such systems. It is precisely their insistence on understanding the individual leader as autonomous that leads them to understand the wholeness of the self-organizing system as such a "reasoning" autonomy. From the perspective of systems thinking, when social and cultural systems are thought of as wholes with humans as the individual agents there is no other possibility than to attribute some sense of ethical responsibility and stability to the organization as a "whole".

The movement has been, then, from

- Kant's understanding of an ideal "realm of ends" ruled by universal laws established by rational individuals;
- to understanding the organized ends of rational individuals as a "whole", that is, as if it were a system in nature;
- to understanding the systemic self-organizing of ends (values and norms) as cultures;
- to understanding cultures as having *inherent* values determining in systemic self-organization the ends individuals strive toward;
- to understanding systemically self-organizing cultures as autonomous;
- to understanding organizations as autonomous just as individuals are ("This utility company polluted our ground water.").

We come full circle to an understanding of authors like Senge:

> The sense of connectedness and compassion characteristic of individuals with high levels of personal mastery naturally leads to a broader vision. . . . Individuals committed to a vision beyond their self-interest find they have energy not available when pursuing narrower goals, as will organizations that tap this level of commitment.
>
> (Senge, 1990: 171)

Thinkers such as Senge, in taking the perspective of social interaction as systemic self-organization, clearly view the rationality of the autonomous individual as a "synergy of reason and intuition" on the basis of which that individual should understand "connectedness to the world" and "commitment to the whole" (ibid.: 171). In the next section I explore the implications of such thinking.

Participation in "living" systems: harmony and inherent values

How is it that management and organization theorists have increasingly come to be unable to resist the notion of an overriding system or "whole" in which we participate and, even further, to attribute the powers of autonomous action to them, regarding them in some sense as individuals?

The continuing influence of positivism

The first example of simply applying scientific research in the modernist paradigm to the level of society is commonly referred to as positivism. It is regarded as having begun with Jean d'Alembert's statement in the "Discours preliminaire" of the *Encyclopédie* that, just as in the physical sciences, the appropriate method in the social sciences should be a preoccupation with "positive truths". "All occupations with purely speculative subjects should be excluded . . . as profitless pursuits" (cited in Golembiewski, 1989: 28). This in effect separates "is" and "ought", "fact" and "value". One can find such splits in the work of authors such as H.A. Simon (1960). The moral aspect, the value, was diminished as an object of interest and finally went unrecognized. Friedrich A. Hayek noted in his treatment of positivism, however, that the positivists could not in the end avoid value constraints in providing direction for their own programme. Almost predictably, positivistic thinkers soon began a quasi-religious mysticism, which eventually included the "discovery" of a "spiritual power" that would "choose the direction to which the national forces are to be applied . . ." (Hayek, 1941: 127). This spiritual power was somehow capable of choosing values itself. What began as a movement to free the minds of men from the tyranny of the past became, in the extreme, the mindless following of a spiritual power guiding the nation.

Hayek also described the encouragement of "methodological collectivism". This was the tendency to treat concepts of society as "wholes", as "definitely given objects about which we can discover laws by observing their behavior as wholes" (Hayek, 1943: 41). This was the only way in which the required direction for the action of the masses on the individual could be known. This was the only way for the positivists to retain control: the methodological collectivism could take only the direction that it is given. This type of thinking appeared in management theory in Frederick W. Taylor's concept of scientific management as summed up in his often repeated statement: "In the past man has been first: in the future the system must be first." As another theorist of scientific management put it:

> Measurement is in fact the criterion of genuinely scientific research. When measurement is possible, science at last has arrived; until measurement is possible research is of dubious merit and even of questionable legitimacy. Facts, research, and measurement are assumed to answer questions not only of "What is the case?" but of "What should be done?" In the spirit of the scientific maxim, "When we can measure, then we know", the assumption is made that measurement "solves problems".
>
> (Waldo, 1948: 58)

Today, with the new scientific insights around theories of systemic self-organization we are faced again with the question of the relation of the natural and social sciences. As Mainzer puts it:

> ... theoretical models of society may have a normative function influencing the future behaviour of its agents. A well-known example was the social Darwinism of the 19th century which tried to explain the social development of mankind as a linear continuation of biological evolution. Actually, that social theory initiated a brutal ideology legitimating the ruthless selection of the social, economic, and racial victors of history. Today, it is sometimes fashionable to legitimate political ideas of basic democracy and ecological economy by biological models of self-organization. But nature is neither good nor bad, neither peaceful nor militant. These are human evaluations. Biological strategies over millions of years have operated at the expense of myriads of populations and species with gene defects, cancer, etc., and have, from a human point of view, perpetrated many other cruelties. They cannot deliver the ethical standards for our political, economic, and social developments.
>
> (Mainzer, 1997: 320)

Thus the very roots of management theory in positivism put the focus on changing *whole* organizations. In a recent (1995) book entitled *Organizational Epistemology* von Krogh and Roos approach organizational knowledge on the basis of the theory of self-reference in autopoiesis, citing F. Varela and N. Luhmann. But I would argue that they misunderstand both authors, especially Luhmann's warning that "the theory of self-producing, autopoietic systems can be transferred to the domain of action systems only if one begins with the fact that the elements composing the system can have no duration" (Luhmann, 1995: 121). Luhmann, like Parsons in his later thought, clearly refutes the possibility that the individual can be the unit, or element, in systemic self-organization. But in their book von Krogh and Roos provide an example of what Mainzer means by applying a non-linear theory developed at the level of the natural sciences in a linear continuation to the social level. It is in effect a theory of action composed of elements with "no duration", no temporal quality. They suggest for instance that organizational knowledge development may be impeded if the process becomes different across scales, which they label self-difference. They cite the example of a vision statement developed by the top management team in a large firm.

> The object was, obviously, to get all organizational members to live up to the vision, thus the intention was to create a self-similar principle: the fundamental principles should be similar on all levels in the organizations.
>
> (von Krogh and Roos, 1995: 154)

The authors were then appalled when it became "embarrassingly evident" that the vision statement was not only virtually unknown further down the hierarchy, but also a source of ridicule. Their conclusion: "Thus, the principles embodied in the vision statement were not similar across scales" and "because the vision statement in some instances was intentionally obscured by some managers, it became de facto self-different" (ibid.). They go on to explain that in organizations there are rules for the usage of certain words that give meaning. These rules are dependent on the social context in which the word appears.

> Rules for the usage of words are dynamic, especially in companies where little formal control is exerted. Managers frequently discard distinctions, introduce new distinctions, use old distinctions in new situations, put new words in new contexts, and use distinctions in a metaphorical sense, etc. Individuals and groups develop their own language that, in turn, influences other individuals' and groups' actions. If such rules, that is, the linguistic tradition, are different for the individuals, groups, departments and the organization, then organizational knowledge development will be impeded. Similarity across scales, on the other hand, reduces complexity and facilitates organizational knowledge development.
>
> (ibid.: 155)

The way in which von Krogh and Roos are "applying" self-organization and self-reference to management theory is a return to the linearity of the positivist application of science to the social level. Again, there is the concern for "wholes" which must be controlled across the organization. These wholes are simply given as the strategies or vision statements of top management.

In the following sections I would like to look at three perspectives on such transcendental or overriding wholes: new concepts of nature, the argument that cultures have inherent values and the attribution of the qualities and action of an autonomous individual to the systemic self-organization of social organizations.

New concepts of nature

Both the mysticism based on the collective methodologies of wholes, which Hayek argues we have inherited from positivism, and the mysticism which Bateson (see Chapter 2) resigns himself to as the ultimate consequence of a third loop of learning in second-order cybernetics, have been the source of multiple and varied appeals to transcendental or all-encompassing "wholes" which influence and to various degrees determine our actions. The scope of such thinking ranges from New Age appeals to mythology, oriental wisdom and various tribal understandings of belonging to attempts to rethink the tradition of metaphysics, such as Wilber's (1995) concept of an absolute spirit similar to that which the German philosopher Hegel failed to demonstrate in order to establish his philosophy as an all-encompassing system of thought. Such attempts do not appeal to systems thinking but are often used as powerful analogies by those who do. They have in common the appeal to escaping the "selfish" aspect of the autonomous individual which we found in the previous chapter to be shared by those basing their concept of the all-encompassing whole on systemic self-organization.

This escape from aspects of the self is the basis for the appeal to ethics in both the mystical and systemically self-organizing references to "wholes". It is an escape from the "grasping self". "The goal of the self is to bring inside the boundaries all of the good things while paying out as few goods as possible and conversely to remove to the outside of the boundaries all of the bad things while letting in as little bad as possible" (Varela, Thompson and Rosch, 1995: 243). Moving to participation step by step means letting go of the grasping self and achieving a concern for others which is present in all fellow participants. For Varela this discipline is to be found in Buddhism. Other thinking of this type attempts to escape the paradox at the core of the experience of the self and not-self by taking a macrocosmic perspective, for example, Kauffman's being "at home in the universe". I find it important to mention the ethical perspective here because it represents a basis for comparison to the ethical position that I will be arguing for in Part II of this book. I will attempt to outline an ethics based on an evolutionary theory of action that can be understood very much in terms of the everyday life of organizations. The paradox of self-organization to be treated in Part II, that of participative self-organization, does not rely on systems thinking and is very different to the kind of paradox-free sphere described, for example, by Wheatley:

> The world of dissipative structures is rich in knowledge of how the world works, of how order is sustained by growth and change. . . . If we plod across this new territory, heads down, our attention focussed on specific features of the land, we may fail to look up and take in the whole of things here. We may fail to sense how life is maintained and how things work together, and we may fail to see the unifying process that embraces great paradoxes. I find pleasure in letting these concepts swirl about me. Like clouds, they appear, transform, and move on.
>
> (Wheatley, 1992: 99)

> The more I read about self-renewing systems, the more I marvel at the images of freedom and possibility they evoke. This is a domain of independence and interdependence, of processes that support forces we've placed in opposition – change and stability, continuity and newness, autonomy and control – and all in an environment that tests and teases and disturbs and, ultimately, responds to changes it creates by changing itself. The traditional contradictions . . . all whirl into a new image that is very ancient – the unifying dance of the great polarities of the universe.
>
> (ibid.: 98–9)

Again it is us who have, as selfish individuals, brought opposition and conflict into processes which influence nature's forces. Such thinking diverts the discussion of ethics away from the social interaction of our everyday lives. Leadership becomes a question of knowing the "hidden" secrets of science in order to achieve control in terms of the "laws" of this all-encompassing whole. This is often referred to as being consistent with Ashby's (1952) theory of requisite variety, for example in Hunt (1996: 15):

> ... the stratified-systems perspective argues that complexity in the leader must be consistent with that in the organization. Therefore, as the task becomes more complex, so must the leader's cognitive complexity develop to provide an appropriate "match".

Such thinking is also typical of those referring to the new leadership emerging in the internet economy, such as McCarthy's (2000: 3) statement that "eLeadership adds another layer of complexity that companies must address in their transition to eBusiness".

Moving from nature as an all-encompassing whole to cultures with inherent values

Earlier in this chapter, I introduced Parsons' concepts of value and norm which were the basis of the functionalism of his theory of social systems. At this point Parsons still saw the individual as the unit of the social system. The regularities of form that can be observed are those of function. "This organization of action elements is, for purposes of the theory of action, above all a function of the relation of the actor to his situation . . ." (Parsons, 1951: 5). The social scientist objectively observes and describes cultural systems as the regularity of functions. The system is described as dysfunctional should one or more of the actors not fulfill their function.

What is now important is the move from the kind of first-order cybernetic system Parsons is describing (where there is an external observer) and the move Parsons himself later made away from assuming that the individual is the unit of the system. In the new concepts of nature based on second-order cybernetics, whereby there is a shift to the notion of an all-encompassing whole in order to supposedly bring the external observer into the system, the question of culture and the transmission of values and norms becomes problematic. As pointed out in the last section, theorists of systemic self-organization of social systems are then forced somehow to view the "heritage" (which Parsons referred to) as the transmission of values which are *inherent* in the all-encompassing whole. Thus the move becomes possible from the notion of the dysfunctional as seen by the external observer to the notion of not participating in the system, as was the case for the organizational theorists treated in previous chapters.

Frederick (1995) has presented an ethics developed on such a basis: an all-encompassing nature with inherent values as the basis for a theory of cultures with inherent values. After reviewing traditional views of the concept of value, Frederick develops, on the basis of his resonance with second-order cybernetics and some complexity theorists, his concept of "original values".

> The original values of business arise as manifestations of natural evolutionary processes. The forms they take reflect the operation of basic physical processes in the universe. This evolutionary embeddedness gives them their distinctive function in organized life and causes them to be an essential component in sustaining life itself. Although . . . these values have an acquired cultural meaning, they are rooted firmly in biophysical and biochemical processes that gave them their first significance. As values, they are emergent from, or extrusions of, these natural processes, only subsequently being assigned a conceptual and culturally symbolic significance.
>
> (Frederick, 1995: 27)

These original values in business are for Frederick, the defining beliefs, relationships, and judgmental processes that make business what it is as a human institution. He identifies three values at the "most fundamental, archetypal level, as economizing, growth and systemic integrity. They make business what it is by being combined and expressed in the minds and operations of a firm's owners, managers, employees, and associated constituencies" (ibid.: 26).

In discussing the structure or form that these values necessarily take on, Frederick introduces a concept of culture which he considers to be radically different from that of anthropologists.

> Clearly, there is a quantum difference between the anthropologist's idea of "culture" and what is popularly called "corporate culture". In spite of this lapse, an understanding of business culture need not rest on a superficial misuse of this powerful concept.
>
> (ibid.: 82)

He understands culture from three perspectives:

- Culture is conceived as consciously transmitted, cumulative, symbolic learning, which enjoys an established continuity with pre-cultural, naturalistic processes and forces. ". . . culture is only another manifestation of the regularity and patterning that accompany the operation of thermodynamic laws" (ibid.: 83).

- Culture is an amalgam of experience-based efforts to solve perceived problems as its human carriers adapt to their environment. "Culture is also a repository – a vast memory storage bank – of previous efforts to cope with the environment" (ibid.: 83).
- Culture gives form and meaning to human values. "Because culture is a phase in natural evolution and because culture has adaptive functions, it extrudes values that reflect human experience in coping with the environment that either sustains or diminishes life" (ibid.: 84).

Such a confident and optimistic presentation of the possibility of participating in this all-encompassing movement of evolution almost succeeds in diverting attention completely from the questions raised in the first chapter of this book: how does it come about that a company culture with thousands of employees is the source of polluting the ground water of their own neighbourhoods? How is it that the employees in such corporate cultures are seen by Sennett as having lost their sense of identity, character and community? In the final chapter of his book Frederick poses these questions himself and, inevitably, given the basis of his notion of an all-encompassing whole, finds the blame in the individual:

> Greed, selfishness, ego-centeredness, disregard of the needs and well-being of others, a narrow or nonexistent social vision, and ethnocentric managerial creed imposed on non-industrial cultures, a reckless use of dangerous technologies, an undermining of countervailing institutions . . .
>
> (ibid.: 277)

Faced with the problem of reconciling this with his concept of culture Frederick formulates the typical "both . . . and" position:

> It may be possible to visualize yet another, even broader and more inclusive realm of valuing phenomena that lends additional normative meaning to business activities. That more extensive value complex is the "culture of ethics. . . . This culture of ethics – this normative seedbed – evolves and functions alongside the societally vital economizing, technologizing, and ecologizing values, and because it is supportive of those values, it carries humankind along against the tides of entropy.
>
> (ibid.: 280–1)

This "both . . . and" argument with its vague "added-on" formulation of a system is considered adequate by Frederick to enable him to cope with the injustice he describes. In the next section on G.H. Mead's theory of cult values I would like to turn to a position that finds the source of the injustices in such a theory of inherent values, which Frederick so enthusiastically advocates.

Challenging the theory of inherent values: conflicts between cult values and functional values

In an essay published in 1914, entitled "The psychological bases of internationalism", Mead reflected on the way in which nations were coming to be spoken of "as if" they were autonomous individuals. He drew attention to the fact that in the midst of the First World War *all* the nations involved were justifying their engagement as self-defence. It struck Mead that self-defence is usually attributed to individuals and not to whole collectives. Furthermore, he wondered about the nature of the process in which all the nations involved were appealing to individual self-defence and in so doing motivating their citizens to give their lives.

Mead's answer was that "Nations, like individuals, can become objects to themselves only as they see themselves through the eyes of others. Every appeal to public sentiment is an effort to justify oneself to oneself" (Mead, 1914: 604). In other words, all of the nations involved in the war had to identify the same cause of the war, namely, self-defence, because at that time it was the only justifiable cause of war. However, Mead argued that, behind the cover of the self-defence justification, there were other much more irrational "cult" values that were driving people to aggressive action.

> There has arisen among the militaristic groups a revival of the cult of Napoleon with an appeal to the glory of combat ... Out of the warlike birth of the German Empire under its hegemony, there has arisen a cult of the strong-armed state ... But today there is not a German who can catch the public ear who will recognize that the cult of Treitschke and von Bernhardi has an echo in the German nation.
>
> (ibid.)

The argument, then, is that the process of individualizing a collective and treating it "as if" *it* had overriding motives or values, such as self-defence or the glorification of combat, amounted to a process in which the collective constituted a "cult". The members of such a "cult" found their behaviour being driven by the cult's values.

Mead saw both ethical and psychological aspects in this process. There was an ethical aspect because of the potential conflict between the cult values and other values that members of the cult might subscribe to. What interested Mead more, however, was the psychological aspect. "It is the feeling of enlarged personality, of the national amour propre, a feeling not so much of what people have or want as of what they are, that militarism supports in national life" (ibid.: 607). The values actually motivating war and the preparation for it reflected attitudes and states of mind. Mead was arguing, therefore, that "cult values", such as self-defence and the glorification of combat, reflected an idealization of the collective, imagined as an enlarged personality that justified the terrible actions people took. The idealization functions to divert people's attention from the ethics of their daily actions. What Mead means by "cult values" then is collective idealizations that divert attention from the detail of interaction in the living present.

Mead made a major change in his theory of "cult values" in an essay published in 1923. He continued to focus on the phenomenon of the diversion of attention to the ideal but he no longer referred to it as "enlarged personality". He recognized that the diversionary function of cult values related not only to negative ideals, which he had cited in the earlier article, but also to positive ideals such as family values, democracy and criminal justice. The influence of cult values in social interaction was thereby generalized and became a major key to Mead's overall understanding of social interaction.

> The cult value of the institution is legitimate only when the social order for which it stands is hopelessly ideal. . . . There are no absolute values. There are only values which, on account of incomplete social organization, we cannot as yet estimate.
>
> (Mead, 1923: 238)

Mead argued that cult values "are the most precious part of social heritage" (ibid.: 237) and that they are functionalized in ordinary everyday action. In other words, idealized values emerge in the historical evolution of any institution and these are ascribed to the institution itself. These idealized cult values become functional values in the everyday interactions between members of the institution. For example, the cult value of a hospital might be to "provide each patient with the best possible care". However, such a cult value has to be repeatedly functionalized in many unique specific situations throughout the day. For example, whether "best possible care" means two doses of medication per day or three, whether a particular procedure is affordable or not. In other words, as soon as cult values become functional values in real daily interaction, conflict arises and it is this conflict that must be negotiated by people in their practical interaction with each other. This is how they are continuously constructing the future.

Mead emphasizes functional values to alert us to the dangers of thinking that cult values are the values of the personalized institution or system that are directly applied as overriding universal norms, conformity to which constitutes the requirement of continuing membership of the institution. This is the usual understanding of a "cult", namely an idealized group with values to which individuals must conform if they are not to be judged selfish or sinful, thereby raising questions about their continued membership of the group. I would argue that when organizations are said to be caring, or to have a soul, then the organization is being idealized as a cult. Instead of focusing attention on the daily, necessarily conflictual functionalization of cult value, this idealization of the organization involves the direct application of the cult values as universal norms abstracted from daily life and people are said to be selfish when they do not conform to them.

Here Mead clearly rejects any theory of "inherent values", such as that espoused by Frederick, discussed earlier in this chapter, and any type of overriding or all-encompassing whole or system, such as those proposed by the management theorists reviewed in Chapters 3 and 4. All cult values, those esteemed by various groups in society as good or bad, as harmful or beneficial, are seen as grist to the mill of everyday social interaction in which they become functional values as the source of the conflicts which both sustain identity and bring about change. Cult values are a vital part of the past and, as they are functionalized in the movement of the living present, social and personal identities are recreated and potentially transformed as people together construct their future. In this chapter, I have been arguing that the direct application of cult values, of universal idealizations ascribed to collectives understood as if they were individuals and to be applied in all circumstances, silences people into conformity. In Part II, I will be developing further the notion of functional values as the articulation of cult values in the context of daily life and the essential negotiation of conflict that this involves.

Mead posed the same question as management theorists did throughout the twentieth century: "Can the world of natural science provide objects for the world of social and moral conduct?" (ibid.: 234). To answer this question, Mead turned to the philosophical tradition that attempted an answer using the concept of teleology. Teleology asks the question: what is causing the movement of a phenomenon? In relation to human action one can put the questioning a number of different ways. What is causing or motivating the striving of human beings? What is the end that is causing or motivating the striving? Philosophers have traditionally sought to answer the question of teleology in terms of a universal, fixed end state. In the discussion here on cult values, this kind of answer amounts to positing that the cult values themselves are the motive or cause of human striving. Mead rejects, as does modern science, this kind of answer to the teleology question.

He argues that those who appeal directly to cult values in determining action in the present are appealing to teleology as it was understood in the past, as some sort of perfect or merely possible world "by fastening its vision upon a clearly outlined distant goal" (ibid.: 241):

> The psychological technique of maintaining such a cult is the presentation by the imagination of a social situation free from the obstacles which forbid the institution being what it should be, and we organize social occasions which in every way favor such a frame of mind.
>
> (ibid.: 235)

Mead's argument is very close to Marx's concept of alienation, whereby the substructure of a society is split off from a superstructure that provides a false sense of legitimacy. But what Mead wants to argue in taking up the theme of teleology is very different. Coming back to his question about whether the world of natural science can provide objects for the world of social and moral conduct, Mead argues that the social world can learn from the scientific to rediscover the *question of causality linked to teleology*. Like Hayek, mentioned earlier in this chapter, Mead is pointing to the need to move away from "collective methodologies":

> Scientific method is not teleological in the sense of setting up a final cause that should determine our action, but it is categorical in insisting upon our considering all factors in problems of conduct, as it is in demanding the recognition of all of the data that constitute the research problem.
>
> (ibid.: 233)

Cult values set up ends, institutions and values that are considered to be inviolable. Mead points out that the causality of teleology, that is, the motivation arising in striving for the good, will necessarily lead to the articulation of cult values as functional values which will in turn necessarily lead to the everyday conflicts of social interaction and not to a false sense of harmony. There are, for example, no overriding systems in which blame disappears (Senge, 1990) and no overriding caring soul (Lewin and Regine, 2000).

Mead focuses on the question that the concept of teleology is asking, i.e. the causality of the ends or purposes that we set, while at the same time distancing himself from the answers given in the past. This is also the main focus in contrasting some complexity theorists and systems thinking in Stacey, Griffin and Shaw, 2000. It is in the participative self-organization of social conflict that values emerge in present experience. I will return to this in Chapter 6.

Summary

In this chapter, I have described how a theory of culture was developed in which culture came to be thought of as an autonomous system of values and norms, which individuals internalized and to which they conformed. Leaders were also conceived of as autonomous individuals who could manipulate and control the autonomous system of culture. It is important to note how this constitutes Kantian "both . . . and" thinking in that there is both an autonomous system and an autonomous individual leader. As is typically the case with "both . . . and" thinking, there is no sense of any paradox in thinking that a system that is supposed to be autonomous is nevertheless thought to be controlled by an individual who is autonomous – the paradox is eliminated in a taken-for-granted way. This theory of culture and leadership was imported into thinking about organizations and subordinated to the dominant paradigm of control.

This theory of culture and leadership has ethical implications that are not usually made explicit. The perspective of the autonomous individual brings with it a particular approach to ethics. Ethical behaviour is understood to be determined by the reasoning individual who tests proposed actions against universal ethical imperatives, which are not affected by natural or social contingencies. Reasoning individuals who think and test their proposed actions against universal principles are truly free. However, individuals who permit their actions to be determined by sensuous desires or personally/socially contingent aims become subject to the laws of nature and so are not free. As this kind of ethics is taken up in relation to organizations an additional implication arises. Because organizations are thought of as autonomous cultural systems, like individuals, the need for ethical choice of action is applied to such reified organizations. Organizations too are required to test their actions against ethical universals. Nowadays, then, ethics as it relates to organizations amounts to *thought*, that is, "scientifically" testing actions against hypothetical universal principles, *apart* from the *action* that follows it. It is important to note that this dominating view of ethics removes the consideration of ethics from the ordinary everyday interactions of people constituting an organization because the ethical universals are not dependent in any way on the social or natural worlds. Ordinary, feeling individuals relating to each other disappear from the sphere of ethics.

Kant's notion of ethics in which the rational, free person tests his or her action against universal ethical principles brings with it an egalitarian view of organizations. All people are autonomous individuals and all who act ethically are individually testing their actions against the same ethical universals. Each person should, therefore, be acting in such a way as to establish laws for an ideal organization or society, that is, one in which everyone is testing their actions against the same ethical universals. The test of an action is against some ideal and it is ideal in that it is independent of the laws of nature, including the passions of the body, and of any particular social arrangements or circumstances existing at the time. In organizations today this kind of thinking is reflected in the taken-for-granted way in which leaders are supposed to set out a vision, that is, an idealized future for the organization, and then empower people, that is, drive leadership down through the hierarchy. In other words they are supposed to allow others to share in their autonomy so that participation becomes participation in the leadership of the leaders. Participation becomes participation in an idealized systemic whole. Those proclaiming organizations to be living systems then link such systemic wholes to the forces of nature, sometimes using the complexity sciences to justify the link. Participation in turn becomes participation in this living whole, often understood as a kind of mystical union. The ethical and moral responsibility of individuals is related to this mystical whole rather than to the everyday contingencies of ordinary life in organizations. Culture comes to be thought of as an overriding, autonomous, harmonious whole to which "good" people must conform. The notion of participation as ordinary interaction between people and the notion of ethical and moral behaviour as our accounting to each other tends to be lost.

Mainstream theories see culture in organizations, then, as transcendental, autonomous, living wholes in which individuals participate and to which they submit. I argue that this view of culture is an attempt to escape the "selfish" implications of the focus on the autonomous individual. Participation comes to mean letting go of the grasping self and submerging in the transcendental whole. The selfish aspect of the autonomous individual is thought to bring opposition and conflict, whereas participation in the whole leaves behind all conflict. This leads to the dangers of mindless following, and remains true even when there is free consent to such following. The idealization of human nature that this involves is quite obvious, particularly when the harmonious whole is linked to nature and leaders are understood to know the hidden secrets of nature as the basis of the control they are supposed to exercise over the all-encompassing whole.

Mead talks about this kind of approach as a feeling of enlarged personality and he pointed to the way in which this kind of thinking diverts attention from what people are actually doing, focusing on some idealization. For him this constitutes a cult. In his early thinking Mead saw such cult values only as negative, but later realized that this evades the paradox between cult values and the functional values expressed in our everyday actions. As functional values ideals are not simply applied to determine current actions irrespective of particular social or natural contingencies. The psychological technique of maintaining a cult is to present to the imagination a situation free from the ordinary obstacles of social life or nature. Cult values set up idealized ends that are considered to be inviolable, a harmonious whole which everyone is forbidden to argue with and if anyone does they are immediately accused of selfishly introducing conflict. When we talk about organizational culture as harmonious wholes and leaders with visions, we are talking about organizations as cults. While we are not able to live without cult values, such as democracy, justice and love of neighbour for example, we need to be aware of the dangers of thinking that we can achieve conflict-free ethical behaviour through direct conformity to cult values. To understand the paradox of cult and functional values in everyday social interaction it is necessary to let go of the modernist concept of the autonomous individual which, as we have seen, leads necessarily to the elimination of the paradox; it is to this which I would now like to turn in Part II as an alternative sense of participation.

A key point I have been making in Part I about the perspective of systemic self-organization relates to the long tradition of thinking about human action in two ways. First, individuals are thought of as autonomous. Then the group, the social, society, culture, values, are all thought of as autonomous wholes, outside of the daily experience of human interaction, causing that interaction. There is a powerful tendency to idealize these wholes, so removing them even further from ordinary daily experience. This has major implications for ethics and the roles of leaders. Ethics becomes "both . . . and" in that there is an ethic for the autonomous individual and an ethic for the whole system. For the individual there is Kant's universal ethical imperative, but sight is lost of the hypothetical nature of this and how it is discovered in action. There is also a universal ethic for the idealized whole, cult values, which tend to be applied directly to action, losing sight of the need for deriving functional values in daily interaction. The result is an ethic requiring participation in an harmonious whole, an ethic of conformity, which displaces attention from the on-going responsibility and accountability we all have to each other in our daily lives. Moving from a systemic self-organization perspective to a participative one, therefore, has important implications for ethics.

Part II
Leadership and participative self-organization: participation in local interaction

Solang du Selbstgeworfenes fängst, ist alles
Geschicklichkeit und läßlicher Gewinn -;
erst wenn du plötzlich Fänger wirst des Balles,
den eine ewige Mitspielerin
dir zuwarf, deiner Mitte, in genau
gekonntem Schwung, in einem jener Bögen
aus Gottes großem Brückenbau:
erst dann ist Fangen-können ein Vermögen, -
nicht deines, einer Welt.

> (R.M. Rilke, cited by Hans Georg Gadamer in the beginning of
> *Wahrheit und Methode*, 1960)

As long as you go on catching what you yourself have thrown,
everything remains a matter of skill and casual gain -;
It is only when you suddenly become the catcher of the ball,
which an eternal fellow player
has thrown to you, to your core, in precise
and practiced rhythm, in one of those arcs
of the great bridges which God constructs;
only then does the ability to catch become a game, -
not yours, a world's.

> (Rilke, freely translated, DG)

The key distinction I am making in this book is that between systemic self-organization and participative self-organization. Such a distinction has become necessary because the concept of self-organization/ emergence has been so vigorously taken up, over the past two decades, in the social sciences, particularly in management and organization theories.

As I mentioned in Chapter 1, some natural complexity scientists, for example Kauffman (1995), are arguing that the concept of self-organization is the same as that developed by Kant over two hundred years ago. Others, including Prigogine and Goodwin (Prigogine and Allen, 1982; Prigogine and Stengers, 1984; Prigogine, 1997; Goodwin, 1997), claim that the concept of self-organization is a new one that signals the end of science as usual. What has happened in the social sciences is very similar (see Chapters 2 and 3). Some organization theorists who are taking up the complexity sciences, for example Marion (1999), claim that we are witnessing the rediscovery of Kant's theory of self-organization. Many of those applying cybernetic theory, especially second-order cybernetics, have taken ideas, including self-organization, from the complexity sciences to support their application of systems thinking to human organizations. Others apply the theory of autopoiesis.

For example, Capra (1996) and Wheatley (1999) think of organizations as living organisms. Then there are other writers, such as Luhmann (1967), who exclude the human subject from social systems altogether. They understand the human subject as a psychic system participating in the social system as such (Habermas and Luhmann, 1971: 317). Of course, these social systems, as systems of meaning, are also concerned with living processes, but the focus is on the autopoietic sustaining of social structure rather than the ordinary interaction of embodied human beings.

As I pointed out in Part I, despite their differences, those referred to in the previous paragraph agree on a concept of *participation*. They develop a theory of participation as the individual participating *in self-organization,* where it is a whole that is self-organizing. Participation then means taking part in a system outside of immediate, ordinary daily interaction between living bodies. This notion of participation as systemic self-organization is the key difference between what these authors are claiming complexity theory means for management and organization theory and the position my co-authors and I are taking in this series, *Complexity and Emergence in Organizations*. What we are drawing attention to is an approach that looks to analogies in the complexity sciences to develop a theory of communicative interaction between embodied human subjects and that implies a very different understanding of participation, namely, that participation *is* self-organization. Here, there is no self-organizing whole outside of immediate, ordinary daily interaction between living bodies. The difference between these two understandings of participation has far-reaching ramifications for understanding communication and conversation.

As soon as one understands participation as individuals participating in self-organizing wholes outside of ordinary interaction, it follows that each individual is split into "good" and "bad". An individual is "good" to the extent that he or she participates in the overriding values of the self-organizing whole and "bad" or "selfish" to the extent that he or she does not conform to the overriding values. Ethics becomes the giving up of individual, selfish and egoistic inclinations in order to participate in the self-organization of the system. The task in Part II of this book is to work out a basis for understanding participative self-organization as the process of sustaining and potentially transforming identity directly in participating in ordinary interaction between people. This requires developing a concept of participation that includes the embodied human being but is not limited to the modernist concept of the autonomous individual. The systemic self-organization theory of communication eliminates the subject, or is based on splitting the individual, because it is unable to deal with the paradox of observer and participant. This theory finds the relief of the convenient taken-for-granted "both ... and" described in previous chapters so that the individual can be both "inside" and "outside" of the system without any sense of paradox. In Part II, I move away from this concept of the autonomous individual and develop an understanding of experience as the paradoxical movement of self-organization which is the living present.

To understand better the difference it might be helpful to return to Table 1.1 in Chapter 1, which lists the differences between systemic and participative self-organization. However, there is a potential for misunderstanding that seems to be almost inevitable in making a list of two contrasting conceptual positions. There is a powerful tendency to look at such a comparison and interpret it as an "either ... or" position. You either have to think in terms of systemic self-organization or you have to shift your thinking to participative self-organization. These are then understood as mutually excluding, even antagonistic, positions. Alternatively, there is an equally powerful tendency to immediately subsume a comparison of the kind given in Figure 1.1 into "both ... and" thinking. In that case you specify the conditions in which it is sensible to think in terms of systemic self-organization and the conditions in which it is sensible to think in terms of participative self-organization. This then enables you to alternate between them. However, I am not setting the two notions of self-organization up as mutually exclusive nor am I suggesting that you can alternate between one or the other depending on the circumstances. Instead, I am trying to signal a movement in thought from one conceptual framework, which patterns thought into "*both* the autonomous individual *and* the collective system of interaction", to another conceptual framework that preserves the contradiction individual-collective but does so in a way that transforms the relationship between the two. Participative self-organization then becomes a new unity, paradoxically containing both individual and collective at the same time. They simultaneously form and are formed by each other. This movement avoids the elimination of paradox.

From the perspective of participative self-organization, I will explore an understanding of selves as emergent persons in social interaction, as an alternative to the modernist understanding of the individual as autonomous. This interaction is understood, in turn, as complex processes of relating. Such processes represent an understanding of experience as the movement of the living present, which is based on a radically different understanding of time to that of systemic self-organization. This temporal concept reveals a spontaneity in the emergence of the person which remains in the tradition of thought about human freedom that understands ethical responsibility and choice in terms of persons.

The chapters in this Part raise the following questions: Why is participative self-organization rather than systemic self-organization more useful in understanding of human interaction? Why does the notion of person help to make more sense of experience than that of the autonomous individual? Why do I argue for the theory of complex responsive processes rather than other theories of interaction? In the following chapters, I attempt to articulate an alternative to using systems thinking to understand organizations. Why? As I have indicated a number of times in Part I, the application of systems thinking is not simply an academic exercise. It is a matter of how power and ideologies are made undiscussable and manipulated.

Kant's genius was reflected in his contribution to supporting the emerging concepts of the individual and the scientific method which, under the banner of enlightenment, meant the end of the autocratic powers of state and church and the alleviating of human suffering. However, these same core ideas that Kant created have now themselves become powerful ideologies in Western thought. What is different in articulating experience in terms of complex responsive processes is that power and ideologies are no longer obscured, but are on the contrary always presumed to be a part of the themes organizing human experience. This experience is articulated as the on-going negotiation of power and conflicting understanding of values and as the co-creating of leadership that includes not only the admirable and exemplary, but the bullies and ruthless conspirators. All of these can be enacted in the movement of the living present, which is our experience. What can be different is that we begin to talk more openly about what is going on.

5 The emergence of persons as selves in society

- Social interaction without the concept of the autonomous individual
- The paradox of time and the emergence of persons
- Local interaction and the emergence of the person
- Complex responsive processes of relating: the movement of experience in the living present

We all have an everyday understanding of ourselves as individuals, as having a self, and we also refer to ourselves in practically the same sense as persons. We perceive ourselves as unique in many ways, in terms of personality, ability, appearance, background, potential, and so on. And of course the fact that we are going to die makes this sense of individuality most poignant. But this use of individual, self and person as referring to some kind of cellular unity began to be seriously thrown into question at the beginning of the twentieth century. Just as scientists succeeded in splitting the atom, various disciplines began to "split" the understanding of the individual. Both "atom" and "individual" have the root meaning of "that which cannot be divided". They had been considered the fundamental units of understanding, but with increasing complexity they were "taken apart", not only as the objects of the scientific method, but also across a broad scope of philosophical reflection.

This is the case, for instance, in the work of the German philosopher Karl Jaspers who, writing in 1931, comments on the focus of human freedom, the self. Jaspers is concerned with

> meaning in relation to the extant situation. It does not float in the void, related to a timeless observer. He will achieve the most decisive forecast who in the present has derived the profoundest knowledge from the experience of his own life. A man gains awareness of what he is through his selfhood in a world in which he plays an active part.
> (Jaspers, 1957: 223)

In other words, experience cannot be understood in terms of the individual alone but in terms of a world in which the individual "plays an active part". "All cannot be found in the individual." It is in the "tension between authority and freedom in which man as temporal life must remain . . ." (ibid.: 228). In this tension the only certain thing is the uncertainty of the possible. And this means for Jaspers that the tension between authority and freedom is characterized by the paradox of the known and the unknown.

> Consequently, there is, at any and every time, a point where the will to the future human existence concentrates itself; and, paradoxically enough, what we make out of the world is decided by each individual through the way in which he comes to a decision about himself in the continuity of his action.
>
> (ibid.: 225)

It is important to notice that Jaspers still holds on to the notion of the individual as the focus of freedom, "the way in which he comes to a decision about himself", but in the paradox this is only possible "in the continuity of his action". Jaspers formulates this unequivocally as the first quote above continues:

> A man gains awareness of what he is through his selfhood in a world in which he plays an active part. He is one who has learned that he completely loses insight into the general course of affairs if he tries to stand outside as a mere spectator aspiring towards a knowledge of the whole.
>
> (ibid.: 223)

George Herbert Mead, in the remarkable breadth of his thought, sought to bridge the natural and social sciences. He was specifically interested in going beyond understanding the individual as a given unit of interaction, which did not mean dividing the individual into parts to become the new units of understanding, but rather understanding the emergence of the individual in interaction. For Mead an expression such as "participative self-organization" would have been a tautology since he understood the term participation to mean organization and organization to mean "self" organization. Like Jaspers, he saw individuals coming to an understanding of themselves in the continuity of their action, in the world in which they play an active part, and he understood this as process, specifically self-organizing process. Going further than Jaspers, Mead argued that our actions lead to genuine novelty so that the world becomes a different world. While Jaspers talks about each individual deciding about himself in the continuity of his action and thereby determining what is made of the world, Mead talks about humans collectively changing the world in their acting and this changing world changing them. In the former case time is understood in a linear way, with the future being a projection of the past, but in the latter, there is a radically different concept of time in which the future, the changing world, is acting back on the past, the humans collectively changing the world, and all of this takes place in the present. This means that Mead sees a different paradox to that mentioned by Jaspers, for whom the paradox was one of freedom and authority based on a static notion of time. Mead sees evolution in terms of a temporal paradox in that the future is not simply the same as the past.

> In the undetermined future of action a new object, a new *terminus ad quem*, can arise, the necessity of which cannot be said to exist in the conditions to which it must conform. . . . The novel element may be very slight, especially in comparison with the given world within which it appears, but in the experience of the individual it was not involved as a necessity of its past. The statement of the abstract motions could not have included the necessity of the particular act. This amounts to the affirmation that all the novelties of living experience are as novelties essential parts in the universe; the fact that when they arose they were unpredictable means that in the universe as then existing they were not determinable, nor in the universe as then existing did there exist the conditions that were the sufficient reasons for their appearing.
>
> (Mead, 1938: 419–20)

For Mead participation in social interaction is not only the basis for the emergence of the identity of individuals but also for the novelty that emerges in the transformation of this identity. Note Mead's definition of novelty. For him, novelty is not necessarily some large change, but it is necessarily unpredictable. In other words, novelty is that which is not merely determined by the past. This is a point of major significance in thinking about organizations. Most people nowadays seem to think that it is necessary to manage novelty by first formulating values and simple rules that create the "right conditions" in which people will act to produce novel outcomes. In Mead's definition of novelty it is clearly impossible to specify in advance any rules, simple or complicated, that will lead to the kind of future novelty anyone may have decided upon in advance.

In this chapter, I first consider the problems created by the "splitting" of the individual as a unit for understanding organization and then turn to a detailed look at Mead's theory of emergence in participation. To get another perspective on this emergence, I will then take up an older tradition of thought that considers the individual as an emergent phenomenon, namely, that which views the "person" as mediating the stability and change that is our experience. I will then look at the implications of this thought in the light of the theory of complex responsive processes and the movement of the living present put forward in previous volumes of this series (Stacey, Griffin and Shaw, 2000; Stacey, 2001).

Social interaction without the concept of the autonomous individual

Jaspers and Mead had no problem in continuing to use the term "individual", in spite of their view that the individual could no longer be considered the fundamental unit of understanding human action. However, since their time, theorists in many different disciplines have come to see the concept of the "individual" as highly problematic, with some claiming that it supports a blinding ideology. This is expressed, for example by the cultural anthropologist Clifford Geertz:

> The Western conception of the person as a bounded, unique, more or less integrated motivational and cognitive universe, a dynamic center of awareness, emotion, judgment and action, organized into a distinctive whole and set contrastively against other such wholes and against a social and natural background is, however incorrigible it may seem to us, a rather peculiar idea within the context of the world's cultures.
>
> (Geertz, 1979: 229)

And the sociologist Norbert Elias has a similar view:

> We speak of the individual and his environment, of the child and the family, of individual and society, or of subject and object, without clearly reminding ourselves that the individual forms part of his environment, his family, his society. . . . Society, often placed in mental contraposition to the individual, consists entirely of individuals, oneself among them. Yet our conventional instruments for thinking and speaking are generally constructed as though

everything we experience as external to the individual were a thing, an "object", and moreover a stationary object. Concepts like "family" or "school" plainly refer to groupings of interdependent human beings, to specific figurations which people form with each other. But our traditional manner of forming these concepts makes it appear as if groupings formed by interdependent human beings were pieces of matter – objects of the same kind as rocks, trees or houses. . . . But this reifying mode of expression greatly hampers and may even prevent one from understanding the nature of sociological problems.

(Elias, 1970: 13–14)

I am here stressing the way in which both Mead and Elias moved away from the notion of the autonomous individual but, nevertheless, retained a notion of individuality as emerging in social interaction without appealing to any whole outside of that interaction. I want to distinguish this from other ways of thinking that also move away from the notion of the autonomous individual but in doing so retain a notion of a whole outside of direct social interaction, or radically deny the concept of individuality altogether.

Systems thinking as an example of the move away from the simple concept of the individual

Systems thinking applied to social systems has its roots in this "splitting" of the individual from the group/social. Talcott Parsons came upon the idea of using cybernetic thinking in terms of social action in collaboration with the anthropologist A.L. Kroeber (Kroeber and Parsons, 1958) who, as an observing scientist, had described the interaction of tribal groups as "cultures". Parsons, together with E.A. Shils (1951), used this coupling of culture with systems thinking to develop a theory of social action that separated the acting individual and the social system. This is a very clear example of what I have been referring to in previous chapters as the "both . . . and" manner of thinking, in which what would normally be taken as paradoxical is resolved by attributing validity to each side of the paradox, but not at the same time. First one and then the other are established as real. For Parsons these realities were the "everyday" acting individual, on the one hand, and the social system, on the other. We have come to take this manner of thinking for granted so that the idea of a system of social action that excludes that "part" of the individual to do with freedom or novel change, as well as that part to do with selfishness, that is, centring on the "ego" as opposed to the interests of the "system", is no longer seen as paradoxical in the sense suggested by either Jaspers or Mead.

However, as mentioned in Chapter 1, this "both . . . and" thinking is a potential intellectual trap because the concepts on both sides retain their character as substantive realities and become reified and isolated. As argued by Elias, each comes to be thought of as in a state of rest. We can notice this in the relief or "rest" we sense when confronted by a paradox and offered such a resolution. As we saw in the thought of the various organization theorists reviewed in Chapters 2 and 3, the "traditional" assumption of the autonomous individual is, thus, not questioned but remains the overriding concern in that it is the characteristic of the "good" individual that is seen as the unit of the functioning system. That which is split off becomes the problem and as such the source of blaming the "ordinary, everyday" individual who is both good and bad at the same time. The trap, in the end, is what I described in Chapter 1 as our world in which we accept *both* being the systems (our bodies, our social interaction, our language) *and* the victims of the systems in that we cannot articulate the paradoxical and contradictory goals that comprise the many facets of our lives as a unified world of experience. We experience ourselves as being part of diverse systems, and because of the habit of taking such splits for granted, we are increasingly inarticulate in the struggle to insist on the fact that they must be reflected as one world in the on-going transformation of how we understand our actions as ethical.

Systems thinking has, in this way, made a key contribution to the intellectual climate constituting the basis for the skeptical position taken by "post-modernist" writers. This skepticism claims that we must now realize that we live in multiple realities or universes that cannot be reconciled. Any sense of unity, or self, leading to paradoxes that cannot be resolved is therefore to be regarded as an illusion.

The social constructionist rejection of the individual

In the intellectual climate influenced by systems thinking, various social constructionist writers have also defined, as their point of departure, the blinding ideology of the individual in Western thought. In avoiding an easy resolution of our tendency to reify both the individual and society, social constructionist thought attempts to focus exclusively on the process of interaction in which society is co-created. Many writers see themselves forced, then, to deny any sense of attributing uniqueness or freedom to the individual. Many turn to Marx and some variation of his notion of process. Others return to thinkers who predate modernism in order to develop ideas that had come to be ignored in the rise of the new sense of self and the individual that characterized the Enlightenment.

An important example of a writer taking this last-named tack is John Shotter (1993a, 1993b) who returns to the rhetorical and ethical theory of the Renaissance writer G. Vico (1668–1744) as a basis for his theory of "conversational realities". In doing so Shotter finds a perspective from which he can bring into focus his critique of the rationalism and individuality of modernism. Shotter argues that the primary human reality is persons in ordinary, everyday conversation. It is in the "indeterminacy, undecidability and ambivalence, in which different people meet each other in the socially constructed encounters in everyday life, that political struggles are their most intense" (Shotter, 1993b: 38). Shotter develops a theory of "taking an active part" very close to that of Jaspers and Mead as mentioned above. He distinguishes "knowing that" and "knowing how" from a third kind of knowing. He refers to this third kind of knowing as "knowing from within" or "joint action". The first two kinds of knowing relate to the description of theories and causal succession, that is, "words already spoken". The third kind of knowing has to do with emergence, that is, "words in their speaking". In ordinary, everyday conversation we do not only choose our next words on the basis of predictions of others' next words. It is just as much that our words are evoked or provoked by the words others are speaking in the continuous, seamless way of conversation. This is very similar to the "continuity of action" that Jaspers refers to, but it avoids the temporal paradox that Mead speaks of as the basis for novelty. In talking of the "continuous, seamless way of conversation", there is an implication of timelessness in the present. In this way, Shotter loses Mead's notion of the time structure of the present, in which people acting in the present do so on the basis of their reinterpretation of their past and their expectations of their future.

Nevertheless, Shotter argues that social constructionism is about a "dialectical emphasis upon both our making of, and being made by, our own social realities" (Shotter, 1993a: 34). He describes a circular process "in which people, rooted in a background and making use of the linguistic resources it provides, act back upon those background circumstances (their 'world') to give or lend them further form or structure" (ibid.: 36) (see Figure 5.1).

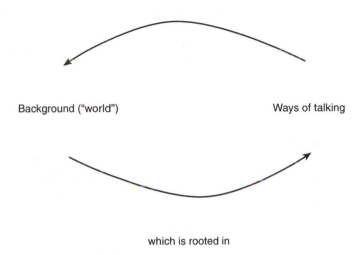

gives or lends further form or structure to

Background ("world")

Ways of talking

which is rooted in

Figure 5.1 *Social realities*

It is the iteration around this circle of social interaction that produces the emergent patterns that become the properties of the whole, which again structure the background.

The important question is whether there is a difference between the kind of whole that Shotter evokes and that which systems thinking has taken over from Kant's concept of systemic self-organization. Shotter, in attempting to define a different ethical position to Kant, develops an "as if" similar to that of systemic self-organization, that is, a whole as a regulative idea or hypothetical reality:

> ... in many of our ordinary, everyday life activities, as we must interlace our actions in with those of others, their actions will determine our conduct just as much as anything within ourselves. The final outcomes of such exchanges cannot strictly be traced back to the intentions of any of the individuals concerned; they must be accounted *as if* "external" to the participants concerned, *as if* a part of an "independent reality".
>
> (Shotter, 1993b: 174)

The individual he is arguing against is the self-contained and centred individual of the rational paradigm of action to be found in Kant and in Parsons, for example. In spite of this exclusion of the individual, however, Shotter retains the notion of a whole external to individuals. There is little difference, then, between his "whole" and Kantian wholes, even though his main interest is in grounding ethical accountability in the actions of people. He describes how the sense of what practical moral identity is really about is lost in both the thinking of most social constructionists and the thinking of those appealing to the rational autonomous individual.

Shotter's theory of joint action, then, repeats the argument of systemic self-organization, namely, that of the scientist who imputes a "mind" as hypothesis into the interaction. He points to Prigogine's work on dissipative structures (Shotter, 1993a: 164) as supporting what he views as communicative self-organization, but he does not refer to the paradox Prigogine draws attention to as the key characteristic of self-organization, that of order and disorder *at the same time*. Shotter's argument relies on the "both . . . and" position of modernism. In an "as if" manner *both* a whole is asserted of which one is a part and in terms of which one has ethical responsibility *and* on the other hand one is caught up in the seamless flow of everyday conversation without any accountable self. By avoiding treating this as a paradox (one is accountable in terms of the system but not accountable in the interaction) it becomes a present without past or future, so that the ethical basis of the individual referred to by Jaspers, where the individual is the source of freedom, and Mead, where the individual is the source of spontaneity and change, is ignored.

The radical denial of the individual found in social constructionist writers, coupled with the sense of multiple "as if" realities resulting from the systems perspective, has become an important factor in the increasingly radical denial of the "self" and a turn to Eastern thought, as well as to what the German philosopher Martin Heidegger referred to as "planetary thinking", by which he meant taking a perspective that incorporates modes of thinking from all cultures on the planet.

The search for an escape from Western individualism in Eastern thought

Varela, Thompson and Rosch's (1995) theory of the emergence of self is difficult for most of us to follow because it moves to a "both . . . and" position based on a proposed reconciliation of Western and Eastern thought. The basic premise is what the German philosopher Fichte suggested was the source of the idealist notion of self. (This will be further developed in the following section.) For Varela, Thompson and Rosch, as for Fichte, the self is not given prior to experience but emerges in interaction with the not-self. The not-self is the interacting others together with the task or purpose of their interaction. For Fichte and for Varela *et al.*, therefore, the emergent self is a rejection of any reified or objectivist notion of the individual self. However, the response to the collapse of an objective self (objectivism or reification) might be to assert the objective nonexistence of the self (nihilism), which rejects the existence of the relative (practical) self altogether. Varela *et al.* find a middle way in Buddhism as a philosophy and practice that appreciates the common source of both objectivism and nihilism. They also find an expression of this in Western thought in what Heidegger referred to as "planetary thinking":

> We are obliged not to give up the effort to practice planetary thinking along a stretch of the road, be it ever so short. Here too no prophetic talents and demeanor are needed to realize that there are in store for planetary building, encounters for which the participants are by no means equal today. This is equally true of the European and of the East Asiatic languages and, above all, for the area of a possible conversation between them. Neither one of the two is able by itself to open up this area and to establish it.
>
> (Heidegger, 1958: 213)

Varela, Thompson and Rosch cite the Japanese philosopher Nishitani Keiji's concept of the world as an objective or pre-given realm and the concept of the self as a pre-given knowing subject. Nishitani argues that to realize the fundamental instability or groundlessness in Heidegger's sense we must "slip out" of this subjective/objective dualism by shifting to the very disclosure of groundlessness. "Within this existential context, we can be said to *realize* groundlessness not only in the sense of *understanding* but also in the sense of *actualization*: human life or existence turns into a question, doubt, or uncertainty" (Varela *et al.*, 1995: 243).

The motivation for taking this perspective is an appeal to ethics. It is an escape from the "grasping self". "The goal of the self is to bring inside the boundaries all of the good things while paying out as few goods as possible and conversely to remove to the outside of the boundaries all of the bad things while letting in as little bad as possible" (ibid.: 246). This thinking moves the "student" step by step, as a discipline, to letting go of the grasping self and achieving unconditional compassion, that concern for others which is present in all people. The parallel to the thinking of, for instance Senge, in the splitting of the self into a good and selfish individual is evident, and the planetary dimension resonates, for instance, with Wheatley and others. It attempts to escape the paradox at the core of the experience of the self and not-self by taking a macrocosmic perspective, and it also has this in common with Kauffman's (1995) expression of being "at home in the universe". Seen from this perspective it is we, as grasping selfish individuals, who have brought opposition and conflict into the processes of nature. Contemplation of this perspective is offered as inspiration to endure a world in which others who do not share that perspective continue to ignore the possibility of participating in nature's true harmony.

Planetary thinking replaces dealing with the paradoxes emerging as ethical conflicts in our everyday lives. Also, it is difficult if not impossible to evaluate and compare the notions of paradox in Eastern cultures without the lived experience of these cultures and their history. The "both . . . and" position becomes one of my experience as opposed to a completely unknown as the "other". This is of course what Varela and his co-authors are suggesting, not viewing it as the "both . . . and" manner of thought but rather as a kind of cleansing journey into complete otherness. This is closely related to the tendency of others who reject both systems thinking and the ideology of the individual and turn, for example, to mythology and metaphysics as an alternative to dealing with the paradox of the world we experience.

Before turning to an alternative way of thinking to the above, I would like to consider briefly the influence that research on the brain has exercised in creating the intellectual climate in which thinkers have taken the positions just reviewed.

The influence of brain research in rejecting the notion of the self

Advocates of cognitivist positions, such as Varela, have of course moved beyond the simpler forms of cognitivism based on brain research in the earlier part of the twentieth century. That research established the first direct connections between sensory organs and neural activity, leading to metaphors of "lenses" and "inner worlds". We came to think of our theories as mental models of the world, as lenses that "we" as selves could change to gain different insights into "reality". More recent research and the theories it spawned, for example, those of McCulloch

(1965), Minsky (1985) and Dennett (1978, 1991), are both influenced by mainstream systems thinking, sometimes including complexity, and are themselves contributing to the argument that any notion of self is an illusion. Again we have *both* the everyday individual with, for "practical" purposes, the "illusion" of being or having a self, and the scientific position that the brain, analogous to colonies of termites, can be fully understood without recourse to any such concept. Minsky, the founder of the Artificial Intelligence Laboratory at MIT, states unequivocally that "according to the modern scientific view there is simply no room at all for 'freedom of the human will'" (Minsky, 1985: 306). He replaces the unity of the self with countless little agents, each mindless on its own, which make up what he refers to as the "society of mind". Dennett (1991) draws an analogy from his observation of ants, termites and hermit crabs to the way that we infer human selfhood. The elaborate structures built by ants and termites seem to reflect the planning and supervision of a single mind. He refers to others (e.g. Marais, 1937) who have imputed a soul to ant colonies. But for Dennett there is no self inside the individual to direct its various and complex functions. He substitutes for this illusion of the self a "center of narrative gravity" around which we spin our tales about ourselves. Again we find radical pluralism with millions of agents but, as Erich Harth (1993: 122) has commented, "In the process of demystifying the brain, Dennett has mystified the ant colony". The same can be said of attempts to explain interaction in organizations by inferring an overriding causality to them as "learning organizations", as having a "soul" or the other forms of all-encompassing transcendent wholeness mentioned in the previous chapter.

Of course, it is one question whether research into the human brain provides analogies discounting the notion of a unified self, and quite another whether such research yields results that factually contradict the possibility of such a concept. If, for instance, we take the metaphor of the lens as the "eye" of the brain, through which it "sees reality", we are implying that there is a unifying "self" or "I" behind the lens, which can change such lenses *in order to* have other insights into the "reality out there". The phrase "in order to" is very important. It implies the striving toward a goal, which is in some way known before changing the lens, even if what is perceived after changing it cannot be known. Such a unified action on the part of the brain is what Hume called into question. He very effectively undermined this view with his scepticism, demonstrating that the notion of self was based only on a series of associations, not on any underlying cause–effect causality. This is in essence the same argument now being presented in a more sophisticated form by writers such as Minsky and Dennett. But the causality of "in order to" is different from that of cause–effect. It is a causality of final causes or teleology, as treated in a previous volume of this series (Stacey, Griffin and Shaw, 2000). Skepticism would imply no unified self on which to base any notion of choice, freedom or ethics. Coming back to the metaphor of changing lenses, this would mean that it makes no difference which lens is used; any given choice could be explained by chance occurrences of cause and effect.

Is the lens metaphor adequate as a metaphor for our experience of ourselves knowing the world? It seems to imply the "both . . . and" argument that we are, on the one hand, knowing subjects, knowing and applying what we know, and on other hand, inhabitants of a world of multiple and unlinked interpretations. Harth (1993) argues that the activity of the brain cannot be viewed so simply.

> What is the difference between seeing a rose, thinking of a rose, and dreaming of a rose? In seeing, a true image is passed from retina to LGN and on to a cortex, where it is gradually dissembled into its various features. In thinking, some of the feature sensitive centers may be simulated from above. The top down connections are there . . . at practically all levels of sensory pathways. In dreaming, I believe, this top down control reaches down further toward peripheral sensory centers where the sensory messages are still more like pictures than codes. This simulated sensory pattern is now reflected back to the cortex, where it is received *as though it had come all the way from the retina*. Images of greater or lesser realism are formed at various levels of sensory processing by feedback from higher levels. The neural loops that generate these mental images are creative in the sense that they allow us to view what isn't really there and to invent what does not yet exist. But they also play a role in the perception of the world around us because they can direct our attention, enhance features deemed significant, and suppress extraneous detail. The loops are self-referent: the signaler and the perceiver are one . . .
>
> (Harth, 1993: 105–6)

What Harth draws attention to from a number of perspectives in his book *The Creative Loop* is a temporal paradox, which he refers to as "bootstrapping". His own inquiry into the activity of the brain presents clear evidence that the argument of skepticism results from an insistence on linear notions of cause and effect, whereas there is irrefutable evidence of another temporal pattern in brain activity. A loop is self-referentially "active" in generating images by becoming an object to itself, in which nothing external to the process is involved (hence Harth's use of the expression "bootstrapping"). The direction of brain research now being undertaken by writers such as Harth supports the conjecture of G.H. Mead, made almost a century ago, that the central nervous system must necessarily be the basis for the temporal paradox he observed in social interaction.

> The complications are very great, but the central nervous system has an almost infinite number of elements in it, and they can be organized not only in spatial connection with each other, but also from a temporal standpoint. In virtue of this last fact our conduct is made up of a series of steps which follow each other, and the later steps may be already started and influence the earlier ones. The thing we are going to do is playing back on what we are doing now.
>
> (Mead, 1934: 71)

In the case of what Mead refers to as the unconscious conversation of gestures, or in the case of the process of communication carried out by means of it, none of the individuals taking part in it are conscious of the meaning of the conversation. Meaning appears in the case of the conscious conversation of gestures. Each of the individuals participating in it is conscious of the meaning of the conversation because that meaning appears *in their experience.* This is for Mead the very meaning of meaning.

> When we speak of the meaning of what we are doing we are making the response itself that we are on the point of carrying out a stimulus to our action. It becomes a stimulus to a later stage of action which is to take place from the point of view of this particular response.
>
> (ibid.: 72)

The social process in this sense constitutes the objects to which it responds, to which it in a sense adjusts. Objects are constituted in terms of meanings within the social process of experience and behaviour through the mutual adjustment of the responses or actions of the various individual organisms involved in that process. This is made possible by means of communication that takes the form of a conversation of gestures in the earlier evolutionary stages of the process and of language in the later stages.

For Mead the central nervous system is the basis for an evolutionary theory of action because of the unique relationship made possible between the future and the past. In initiating an act with a gesture this relationship makes it possible for the response to be reflected back to the gesture, so affecting the individual making the gesture, who can then select among various "responses" to the response. This can change the gesture as well in what becomes the overt process of the social act.

> Human intelligence, by means of the physiological mechanism of the human central nervous system, deliberately selects one from among the several alternative responses which are possible in the given problematic environmental situation; and if the given response which it selects is complex – i.e. is a set or chain or group or succession of simple responses – it can organize this set or chain of simple responses in such a way as to make possible the most adequate and harmonious solution by the individual of the given environmental problem. . . . That which takes place in the present organic behavior is always in some sense an emergent from the past, and never could have been precisely predicted in advance – never could have been predicted on the basis of a knowledge, however complete, of the past, and of the conditions in the past which are relevant to its emergence; and in the case of organic behavior which is intelligently controlled, this element of spontaneity is especially prominent by virtue of the present influence exercised over such behavior by the possible future results or consequences which it may have.
>
> (ibid.: 98–9)

It is this spontaneity of selection that makes possible the further development of an individual to a self on the basis of what Mead refers to as the dialectic of the "I" and "me". Mead assumes the possibility of what Harth refers to as "bootstrapping" and the "creative loop"; this is not merely an analogy but a necessary precondition for the evolution of processes of social interaction. In the following section I will present Mead's important development of the "I – me" dialectic and, in the section after that, I will look at the perspective of John O'Donohue who has re-examined Hegel's concept of the person in order to establish, as Mead does, an alternative to understanding interaction in terms of autonomous individuals.

So, the position I am taking from the perspective of the thought of Mead and Elias and from recent brain research does not deny the individual and does not retain the notion of a whole. It sees the individual as a person, self or identity emerging in social interaction, forming and being formed by that social interaction. In the next section, I explore Mead's theory of how this happens.

The paradox of time and the emergence of persons

Mead's thought, along with that of John Dewey, William James, and Charles S. Peirce, falls into a movement of philosophical thought known as pragmatism. Mead and James were concerned with questions arising from theories attempting to found psychology as a science independent of philosophy. Mead studied in Germany and brought to these questions an extraordinarily broad perspective based on his knowledge of both philosophy and the natural sciences. His thinking is based firmly on evolutionary theory. For Mead this means that thought itself moves and that evolutionary theory is itself evolving. The first formulation of evolutionary theory is that of Aristotle. Based on observation of nature, Aristotle describes the evolution of plants from one form to another, but there is no question of a new form emerging.

For Mead the question of the genesis of a new form emerged itself as a new form of evolutionary theory for the first time at the beginning of the nineteenth century. Movements of thought at this scale emerge from historical events that they at the same time precipitate. Societies are shaken from the foundations and this makes possible longer periods of stability. These foundations are the theories that are in a real sense the stories told about the nature of the world and humankind's place in it. The idea of the autonomous individual was emerging in the eighteenth century and the attempt to make this autonomy concrete took the form of the French Revolution. This led to the excesses of Napoleon, who spread the destruction of the old order across Europe while establishing a despotic regime internally. Mead argues that it is as people began to build a new order on the ruins of this destruction that a new consciousness of the self emerged, which became the basis for the further evolution of evolutionary theory.

The paradox at the core of evolutionary theory

The destruction of the old order in Europe included the metaphysical basis of philosophy. As philosophers such as Fichte, Schelling and Hegel responded to this situation, they reflected on experience for the first time as a process. For them, the forms that Kant had viewed as unchanging categories of reason shaping reality were now understood as emerging in the *process of experience,* understood as a process of overcoming antinomies, that is, the contradictions arising in rational thought. They conceived of logic as dynamic rather than static. For Kant, the antinomies were the attempts of the mind, in its reasoning and understanding, to go beyond experience. The question of freedom was such an antinomy. One argument was that humans were characterized by a necessary causality based on freedom. Another was that there was no such thing as freedom because everything that happened was according to the laws of nature. Kant's solution to this antimony was to split the world in two: freedom, for Kant, could not be known in the *phenomenal* world, but only in the *noumenal* world by means of such postulates as the categorical imperative. Fichte, however, recognizes an experience of freedom in our actions. The antinomies are also recognized in the process of passage from a free self over into the field of experience. *These "contradictions" characterize for him the very experience of the self.*

The self is then no longer conceived of in the medieval sense as a soul that was born into the world with the body. For Fichte the very existence of the *self* (or subject) implied a *not-self* (or object), which can be identified with the self. In other words, the self can only be understood in terms of its contradiction, the not-self, which is the others and the historically shaped task or purpose of their interacting. The self as subject can only be understood as reflexive movement in relation to the social. This is for Mead the key move toward a new understanding of the self as a process:

> You have seen that the term "self" is a reflexive affair. It involves an attitude of separation of the self from itself. Both subject and object are involved in the self in order that it may exist. The self must be identified, in some sense, with the not-self. It must be able to come back at itself from outside. The process, a process within which both of these phases of experience lie, a process in which these different phases can be identified with each other – not necessarily as the same phase but at least as expressions of the same process.
>
> (Mead, 1936: 88)

In his moral philosophy Fichte moves beyond Kant's understanding of moral experience. For Kant, the individual identifies himself with his duty in moral experience. As discussed earlier, our actions are tested by the categorical imperative, by asking whether or not we can make a universal law of our proposed action, a maxim which all can follow. Fichte identifies the self with the *task* to be performed. The reality of moral experience is that "one finds before him something to be done and then, in the doing, finds himself identified with it. . . . And the accomplishment of the task, the doing of the duty, realizes the individual" (ibid.: 89). One does not get at him/herself simply by turning upon him/herself the eye of introspection. One realizes him/herself in what he/she does, in the ends that he/she sets up, and in the means he/she takes to accomplish those ends. "This process, according to Fichte, is what is continually taking place. The self throws up the world as a field within which action must take place; and, in setting up the world as a field of action, it realizes itself " (ibid.: 90).

What is important for Mead is the tension between the self and not-self. The world of meaning arises out of the individuals that live in it. And yet, this world of physical things is there, and it is there before the self comes into existence in it. In fact it seems to be a condition for the existence of the self. Mead rejects the attempt by Fichte and other idealist philosophers to contain the self and not-self in an absolute self as an organization and realization of all selves. For him this attempt would mean the containment of the self and not-self in an individual, albeit an absolute individual. This for Mead does not reflect the primary experience of the individual in the world.

> Our scientific picture of the world is independent of the individual who inhabits it. He comes into it, and it may be the scene of his endeavor. It may take on his values, the values of society, but still it is there in advance of him. It does not seem to be dependent on him in any way.
>
> (ibid.: 91)

It was in this period that evolutionary theory, as we know it today, first appeared in the hypothesis of Lamarck and later in that of Darwin. And what they formulated is the conception that humans and all that human means – self-consciousness, values – are dependent upon the prior development of a physical universe. Nature is in a radical sense the not-self, the unknown, just as for Fichte moral life was the constant transcending of the not-self which is to be made part of the self. The antinomical contradiction is there but in a different form from that of Kant, for whom it indicates the limits beyond which knowledge cannot go. Fichte maintains that contradiction represents an *actual move in the development* of reality, of the self.

> The self grows by overcoming those obstacles, by making them its own interests. That assumption that reality is a process of development, the development of the self, is the first step in the idealistic dialectic. That is what reality is. And this development takes place over obstacles or contradictions.
>
> (ibid.: 94)

Instead of locating how humans know anything in innate categories, therefore, Fichte, Schelling and Hegel understand human knowing to be a dynamic movement of the self engaging with, or moving through, not-self, which is nature and other humans interacting for a purpose. In other words, knowing and knowing selves is social process.

Evolutionary theory and ethics

For Mead there is an essential link between evolutionary theory and the paradoxes of individuals in social interaction. The self is that experience that we attain only by becoming, in a sense, not-selves. We cannot get the experience of ourselves as selves except in so far as we take the attitudes of others and regard ourselves from that point of view. This is the core of the theory Mead was to develop over three decades. In his essay "The philosophical basis of ethics" published in 1908, Mead further defines the link between the emergence of evolutionary theory and the question of ethics. In addition to the traditional understanding of ethics as conscious control over action before it is taken by evaluating the ends of the proposed action, Mead draws attention to the situation where the individual and the environment (the not-self) mutually determine each other.

> Not only can we trace in the history of thought the evolution of the conception of evolution, but we find ourselves with a consciousness which we conceive of as evolved; the contents and the forms of these contents can be looked upon as the products of development. . . . The very time process as well as the space of the universe lies in experience which is itself presented as the result of an evolution that arises in and through spatial conditions, which is first and foremost a temporal process. . . . It has become evident that an environment can exist for a form only in so far as the environment answers to the susceptibilities of the organism; that the organism determines thus its own environment; that the effect of every adaptation is a new environment which must change with that which responds to it. The full recognition, however, that form and environment must be phases that answer to each other, character for character, appears in ethical theory.
>
> (Mead, 1908: 73–4)

Mead is very much aware of the paradox of evolutionary theory from an ethical point of view: the motive in the ethical sense does not arise from the relations of the ends toward which the activities are aimed in advance, but rather the motive is the recognition of the end as it arises in consciousness. This means that "the moral interpretation of our experience must be found within the experience itself" (ibid.: 76). There is, for Mead, a paradox at the very core of evolutionary theory. It is a paradox of the known/unknown, which he sees in Fichte's self/not-self, and in Darwin's concept of nature. In terms of social action the evolutionary process consists of the mutual determination of the individual and his/her environment – not merely the determination of the individual by his environment.

> The moral necessity is that all activity which appears as impulse and environment should enter into the situation, and there is nothing which ensures this completeness of expression except the full interrelationship of the self and the situation.
>
> (ibid.: 77)

Evolution as a general idea

This interrelationship as a unity of process is Mead's conception of evolution as a general idea. It is a life-process that flows in different forms, taking on now this form, now that.

> Given such a conception as this, it is possible to conceive of the form of the plant or the animal as arising in the existence of the life-process itself. It is very important that we should get the conception of evolution that is involved in it and distinguish it from the earlier conception in its philosophic form. We are concerned with a theory which involves a process as its fundamental fact, and then with this process as appearing in different forms.
>
> (Mead, 1936: 163)

This evolutionary idea was developed in philosophy first by Fichte as the self/not-self and later by Hegel in terms of subject and object. In order to be both subject and object there must be the process of passing from one phase to the other. This is a dynamic relationship, a process that appears now in this phase, now in that. The self can exist only in so far as it is experienced as a subject and for that to happen a subject must be an object to itself. And objects can exist only as objects for a subject. What the idealist philosophers did was to fuse these two phases of experience, the self-experience, on the one hand, and subject-object experience, on the other. This enabled them to insist that not only did the subject involve an object but also, at the same time, that the object involved a subject.

> This, then, was the central process for them: the self, the not-self, are expressions of a single process, and in this also is found the subject-object relationship in which both terms are always mutually involved. Just as there can be no self without a not-self, so there can be no subject without an object, and vice versa.
>
> (ibid.: 168)

Mead insisted that one must first explain the emergence of consciousness. Mead's project was to explain the interiorization of subject and object as consciousness, as having emerged from an evolutionary process, the process of social action. He wanted to demonstrate the truth of Hegel's insight that it is only in the organization of society that the individual could ever attain any control over his environment. The speech he uses, the very mechanism of thought, are social products. However, Mead rejects Hegel's notion that this is the process of the self realization of an absolute spirit or self.

> One's own self is attained only through his taking the attitude of the social group to which he belongs. He must become socialized to become himself. So when you speak of this evolution, of its having reached a certain climax in human form, you must realize that it reaches that point only in so far as the human form is recognized as an organic part of the social whole.
>
> (ibid.)

In his treatment of the evolution of evolutionary theory at the beginning of the nineteenth century Mead established a view of this theory as

- radically dealing with the known-unknown: nature which was there billions of years before the appearance of man, and the not-self as necessary for the process of social evolution;
- emerging from paradox, specifically the paradox of the self/not-self;
- facing the temporal paradox in ethical theory of the emergence of motives *in the process of the act*;
- the evolutionary emergence of the individual from society.

Surprisingly it is to behaviourism that Mead turned to found this theory in terms of social action.

Behaviourism and the emergence of mind

The development of pragmatism was very much influenced by the differing reactions of Dewey, James and Mead to Watson's concept of behaviourism. They shared an interest in the unity of the action of the central nervous system. Considering all the stimuli that reach the brain in all its parts, it seems almost inexplicable that we still get unitary action. While James developed a dynamic theory of consciousness as flowing, very similar to that developed by Husserl as inner-time consciousness, Mead found in behaviourism as he understood it a possibility to develop further his theory of the social act. Because he viewed evolution as a general idea, he worked on the assumption that the circular time structure he observed there must also be the basis for the activity of the central nervous system. He therefore rejected the behaviourist concept of stimuli and response as two different acts in the relation of cause and effect. He regarded these as phases of one act and on this basis further developed his understanding of the act as a process of self in relation to not-self. Coming from evolutionary theory he was also of course interested in attention and selection. Attention was, for Mead, an organizing process as well as a selection process.

> When giving attention to what we are going to do we are picking out the whole group of stimuli which represent successive activity. Our attention enables us to organize a field in which we are going to act. Here we have the organism as acting and determining its environment. It is not simply a set of passive senses played upon by the stimuli that come from without. The organism goes out and determines what it is going to respond to, and organizes that world.
>
> (Mead, 1934: 25)

There is an interesting parallel here to the computer simulations of behaviour based on algorithms, such as Craig Reynolds' (1987) simulation of the flocking of birds. The rules which are given to the individual "agents" are acts with the kind of phases Mead describes. For example two of the rules are:

● The agents should seek the centre of mass of other nearby agents.
● The agents should attempt to match the velocity of nearby agents.

The agents as units of activity are not self-contained, but even in this completely deterministic system, in the behaviourist sense, what is observed as a result is actually a process with phases of stimulus on the basis of response and response on the basis of stimulus. One agent cannot act alone and is therefore not an agent apart from the relationship to others. For Mead the mistake of Watson's behaviourism was only to see the result. Mead was interested in developing what, for him, was a genuine behaviourism as process, from the inside if you will, whereby mind emerges in such a process.

The conversation of gestures

To understand the emergence of mind and to distinguish his thought from that of Watson, Mead introduced the concept of gesture. Gestures are the beginnings of social acts, which are stimuli for the responses of other forms. Taking the example of a dogfight, the action of one dog in getting ready to attack another becomes a stimulus to the other dog to change its own position or its own attitude. This is for Mead a conversation of gestures.

> In this case we have a situation in which certain parts of the act become a stimulus to the other form to adjust itself to those responses; and that adjustment in turn becomes a stimulus to the first form to change his own act and start on a different one. There are a series of attitudes, movements, on the part of these forms which belong to the beginnings of acts that are the stimuli for the responses that take place.
>
> (Mead, 1934: 43)

Mead is pointing at this elementary level to the paradoxical temporal structure of the evolutionary theory of action. The initial gesture changes on the basis of the response and all of this together makes up the phases of the act. A stimulus alone is not an act. This is depicted in Figure 5.2.

Mead next points out that in humans, the gesture not only calls forth a response from another, but also calls forth the same response in the maker of the gesture. In this way, the gesturing individual can know what he or she is doing. This capacity, to call forth in oneself the same response as in another, imparts to the gesture the characteristic of a symbol in that it points to the potential meaning of the social act. Mead calls this a significant symbol. This is a symbol which answers to a meaning in the experience of the first individual and which also calls out that meaning in the second individual. "Where the gesture reaches that situation it has become what we call 'language'. It is now a significant

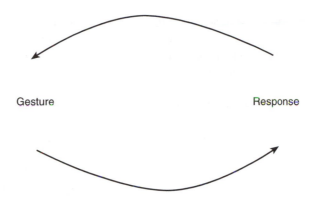

Gesture   Response

Figure 5.2 *The social act*

symbol and it signifies a certain meaning" (ibid.: 46). Only in terms of
gestures as significant symbols is the existence of mind or intelligence
possible; for only in terms of gestures that are significant symbols can
thinking – which is simply an internalized or implicit conversation of the
individual with himself by means of such gestures – take place. For Mead

> ... selves must be accounted for in terms of the social process, and in
> terms of communication; and individuals must be brought into
> essential relation within that process before communication, or the
> contact between the minds of different individuals, becomes possible.
> The body is not a self, as such, it becomes a self only when it has
> developed a mind within the context of social experience. . . . Mind
> arises through communication by a conversation of gestures in a
> social process or context of experience – not communication through
> mind.
>
> (ibid.: 50)

Significant symbols and the emergence of the self

Humans, then, can unconsciously experience themselves in the place of
others and act as they act, and they are capable of experiencing
themselves as others experience them. This kind of self-reference is
clearly visible in sports, for example, when a basketball player fakes
passing the ball, so initiating in the other expectations that are then
quickly changed. This is the condition for the possibility of language, the
vocal stimulus, emerging from human experience and this same process
is essential to the development of self-consciousness and the appearance

of the self. Watson and other behaviourists did not take into account all that is involved in this process. They did not recognize that the stimuli are the essential elements in elaborate social processes and carry with them the value of those social processes.

> In dealing with the communication we have first to recognize its earliest origins in the unconscious conversation of gestures. Conscious communication – conscious conversation of gestures – arises when gestures become signs, that is, when they come to carry for the individuals making them and the individuals responding to them, definite meanings or significations in terms of the subsequent behavior of the individuals making them; so that, by serving as prior indications, to the individuals responding to them, of the subsequent behavior of the individuals making them, they make possible the mutual adjustment of the various individual components of the social act to one another, and also, by calling forth in the individuals making them the same responses implicitly that they call forth explicitly in the individuals to whom they are made, they render possible the rise of self-consciousness in connection with this mutual adjustment.
>
> (ibid.: 69)

The unity of mind, of self and of self-consciousness

For Mead, the emergence of a self and human communication is based on the fact that individuals are capable of behaviour in which an individual can become an object to him/herself. Our communication is directed not only to others but also to ourselves. The self, as that which can be an object to itself, is essentially a social structure and emerges in social experience. This is not to deny that once a self has emerged, one can abstract from the social process and carry on a conversation of gestures within one's own mind. This is for Mead the essence of thinking, and it has emerged from social action and is preparatory for action. But the *object* of the thought process is social in origin:

> I know of no other form of behavior than the linguistic in which the individual is an object to himself, and so far as I can see, the individual is not a self in the reflexive sense unless he is an object to himself. It is this fact that gives a critical importance to communication, since this is a type of behavior in which the individual does so respond to himself.
>
> (ibid.: 142)

The social experience determines how much of the self gets into communication. We carry on different relationships and are different things to different people.

> There are parts of the self which exist only for the self in relationship to itself. We divide ourselves up in all sorts of different selves with reference to our acquaintances. . . . There are all sorts of different selves answering to all sorts of different social reactions. It is a social process itself that is responsible for the appearance of the self; it is not there as a self apart from this type of experience.
>
> (ibid.)

But there is an organization of the self as a whole in reference to the community to which we belong. The various "selves" which make up the complete self are the various aspects of the structure of the social process as a whole. But for Mead the unity of the mind is not identical with the unity of the self:

> The unity of the self is constituted by the unity of the entire relational pattern of social behavior and experience in which the individual is implicated, and which is reflected in the structure of the self; but many of the aspects or features of this entire pattern do not enter into consciousness, so that the unity of the mind is in a sense an abstraction from the more inclusive unity of the self.
>
> (ibid.: 144)

The question of the emergence of unity, the wholes of the objects, is essential to understanding the evolutionary theory of action. The sense we have of the mind as a given whole is an abstraction from the social process, the interactive tension of the "known–unknown". The known–unknown is the otherness encountered by the self, or subject. Here Mead is expressing the thought of Fichte, Schelling and Hegel discussed above. The gesture is the action of the self or the subject in relation to the not-self or the object, that is, the others engaged in on-going purposeful action in a natural context. The response refers to the action of not-self and the unity of self/not-self is the social act, the social process in which meaning arises, including the meaning that is the self. This is depicted in Figure 5.3.

This conception of the self as emerging in the social process, which is the interaction of selves is profoundly different to the notion of the autonomous individual or, indeed, any notion of an innate self. Instead of being given by inheritance or given in any other way, Mead's argument

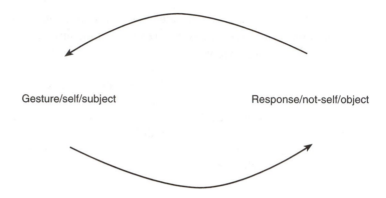

Gesture/self/subject   Response/not-self/object

Figure 5.3 *The unity of the social and the self*

posits that selves are formed in social interaction at the same time as they form this interaction. This paradox of "forming and being formed by" is thus at the heart of the emergence of self and society, and thus becomes a basis for holding the tension of paradoxes, for example, that of participant and observer. Both the self and the social are the same process, with the only distinction being that the former is a private role play or silent conversation while the latter is a public "game" and vocal communication. From this perspective, there is no "whole" outside of the interaction between selves. There is only the human experience of interaction or relating. This explanation, therefore, requires no appeal to anything transcendent like a group mind, a common pool of meaning, culture as a system of values causing interaction. This means that a very different notion of participation is involved. In the perspective of systemic self-organization, participation means the participation of individuals in some system such as culture. Mead's argument is an example of participative self-organization where *participation means the direct experience of relationship* between human beings, not the participation in something outside their direct relationship.

Mead regarded the unity of the self as depicted in Figure 5.3 as "inclusive" because it includes both unconscious and conscious aspects of human relating. He then provided an explanation of the emergence of consciousness, which he calls mind, in social interaction. Consciousness or mind is the capacity to call forth in oneself the same response as in the other. This is depicted in Figure 5.4, where the gesture is now made by the self to itself. The self not only calls forth in itself the same attitude as in the other, that is, takes the attitude of the other, but also takes the attitude of the generalized other, or the group.

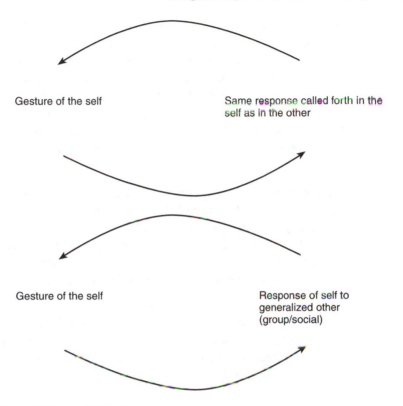

Gesture of the self

Same response called forth in the self as in the other

Gesture of the self

Response of self to generalized other (group/social)

Figure 5.4 *The unity of mind*

With the concept of the generalized other, self is described in a sense that goes beyond merely taking the attitudes of other human individuals toward oneself and toward one another in a social process. Going a step further the self takes the attitudes toward the various phases or aspects of the common social actions in which individuals are organized as groups.

> This getting of the broad activities of any given social whole or organized society as such within the experiential field of any one of the individuals involved or included in that whole is, in other words, the essential basis and prerequisite for the fullest development of that individual's self. . . . And on the other hand the complex co-operative processes and activities and institutional functionings of organized human society are also possible only in so far as every individual involved in them or belonging to that society can take the general attitudes of all other such individuals.
>
> (ibid.: 155)

This self is understood as fully developed and capable of participation and communication in the organization of social or group attitudes. It emerges then as a self in the sense of an individual reflection of the general systematic pattern of social or group action. Participation at this level is in tension with the "generalized other" as a known–unknown – patterns which enter "as a whole into the individual's experience in terms of these organized group attitudes which, through the mechanism of the central nervous system, he takes toward himself, just as he takes the individual attitudes of others" (ibid.: 158).

The emergent whole is not given in experience. Mead uses the term "other" always in the sense of the known–unknown. It is only by abstracting from the social process that we can speak of mind or self as a given object. Mead again and again refers to the central nervous system as the necessary prerequisite for emergence. As we have seen earlier in this chapter this is very much in agreement with brain research today (Harth, 1993).

However, what Mead is above all interested in, is founding an understanding of self-consciousness as process which emerges in the individual in participation and communication with the others, that is, an unknown, a not-self. What Mead meant by self-consciousness is:

> an awakening in ourselves of the group of attitudes which we are arousing in others, especially when it is an important set of responses which go to make up the members of the community. It is unfortunate to fuse or mix up consciousness, as we ordinarily use that term, and self-consciousness. Consciousness, as frequently used, simply has reference to the field of experience, but self-consciousness refers to the ability to call out in ourselves a set of definite responses which belong to the others of the group.
>
> (Mead, 1934: 163)

The dialectic of the "I" and "me": Mead's concept of participation

Selves can only exist in definite relationships to other selves. The individual possesses a self only in relation to the selves of the other members of the social group. The structure of his/her self expresses or reflects the general behaviour pattern of the social groups to which he/she belongs, as do the selves of the other members of the groups. But Mead's concept of self-consciousness goes beyond the mere organization of social attitudes. To clarify this further, he describes the self from the point of view of the moral necessity of the act, that is, from the perspective of the participation of the individual as a dialectic between the individual's sense of acting as an "I" and a "me". The "I" is always present in the moment of acting but is never given in the experience.

> The "I" responds to the gesture of the "me", which arises through the taking of the attitudes of the others. Through taking those attitudes we have introduced the "me" and we react to it as an "I". The "I" of this moment is present in the "me" of the next moment. There again I cannot turn around quick enough to catch myself. . . . It is because of the "I" that we can say that we are never fully aware of what we are, that we surprise ourselves by our own action.
>
> (Mead, 1934: 174)

The "I–me" dialectic is depicted in Figure 5.5.

The "I" is a known–unknown for the "me". We identify with the "I", but it is not a given whole. It emerges as a unity of movement, as a unity of process, in response to the "me". The "I–me" dialectic is then in the present of the act, where the movement of the living present recreates the history, or past, together with the expectation of the future, out of which the individual initiates the act. In this movement, the response of the "I" is unknown. The response in the immediate experience is uncertain and this is what constitutes the "I". The response, when it becomes known after the act, can prove to be the usual response, but it can also be different and novel, a known–unknown. It is unknown before it emerges but known in the sense that it will emerge in the act, which is always for the sake of identity, the sense of the unity of the self and

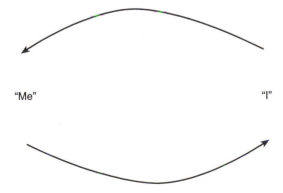

"Me"   "I"

Figure 5.5 *The unity of self-consciousness*

society/culture/organization of which the self is a member. Mead has thus provided a basis for an ethics based on freedom and on creativity. This basis is his evolutionary theory of action, the experience of self in a social process of the known–unknown. In acting, our understanding of the past can change on the basis of a different response emerging from the "I" in the present moment of participation.

Change in societies, cultures or organizations will usually only come about gradually: no one individual can reorganize the whole society, but each one is continually affecting society by his/her own attitude because he/she does take up the attitude of the group and responds to it, and that response can change the attitude of the group. "This is, of course, what we are constantly doing in our imagination, in our thought; we are utilizing our own attitude to bring about a different situation in the community of which we are a part" (ibid.: 180).

The iteration of identity and difference

The originality of Mead's thought results from his refusal to ground his psychology in a concept of consciousness as being in any way a given thing or field as a basis for understanding the self. In taking this position he moves from the paradigm of systemic self-organization to the paradigm of participative self-organization. "Anything that as a whole is more than the mere form of its parts has a nature that belongs to it that is not to be found in the elements out of which it is made" (ibid.: 329). Consciousness as such refers to both the organism and its environment and cannot be located in either of them. It is given only in its emergence – from the interrelation of form and environment, involving both of them at the same time. It is in this sense that Mead understands selection. Selection takes place in the interrelationship but cannot be understood as being in any way done by some "thing" that is given. The systemic self-organization paradigm posits a system as a given whole that is selecting in terms of adaptation to its environment. Mead argues that theories which view consciousness as being in any sense a "field", as is the case with W. James and the gestalt theory of W. Kohler, remain in what I am calling the systemic self-organization paradigm. In Mead's sense, they are for this reason unable to explain the radical nature of the emergence of the self as a basis for consciousness. For this reason, Mead's thought can be interpreted as moving to the paradigm of participative self-organization in very much the same sense as the theories of complexity and self-reference now emerging from the natural sciences.

> So we state the environment not in terms of the form but the form in terms of the environment. Nevertheless, the only environment to which the form responds is the environment which is predetermined by the sensitivity of the form and its response to it.
>
> (ibid.: 246)

The fallacy of imitation

Mead's thorough treatment here of the emergence of mind is important today in arguing against thinkers who tend to look at the result of self-organization as products which can be acquired by imitation. Mead pointed to how theories of imitation collapse the process of gesture–response into a result or product. Referring again to the example of the flocking birds, the familiar explanation when birds are observed in nature is that the birds are imitating others' behaviour, usually that of a leader. What is actually going on is a process of conversation of gestures. Mead argues that, while in humans there is evidence of imitation, there is very little evidence of it in other animals. "Imitation seems to belong to the human form, where it has reached some sort of independent conscious existence" (ibid.: 59). Imitation as a mere tendency on the part of an organism to reproduce what it sees or hears other organisms doing would be impossible in Mead's opinion.

> As soon as you recognize in the organism a set of acts which carry out the processes which are essential to the life of the form, and undertake to put the sensitive or sensory experience into that scheme, the sensitive experience, as stimulus we will say to the response, cannot be a stimulus simply to reproduce what is seen and heard; it is rather a stimulus for the carrying out of the organic process. . . . They are acts which go beyond the organism taken by itself, but they belong to co-operative processes in which groups of animals act together, and they are the fulfillment of the processes which are essential to the life of the forms. One cannot fit into such scheme as that a particular impulse of imitation .
>
> (ibid.: 60)

A summary

I have been arguing for a move from the notion of the autonomous individual with innate capacities, while avoiding any notion of wholes or the radical denial of the individual, to an understanding of the individual in terms of social process. This move has immediate ethical implications. It shifts the thinking away from a view of organizations as "wholes", to be found in the thinking of both those who uphold individual autonomy and those radically denying the existence of the individual, to focusing on direct interaction between individuals who form and are simultaneously formed by social process. The spontaneously creative and destructive individuals emerging in social process have to be responsible individuals and this is the basis for the view of ethics that I take in this book. I have shown how Mead retains the notion of responsible individuals who emerge in the social process, but who always have the freedom to choose their next acts. They have this capacity because they have the capacity, rooted in their bodies, to take the attitudes of others, indeed of society. They can know and so must be responsible for their own conduct, even though none of them can individually determine the outcomes of what they together do. The capacity to know and hence to choose is rooted in the capacity humans have for self-consciousness, that is, their ability to become objects to themselves in their acting as an "I–me" dialectic. This dialectic is the source of spontaneity, creativity and the freedom to choose in the form of the I response to the me. This is the basis of an ethics of individual responsibility in a social process, that is, in the detail of local interaction in the movement of the living present.

What is striking about this way of thinking is that it avoids the positing of an autonomous individual who objectively tests actions in thought against universal imperatives and then acts. It also avoids the radical denial of the individual and the consequent basis of ethics in transcendental wholes or in the community of "we". Instead, ethics, good conduct, is the social process of individual participants knowingly interacting with each other and having to account to each other in an on-going, ordinary, everyday way for the detail of what they do in their local situation in the living present. And since leadership is essentially a question of good conduct, of ethics, Mead's perspective also shifts thinking about leaders as autonomous individuals and leadership as provided by transcendental wholes to a notion of leaders participating in the social process of interaction in local situations in the living present.

Implications in Mead's thought for the concept of leadership

In Chapter 4, I examined the relation of the theory of "point of reference" developed in cybernetic theory as the basis for the concept of leadership found today in mainstream theories of management action. It is a clear example of the major influence that the natural sciences can have on theories of action, both implicit and explicit, in the social sciences. Mead's theory of action, in moving to the paradigm of participative self-organization, is in complete contradiction to that of systemic self-organization. Mead reflects clearly on the implications of his concept of action for understanding leadership. This is based on the importance of each individual in interaction.

> As a man adjusts himself to a certain environment he becomes a different individual; but in becoming a different individual he has affected the community in which he lives. It may be a slight effect, but in so far as he has adjusted himself, the adjustments have changed the type of the environment to which he can respond and the world is accordingly a different world.
>
> (Mead, 1934: 215)

Mead points out what we all experience very clearly when a new member joins a small group of which we are a part. The group as process changes.

Leadership is then understood in terms of the "I–me" dialectic. It is the expression of the spontaneous "I", which is not given in experience. In this sense the leader is acting "with reference to a form of society or social order which is implied but not yet adequately expressed" (ibid.: 217). This statement could be misread, from the standpoint of systemic self-organization, as an argument for "vision". However, what Mead is referring to here is that the leader, in the course of his/her life, has acquired a greater spontaneity, a greater ability to deal with the "not-self", the on-going purpose or task that others are interacting for. The leader is an individual "who is capable of entering into the attitudes of the other members of the group. Figures of that sort become of enormous importance because they make possible communication between groups otherwise completely separated from each other" (ibid.: 256–7).

Local interaction and the emergence of the person

Mead developed the elements of what became his theory of the social act during his studies in Germany in the latter part of the nineteenth century. During that time there he lived through a number of events that, with hindsight, could be seen as leading up to the First World War. His interest in the implications of his social theory for understanding these events is reflected in his essays during this period. I took up an example of this in speaking of cult and functional values in the last section of Chapter 4. As in his reflections on leadership mentioned above, Mead increasingly looked for the source of large-scale political events in everyday social interaction as participation in local events. He increasingly wrote of values, which he understood as both cult values and functional values, being sustained, passed on and becoming determining factors in our actions only in terms of local interaction. The cult values that seem to transcend this local interaction do not do so in any real sense, but only in an ideal sense which can only become real in the functional reality of the living present. As mentioned above, Mead found a basis for an understanding of the present, which became the foundation of his theory of the social act, in the development, by Fichte, Schelling and, especially, Hegel, of a new understanding of process as a reaction to Kant's theory of human experience. Mead took up their concept of experience and understood it as being "in the present", which he understood as the movement of process. He did this in the light of the pragmatic notion of the scientific method and the challenge presented by Watson's behaviourist notion of stimulus and response.

The relation of Mead's thought on social interaction and ethics to his experience of the First World War and the events leading up to it have a parallel in T.W. Adorno's reflection on his experience of the Second World War. Together with Max Horkheimer in *The Dialectic of Enlightenment* (Horkheimer and Adorno, 1947) he reflected on the failure of the ethics of reason and idealism, which had dominated thought since the beginning of modernism, to prevent or stop the atrocities of the fully instrumentalized, large-scale genocide of the holocaust. Reflection on the implications of this failure dominated Adorno's thought not just for years but for decades. He produced an important statement on these matters in 1951 in a book entitled *Minima Moralia*. He pointed to the end of any position based on "universal ethics" since the experience of the holocaust had demonstrated that all such ethics can be instrumentalized to achieve the ends of unquestioned power. The alternative he offered was a "minimal" ethics, as opposed to the edification implied in the former "greater" ethics of the idealized universality of human reason. We find such an ethics in the smallest detail of our everyday lives, especially in language, as evidenced in the anecdotes and stories which make up the *Minima Moralia*. The gesture of this minimalist ethics in the first post-war years had an enormous effect on the writers of that generation.

Adorno's overriding moral "precept" is that "the whole is that which is not-true". The foundations of fascism lie in a fascination with that which is, in and of itself, the "whole" in which people find their identities as "parts". It is in this fascination with the idealized whole, and peoples' identification of themselves as parts of it, that ethics fails. This happens because there is no questioning of the whole as such, only the instrumentalizing and optimizing of "selves" as parts in service of the whole. The focus here turns out to be on local interaction, but in a very different sense from that which I will be examining as the "living present" in the final section of this chapter. Here the local interaction is alienated from a genuine living present because it is in the service of a whole that is not part of the experience of the present. To retain the emphasis on sustaining the whole one must impose a preconceived meaning on local interaction. This in turn results in understanding the "present" in a detached way because it has, in a very real sense, been predetermined. The whole is clearly predetermined even when it is defined as a vision of the future, as was the case with the utopian future for an idealized human community put forward by both fascism and communism.

Adorno clearly stated his debt to Hegel's thought in what he attempted in the *Minima Moralia*. I understand him to be referring to the same insight concerning time that Mead also took from Hegel as the basis of his theory of the movement of the social act. This "dialectic" is subtly demonstrated again and again by Adorno in the aphorisms and stories that make up the *Minima Moralia*. This is indicated in his premise that "the whole is that which is not-true". This is not meant as a simple negation since it would negate itself as such, claiming a standpoint of a "whole" from which to make such a statement. Adorno is drawing attention to the movement of the negation of negation. In stating that a given whole, or object is true as such and in itself, the speaker affirms the simple negation of himself, finding truth in an object or other. In maintaining that a whole or other is not true *as such and in itself* Adorno focuses on the subject–object relation. We find ourselves in the negation of the simple negation. The whole or other becomes the motive of the further movement of negation which shows this motive not to be true as the whole it seemed to be. In social interaction we are all doing this, so that the "truth" that we maintain, in "bumping up against" wholes claiming to be self sufficient and simple in themselves, reveals a process of on-going definition of that which is true in the conflict of the present moment. This is very similar to what Mead (Chapter 4) was referring to as the interpretation of cult values as functional values in the present, which generate the rich and productive conflicts of everyday interaction.

John O'Donohue (1993) is another writer who has recently taken up the same kind of dialectic and process, that is, the concept of time that is the basis of Hegel's understanding of the movement of experience in his phenomenology of mind. In attempting to establish an alternative position to that of the modernist idea of the individual, O'Donohue has returned to the concept of "person" and argued that Hegel reaffirmed this tradition in himself rejecting the notion of a society of autonomous individuals. O'Donohue argues, as did Mead, that Hegel held that persons emerge in the mediation of society in local interaction and that neither can be thought of without the other. We lose sight of this when we reduce time to only a segment of its circular quality as memory of the past in terms of our on-going construction of the future in the experience of the present. By taking only a segment of this time to express intention and experience in terms of the individual we reduce ourselves to observers of experience, which is to say that we detach ourselves from the emergence of our own identity. Before turning to a consideration of the movement of the living present as complex responsive processes, it is worthwhile looking more closely at O'Donohue's perspective on the person since he emphasizes an important aspect with regard to time, namely, that of recognition.

The tradition of thinking of the person as an emergent phenomenon

O'Donohue examines in detail and rejects the pervasive focus on the individual in Western thought, including the phenomenology of intersubjectivity, dialogue and Buber's "I–thou" (O'Donohue, 1993: 21–41). He also rejects attempts to bring such an interpretation of the individual into Hegel's thought. O'Donohue takes up the concept of person in Hegel's *Phenomenology* as reviving a tradition that has its roots in ancient Greece.

The concept of "person" gradually developed the sense that it has for us today in the clash of the "world" of the Greeks with the Latin culture of ancient Rome. In ancient Greece the word for person combined a word referring to the mask of actors, and hence their role, with a word conveying a meaning similar to "foundation", "support" or "substance". Throughout the years those taking up the concept of person have tended to emphasis one or the other sides of this duality (1993: 13–15): some see person as representing the stability of individuality, while others understand person as relational dealing with changing appearances and being a part of a larger context.

The later Latin definition of Boethius, "Persona est naturae rationalis individua substantia" (person is the individual substance of natural rationality), proved to be definitive for many centuries in reducing the concept to one side of this bipolarity, that of stability and containment. This was to have great influence on Aquinas, indeed, on all of Scholastic thought and rationalism. Descartes contributed to this in splitting off the person from the larger context through the methodical skepticism of his "I think, therefore I am". A key motive and theme of German Idealism then became a response to this and an attempt to revive the bipolarity of the understanding of the concept of person that would again include its relational sense. Kant sought to reconcile this with the empiricism of Hume and Locke in his transcendental categories, but Fichte, Schelling and Hegel carried the relational sense much further. Hegel in his *Phenomenology* presented a theory of self-consciousness that is, in effect, the movement, within thought itself, of the dualism that had for so many centuries been expressed in the concept of person. Hegel argues for a notion of time that is echoed in Harth's notion of "bootstrapping" mentioned earlier in this chapter:

> The neural loops that generate these mental images are creative in the sense that they allow us to view what isn't really there and to invent what does not yet exist. . . . The loops are self-referent: the signaler and the perceiver are one.
>
> (Harth, 1993: 105–6)

For Hegel, the concept of the person is about movement, unfolding, differentiating and integrating. It is the on-going emergent mediation of the individual and the social (O'Donohue, 1993: 93). This leads necessarily to the paradox that the individual is only such in and through the social and the social is only such in and through the individual. For this reason it is in no sense static, which means that experience can be neither simply private nor abstract. The social mediation of person means that the person, as emergent, is not something apart from the larger context and cannot emerge in itself alone. The person emerges among other persons as the unfolding of reality. Relation and difference mutually intensify one another in the iteration of creating identity. In this regard it is important to look again at the question of time in O'Donohue's treatment of Hegel's concept of recognition, a key aspect which complements Mead's understanding of the "I–me" dialectic.

Person, identity and time

In his examination of Hegel's concept of time as the basis of his dialectic, O'Donohue emphasizes the importance of holding onto two questions that Hegel addressed simultaneously. Hegel is asking what the source of the emergence of the self is and, at the same time, how the self emerges as the self over time. This double question reflects the double meaning that the word recognition has in the English language. On the one hand, it refers to the source of the recognition, that is, an on-going identity of the self that is the basis for recognition of the "familiar". On the other hand, it refers to that which the self "gives" recognition to as such. Again we have the polarity of the person as in one sense the stable source of the on-going interaction over time and, in another sense of the person giving recognition to difference in others. In the latter sense of recognition we see again the theme of the mutual co-creation of the individual and the social over time.

It might be more helpful to understand this if we leave for a moment the lofty heights of German idealism and look at something as "everyday" and mundane as Peter Senge's Beer Game. Senge has made a rather extraordinary move in proposing playing this game and reflecting on it as a way of gaining more insights into what he is trying to understand as the dynamics of systems. In looking at it here, I would like to point to what Hegel has said about time and what Norbert Elias has said about game theories and social processes. This will in turn have implications for the conclusions other complexity writers are drawing about the "simple rules" of computer simulations. The Beer Game and the computer simulations present an understanding of time and process that is completely at odds with the movement of process that Mead, Adorno and O'Donohue draw attention to in the phenomenology and dialectic of Hegel.

Senge very rightly uses the experience of playing the Beer Game to focus on time. Games seem to be "timeless"; they can be taken off the shelf and played at any time, the rules simply "play themselves out again". On the other hand, Senge wants to draw attention to something in the nature of games that also interests Mead and Elias. In the Beer Game there are four positions, namely retailer, wholesaler, distributor and production company. Each position moves forward in time beginning with very simple rules of regular ordering, buying and selling. Small variations eventually amplify in the system over time and the individual players develop mental models of what is causing this and how it will further "play itself out". What is different from computer simulations is that the players, as human individuals, introduce enormous complexity into the potential for meaning. At this point the difference in what is being referred to as time by Hegel becomes apparent. Hegel's concept is not the external linear progression of the measured time of observation, but the non-linear, circular time of participation in the negotiation of meaning. Senge avoids this question by looking at the game from the aspect of the mathematical modelling of various results to address questions such as optimization. He also avoids the question in that the meaning made by those playing is reduced to mental models of the game, which are also analyzed in terms of efficiency and optimizing. There is nothing in this about the negotiation of meaning in a circular back and forth manner between participants as in Hegel's concept of time. Instead there is the linear time of the progression of the game as in the mathematical model of ordering and inventory keeping, and the similar linear progression of time as individuals change their mental models of the game.

How is it that the aspect of time which Hegel (along with Mead, Adorno and O'Donohue) are interested in is avoided here? Elias points to two aspects of games that become reified as given wholes and contribute to a blindness concerning emergence: the assumption that rules are universal, and the assumption that what is "good" is only that which contributes to sustaining the rules as they are at any given time.

> Rule-governed human relationships cannot be understood if there is a tacit assumption that norms or rules are universally present from the outset as an unvarying property of human relationships. This assumption bars the way to asking and observing how and in what circumstances contests which are played without rules transform themselves into relationships *with* set rules.
>
> (Elias, 1970: 75)

> The concept of "function" . . . contains an inappropriate value judgment which, moreover, is made explicit in neither interpretation nor use. The inappropriateness of the evaluations is due to the fact that they tend – unintentionally – to use the terms for those tasks which are "good" for the "whole", because they contribute to the preservation and integrity of the existing social system. Human activities which either fail or appear to fail to do that are therefore branded as "dysfunctional".
>
> (ibid.: 77)

Participative self-organization appeals to a concept of time as process. The temporal structure of the on-going negotiation of meaning points to a causality of transformation. This temporal process is self-referential and leads to the emergence and transformation of the patterns that become "rules" and habits of interaction. It would almost seem that the linearity of cause and effect was reversed here in some way. The goals toward which groups are striving become a cause of interaction. But this can be completely misunderstood if one takes the perspective of cause and effect in terms of the "whole". This is the problem of the simple causal reference to visions and dreams. Posited as simple rules or statements, they alienate those involved from the present, that is, from the negotiation of conflict which is the sole basis for the emergence of patterns of behaviour, whether good or bad. Making such evaluations in advance disguises the motives and ideology of those doing so. This point will be taken further in Chapter 6, but first in the final section of this chapter, I would like to further develop the concept of participation as complex responsive processes and the present as the living movement of the negotiation of meaning.

Complex responsive processes of relating: the movement of experience in the living present

The first two volumes in the series *Complexity and Emergence in Organizations* (Stacey, Griffin and Shaw, 2000; Stacey, 2001) draw upon a particular strand of work in the natural complexity sciences (especially Prigogine, 1997; Goodwin, 1997) as a source of analogies for human action. These analogies are understood in terms of perspectives on human society and human psychology that I have been discussing in this chapter (the thought of Mead and Elias) to formulate a theory of organization and management called complex responsive process of relating. This section provides a brief summary of this theory taken from Stacey (2001).

Complex responsive processes of relating are temporal processes of interaction between human bodies in the medium of symbols patterning themselves as themes in communicative action. These themes are continuously reproducing and potentially transforming themselves in the process of bodily interaction itself. The themes of communicative interaction are also understood as the emergent enabling constraints (power and leadership) within which individual and collective identity and difference is perpetually constructed as continuity and potential transformation. It is interacting persons who form and are formed by these themes.

The themes and variations of communicative interaction and power relating are iterated in the living present. Instead of just being a point that separates the past from the future, the present has the temporal structure of gesture–response between living bodies in the medium of symbols, as discussed earlier in this chapter. The turn-taking/turn-making process of conversational communication patterns itself as narrative and propositional themes, forming while being formed by bodily interactive communication at the same time, leaving behind the traces of history. Communicative action, patterned as official ideological themes, sustains current power relations and leadership positions, thereby giving rise to the dynamics of inclusion and exclusion, which are associated with the evolution of unofficial ideologies that challenge official ideology and so current power relations and leadership positions. Communicative interaction is also patterned as ethical and motivational themes. Ethics is then understood as the patterning of interaction in the living present. Ethical and motivational themes form persons at the same time as persons in their interaction form the themes.

It is in this living present that the future is perpetually being constructed. Mead (1938) used the term "specious present", that is, the forming present, to signify the time structure of forming while being formed at the same time as the inclusion of the past and the future in the experience of the present. Husserl (1960) pointed to the same temporal structure when he used the terms "living present" as on-going potential and "life world" as the context. Wittgenstein (1980) referred to a similar notion as "the background" or "the hurly burly" of everyday life and the same thought is to be found in Shotter's (1993a) emphasis on ordinary, everyday conversation. Focusing attention in this way on the living present places the constructive role of ordinary, everyday communicative interaction between people at the centre of one's understanding of how organizations evolve in ethical and unethical ways. The process is one in which people negotiate and account for their immediate actions to each other in ordinary conversation with its turn-taking/turn-making, gesture-response structure. This is simultaneously a process of sustaining and shifting ordinary, everyday power relations and judgments on good conduct.

Communicative interaction in the living present is action of a local nature. Such communicative interaction consists of acts of one body directed to others, and to themselves, in a particular situation at a particular time. The themes patterning interaction are themes local to those who are interacting and attention is therefore directed to themes emerging in local interaction between people rather than thinking in terms of themes across global situations. Whatever the global themes one might want to articulate for an organization or a society, they have reality only insofar as they are expressed in local situations in the living present. Ethical and unethical themes do not "exist" outside of bodily interaction and bodily interaction has to be local.

Themes patterning communicative interaction

The most obvious themes, not surprisingly, are those that reflect the official ideology as formal-conscious-legitimate themes. These are the publicly proclaimed visions, values, simple ethical rules and cultures of an organization, as well as its hierarchically defined roles, policies, procedures, plans and so on. They all sustain current power relations, indeed that is usually their purpose, although official ideology may from time to time include policies aimed at shifting power relations, for example, by positive discrimination. Furthermore, it is well known that these formal-conscious-legitimate themes are not sufficient on their own for an organization to function and it is widely recognized that informal-conscious-legitimate themes pattern communicative interaction. Many of the cultural themes that pattern interaction are below the level of awareness so that informal-unconscious-legitimate themes also play a part. These themes are continuously reproduced with minimal variation as habits, customs and traditions. This is what institutionalization means.

However, this largely institutionalized configuration of patterning themes, the official ideology they express, the current power relations they sustain, and the ethical principles they articulate, must all have arisen at some point in the past as changes from other configurations. Furthermore, current configurations may well change, or they may remain the same despite efforts at change. In other words, power relations and leadership positions shift, or fail to shift, as changes emerge in the thematic patterning of communicative interaction. Organizational change is change in power relations, is change in the conflicting constraints of relating, is change in communicative interaction, is change in the communicative themes patterning the experience of being together. But how does this change occur?

People in organizations interact with each other in the living present in ways that are patterned by informal-conscious/unconscious-shadow themes at the same time as that experience is patterned by the legitimate themes already referred to. These themes may have qualities of spontaneity and many will reflect unofficial ideologies, conscious and unconscious, that may well undermine official ideology and so shift power relations. As such shifts emerge they are reflected in emergent changes in formal-conscious-legitimate themes. It must be remembered that none of these themes are stored anywhere but, rather, they are continually reproduced and potentially transformed in the on-going relating between people in the living present. It is not that formal-conscious-legitimate themes are of one kind, say intentional and designed, and informal-unconscious-shadow themes are self organizing/emergent. All are aspects of self-organizing processes of continually reproduced and potentially transformed communicative interaction, where intentions, designs and ethical principles are themselves themes. They differ in their public visibility and in their fluidity but they are not different in kind and they are never separated from each other. They are dynamically interlinked processes of evolution.

Although different aspects of themes patterning experience are simultaneously and inextricably interlinked aspects of the same process of symbolic interaction, they are often contradictory and conflicting. In effect, they often serve completely different purposes. Legitimate themes, whether they be formal or informal, conscious or unconscious, are largely habitual. They have arisen in previous communicative interaction and are being reproduced in communicative interaction in the living present with relatively little variation. It follows that they are stabilizing and largely constructive of continuity. They are constraining in a particular way, namely, one that, in reflecting official ideology, sustains current power relations. In their constraint, legitimate themes enable repetitive joint action. Whether conscious or unconscious, shadow themes (always informal) are much more spontaneous and reflect unofficial ideologies, which may either sustain or threaten current power relations. For example, the official ideology may espouse equal opportunity policies while unofficial ideologies, making it feel natural to continue discriminating against women and minorities, sustain current power relations. On the other hand, shadow themes may express unofficial ideologies that covertly undermine official ideology and so threaten current power relations. It is in this potential for conflict between shadow and legitimate themes that the potential for transformation arises because transformation always involves some shift in power relations, some shift in current identity.

The currents of communicative interaction, therefore, do not constitute some harmonious whole and the living present is as much about conflict and competition as it is about harmony and cooperation. Indeed, without this paradox there could be no transformation. Looking backward or forward, no one is able to articulate fully what the themes were or how they linked into each other in reinforcing and contradictory ways. Each articulation is an act of interpretation in the living present as part of communicative interaction in the living present. Each act of interpretation in the living present reconstructs the past, potentially changing its meaning. Furthermore, no one can articulate all the themes in the process of communicative interaction in the living present of a particular local situation, each interpretation being yet another gesture in the on-going flow of gesture–response. It is even less possible for anyone to articulate all the interacting themes across an organization, an industry or a society. Again, any attempt is simply a localized interpretation in the living present.

Nevertheless, coherence emerges in the vast complexity of communicative interactions across enormous numbers of local situations because of the intrinsic capacity of self-organizing interaction to pattern itself coherently. That this is possible is demonstrated by the work of some complexity scientists. However, the pattern of this coherence is not predictable in advance and it involves both destruction and creation, both stability and instability.

Local nature of interaction

Communicative interaction always takes place in specific local situations in the living present. The local nature of these situations is often not hard to see, but particularly when it comes to managers and leaders at the top of an organizational hierarchy, the local nature of interaction might require some explanation. After all, it is supposed to be the role of the chief executive, for example, to act in relation to the whole of an organization. However, closer examination of what a chief executive actually does, points to another interpretation. A competent chief executive will indeed be thinking and talking about the organization as a whole but to whom does he or she talk in this way? A chief executive, like anyone else in an organization, talks most frequently about matters of greatest concern to a relatively small group of trusted others. The chief executive's important communicative interactions take place, therefore, in the local situation of other senior executives. Their communicative interaction is patterned by the processes of themes shaping themes, formal and informal, conscious and unconscious, legitimate and shadow, just as anyone else's is.

There are, of course, differences as well as similarities between the processes of communicative interaction involving a powerful chief executive and those involving the much less powerful. When a chief executive makes a public gesture it potentially calls forth responses in much larger numbers of others than is the case with the less powerful. However, just what those responses will be cannot be arranged by the chief executive, as anyone in that position knows only too well. The meaning of the chief executive's gesture and its impact on the organization will emerge in many local situations, including his or her own, in the living present of conversations around the globe. No one can determine the dynamic of interaction within an organization because that dynamic depends upon what others both within that organization and in other organizations are doing. In other words, an individual, or a group of individuals, powerful or otherwise, can make gestures of great importance but the responses called forth will emerge in local situations in the living present where an organization's future is perpetually being constructed. This is not to say that powerful managers, such as chief executives, have no effect on the "whole" organization. Clearly, they often have major, widespread effects. However, what a chief executive does emerges in his or her local communicative interaction and the nature of the impact on the organization emerges in many other local situations, all in the living present. The focus of attention, in trying to make sense of what happens, shifts from the chief executive's statement or new tool to the processes in which the statement or tool arises and to the widespread local situations in which they have their effects. Instead of taking it for granted that powerful chief executives actually individually change organizations directly through their intended actions, the complex responsive process perspective invites one to explore the communicative processes in which the mere presence of, the images of, and the fantasies about leaders all affect local processes of communicative interaction in the living present.

This perspective immediately focuses attention on the importance of local communicative interaction in the living present, particularly its thematic patterning, its gesture–response-structure and its reflection in ideologies and power relations. Ethics, the nature of good conduct, is understood in terms of the themes patterning interaction, which is forming and being formed by interacting persons.

6 Leadership and ethics:
emergence in everyday social interaction

- Ethics: the emergent structures forming human experience
- Contrasting time and causality in two theories of experience
- Cult leadership versus functional leadership: recognizing diversity through conflict
- Summary

> Though it is unplanned and not immediately controllable,
> the overall process of development of a society is not in the least
> incomprehensible. There are no "mysterious" social forces behind it.
> (Elias, 1970: 146)

We have inherited from modernism, with its emphasis on the autonomous individual, an idealist ethics of universals and the idea that leaders are quite literally "out" of the ordinary. I have argued in this book for a refocusing of our attention on the meaning we are making every day, in every moment in the living present. In this chapter, I would like to look at the question of ethics at this everyday scale and draw attention, in doing so, to the accompanying "everyday" emergence of leadership.

Ethics: the emergent structures forming human experience

What is the close correlation between leadership theory and ethical theory about? Both are concerned with the future, and specifically with action into the future. This implies that they are both very much about "who" is acting into the future. In other words, will the identity of this "who" remain intact in this act into the future? Both leadership and ethics have in common very firm ideas about the temporal sequence of this action into the future which we in the Western world have come to hold over the past two centuries of modernist thinking. It is the very core of what we believe about both ethics and leadership. There is a dominantly held belief that in our everyday exchanges with others we are autonomous individuals, each of whom is capable of making rational decisions based on reflection apart from and before the action itself, weighing the consequences of the outcomes and deciding whether to proceed or not. The dominant temporal view we so firmly hold is that first we reflect and then we act. We do this on the basis of a "contract" with all other individuals according to which each of us will be held responsible for the act that is "carried out" after rational reflection. Leaders are those who are somehow able to understand the consequences better than others or have proven themselves to be worthy of imitation because of the superior quality they display in taking this contract with others seriously. Others, therefore, voluntarily agree to follow them as their contribution to sustaining the identity of all in whatever kind of group they all happen to be in, large or small. We seem to believe that over the years, practices, rules and laws become clearer as they take various codified forms to which we refer in our reflection. Should the individual not be able to find a clear reference for a proposed action in such codes, it is nevertheless believed that he or she can use reason in the light of the "contract" with others to decide on any proposed action. The basis of ethical reflection, then, is referral to the codes and rational decision making. If we fail to refer to the codes, or we fail in our rational reflection before we act, then we are culpable.

In Chapter 1, I referred to the plot of a recent film about a utility company contaminating the water supply of surrounding residential communities. In the terms I have just described, it is clear that ethical responsibility lay with those in senior positions who attempted to cover up the story. They did not keep the contract. They did not take the action required by ethical codes or ethical reasoning. But I also pointed out that we have now come to look at the organization as a whole, referring to it as if it were an individual acting with intention, and therefore also being ethically responsible in the same way as the autonomous individual. Throughout the film, anger is expressed at "it". This has been taken over in our legal system in that organizations are "incorporated" and legal action must be directed at "it". This makes it possible to hold leadership and ethical theories based on codes and reason. The film is but one of many which are openly critical of the "system". Those viewing it enjoy the experience of some senior executives getting caught in the end and of the person who pursued justice appearing as a heroine. Perhaps one of the reasons that the film is both so popular and enjoyable as a plot is that it reassures the audience that in spite of everything our "world" is still okay. Basically we do not need to change our thinking about ethics or leadership. We only need more individuals who play according to the rules as they are and become heroes or heroines. And of course the heroine here gets a large financial reward, so the happy end is complete.

But a key question still remains: how is it that such films enjoy great success in commercial and entertainment terms, but in the end make no difference to the everyday social behaviour of those working in organizations of the kind they portray? The question does not arise as to how it was possible that so many people were involved in contaminating their own water supply over a number of years, and as to how so many others knew about it and did nothing. Because the view we have of ethics and leadership is so deeply engrained, we have a "blind spot" in that we have a taken-for-granted habit of ignoring such questions. I also mentioned the very successful book by Richard Sennett in which he describes the corrosion of character and local communities resulting from the business and personnel practices of large organizations in which individuals lose a sense of identity. Again, such books appear regularly and are read by large numbers of people, but there is no evidence of changes in behaviour or in the basic notions about ethics and leadership. One has the sense that the organization, "it", should decide to change and proceed to do so.

I have argued that the reason for this lack of change is that, despite the radical nature of their criticism, these films and books actually reaffirm a way of thinking that is at the root of the social behaviour they are criticizing. This way of thinking is so taken-for-granted and pervasive that it is extremely difficult to find a perspective from which to draw attention to it. In this book I have tried to establish such a perspective, which I have called participative self-organization. Since ethics is so fundamental I will begin there.

What is ethics?

Ethical theory is concerned with the structures required to sustain identity. These structures can be understood in two senses, reflected in the differentiation between ethics and morals, closely related to the different senses in which one can understand the notion of person. As I pointed out in the last chapter, the original notion of person combined a duality referring to the mask of actors (inferring roles and changing appearances), on the one hand, and to substance and foundation, on the other. The former meaning refers to the changeability of person, while the latter refers to the core of stability and continuity of the person. This duality of change and continuity is at the core of what identity is about. When speaking of ethics, we tend to emphasize more the fact that the identity is what it is because it has the capacity to deal with change, whereas moral codes and philosophies have tended to refer to the stability and substance at the core of identity. It is the latter aspect of person and the connected aspect of moral codes to do with stability that has been elevated in modernism to become the theory of ethics. The strength of modernism and its concept of science led to the way in which it made visible a particular perspective on structure and order, as the basis of the age of enlightenment. But modernism achieved this at a price, which became evident over the ensuing two centuries. Like all strengths, in excess or when made exclusive, they increasingly become weaknesses. Modernism can point to order but it has lost the sense that change necessarily entails disorder and destruction. Modern ethical theory, and the associated leadership theory derived from it, has the same strengths and weaknesses and, therefore, the same tendency to ignore the changeability of persons and the ethical aspects of dealing with change.

The particular focus on order that enables modernist scientists to discover what they then describe as reality means that they must, as observers, be detached from what they are observing. As I described in Chapter 1, this has become our taken-for-granted everyday world. And it has become the basis for our theory of ethics and our everyday theory of leadership. The distinction "everyday" is important here. We have split what the concept of person and identity tries to bring together, a duality of change and stability. Ethics has come to be regarded *both* as the stable pole of universal principles, *and* it is complemented by theories of such as that of leadership which are in effect ethical theories of "everyday" interaction. The two poles of the duality have become split into the "both . . . and" way of thinking I have described in Chapter 1 and referred to throughout this book. The paradox of stability and change at the core of the notion of identity is resolved so that we no longer notice it.

One possible reaction to this emphasis on the stable pole in theories of ethics and leadership which has gained prominence is a factor in what is known as postmodernism. The paradoxical tension of stability and change in understanding the person and identity, and therefore ethics and morals, is declared illusory and the proof submitted for this is the failure of modernism. Any attempt to unify a sense of self is met with skepticism, and the results of modernist sciences are turned against the very spirit of modernism evidenced in the rational autonomous individual. This skepticism demonstrates virtuosity in the ability to move from one side of the "both . . . and" position to the other. As soon as any "opponent" tries to demonstrate the truth of any one position, the skeptic moves to the other. In effect this skeptic can deflate the strength of modernism, turning it into a weakness, should anyone attempt to maintain it as a strength, and inflate the weakness should anyone attempt to take that position.

In contrast to such skepticism, Mead and others I have mentioned are proposing to take modernism seriously and transform it from within. This means holding on to the limitations of modernist thought, which have emerged over the decades, and asking what it is that is causing us to see such limitations. What Mead is proposing is a different way of thinking about everyday social interaction, not as observers of experience but rather as participants in experience, the nature of which is self-organizing sense making. He is drawing attention to what we are doing everyday in all our actions and arguing that we have developed the habit of ignoring it. How could this be possible? How could we have become blind to something so obvious? Mead's argument is quite simply that we have developed the habit of regarding the present as something apart from the future and the past. It has become a habit of thought for us to think ourselves as also being apart from our experience as the present movement of time. Largely due to the success of the scientific method, and especially in the form of the recent dominance of systems thinking, we have come to regard ourselves as both having experience and also being able to detach ourselves from this experience, to manipulate and change it by applying scientific thinking. This has come to be synonymous with our understanding of management. I will return to Mead's concept of experience in the next section, but first I examine his thinking on ethics in terms of the development of ethical theory over the centuries.

Mead does not regard his view of the emergence of the social and moral order, that is, the structures that are viewed by all as sustaining society and that are the most important factor in its survival, as having always been the "structure" of ethics itself. Ethics too has been evolving for over 2000 years and has been shaped by the large-scale economic, geological and societal shifts, which seem to occur every two or three centuries. He understood the particular view that he took as having begun around the beginning of the nineteenth century. What then is ethics? What is it that has somehow remained the same throughout these evolutionary transformations?

These seem to be straightforward questions. Given that we have been using the term ethics for over two thousand years, we should be able to answer them in a straightforward fashion. The answer might be that ethics is the customs, practices, cultures, principles, codes, laws and so on, which emerge and become the "solid reality" of codes that seem to be an unchanging subject matter. Thus we tend to lose sight of the change side of the duality because of the long periods of relative stability, which lead to the impression that ethics somehow escapes evolution and has the universal character spoken of by Kant.

Today, however, as the globe becomes more and more of a "village" because of advances in communication, we are constantly reminded of the plurality of cultures, religions and other groupings, which are guided by greatly varying beliefs and codes of behaviour. Whatever their moral principles may be, they all evolve in the everyday social exchange that was first referred to by Aristotle as "ethics". He wrote two works on ethics but the most famous and influential was named, after his son, the *Nicomachean Ethics*. Ethics in ancient Greece had become teachings about customs and developed into very practical institutions teaching people how to live. In this sense it encompassed what we refer to today as culture and politics. In the *Nicomachean Ethics* Aristotle drew these teachings together with a very particular goal in mind. He was attempting to renegotiate some of the customs which regulated who was able to remain in the "polis" of Athens as a citizen and who was not. He reflected on the goals of the state and on who was to be considered a citizen in terms of these goals. In the end he lost the argument and because he had not been born in Athens he was eventually forced to leave. In the Middle Ages, ethics became formalized in metaphysical systems and took on the form of a philosophical science at the universities. It is this form of ethics that was reconciled with the new concept of the individual in modernism and became the basis of the study of ethics at universities as we have inherited it. We find it difficult to recognize in this the original theme, which was about the identity of given groups and the practices which served to sustain this identity with both its continuity and its change. Instead, ethics has developed, in the extreme, a focus on stability and universality. During the Renaissance much of what had been treated as ethics was dealt with as the teachings and practice of rhetoric.

Without doubt the themes of culture and leadership are theories of ethics. They represent a platform for the discussion of the survival and evolution of the most powerful organizations in our world today. But this discussion reflects the split of theory and practice, of the academic study of the social sciences and the world of those who regard themselves as being persons of simple and direct action. This is again the "both . . . and" way of thinking which gives up on any attempt to regard theory and practice as two aspects of the same thing.

This is one of the reasons why, despite the enormous advances in technology, there has been so little change in our thinking of leadership as a theory of ethics. It is still very much focused on the concept of the autonomous individual as developed in the modernism of the past 250 years. It is still, in a very much taken-for-granted manner, spoken of in a language sounding similar to that of mythologies in speaking of the power of individuals. Examples can be heard daily in financial news programmes about one man or woman succeeding in "turning around" corporations having hundreds of thousands of employees in hundreds of locations around the globe. The pay scales of senior executives in Western societies reflect such myths about the capability of single persons in large-scale operations. It comes as no surprise that the key market of management literature focuses on this centre of power. The literature on leadership is, however, based on a very few central tenets which can be "packaged" in an infinite variety of seemingly different messages. I have been arguing in this book, as have my co-authors in this series on *Emergence and Complexity in Organizations*, that recent findings in the natural sciences undermine concepts that have been taken from the natural sciences to support key notions of what organizations are and how they change.

The ethical theory Mead is proposing as an alternative

Mead points directly to the split in our understanding of ethics:

> There may be, indeed, intellectual processes involved in stating this moral order, but such statement is confined, in the nature of the case, to apologetic and speculative thought, to thought which cannot be a part of the immediate moral consciousness.
>
> (Mead, 1908: 314–17)

He argues against Kant's notion of ethical universals as in any sense "fixed realities", apart from and before action and against which human conduct is to be judged as ethical or not. This would imply that the meaning of an action could have been known in advance. Instead, he is suggesting that the ethical interpretation of action is to be found in the action itself, in the on-going recognition of the meanings of actions that could not have been known in advance.

> The first implication that flows from this position is that the fundamental necessity of moral action is simply the necessity of action at all; or stated in other terms, that the motive does not arise from the relations of antecedently given ends of activities, but rather that the motive is the recognition of the end as it arises in consciousness. The other implication is that the moral interpretation of our experience must be found within the experience itself.
>
> (ibid.)

> That continual recognition requires new points of view that emerge in the conflictual interaction in which the future is perpetually being created. In other words, ethical meaning does not reside in external universals to be applied to interaction but, rather, ethical meaning continually emerges in the interaction itself. Ethics are being negotiated in the interaction.
>
> (ibid.)

Moral advance for Mead then consists not in adapting individuals to the fixed realities of a moral universe, but in constantly reconstructing and recreating the world as the individuals evolve. The quotes above are from an essay written in 1908. In the next section I examine his thought in an article written in 1923 after the experience of the First World War. He had come at that time to a more fully developed theory of the nature of experience as the basis of ethics. He speaks then of his theory of the present, which I explored in the previous chapter, as what he means by the expression "immediate moral consciousness".

The First World War had a profound effect on Mead. He had lived in Europe, mostly in Germany, for long periods in the last decades of the nineteenth century and had experienced the events which with hindsight could be seen as leading up to the war. In his earliest writings it is clear that ethics is at the centre of his thought and the experience of the war caused him to revise some of this earlier thought. Nevertheless a genuine optimism remained in his thought, as well as in that of John Dewey, concerning ethics. They were still very much influenced by the general sense that the United States was a new world that, on the basis of vastly extending education at all levels, would be able to solve many of the problems of the "old world". They were in this sense still under the influence of the Enlightenment as a belief in reason, even though both thinkers were very much aware of the limitations of the focus on the individual. Mead was also optimistic that the emerging growth in businesses in both size and geographical extension would have positive effects; prosperity and new possibilities of creative interaction would also in turn influence education.

The war did move Mead, however, to look again carefully at reason and examine its role in the years leading up to the war. He noticed how important the tendency to idealize in a cult manner had been in groups expressing a growing sense of militarism in Europe. Since he understood social interaction in terms of a conversation of gestures and the "I–me" dialectic, he began to emphasize the way these idealizations must be functionalized in the everyday conflicts in which we are always negotiating the future on the basis of the past.

The idealizations Mead is referring to can, if they are detached from the everyday present of social interaction, be reified and instrumentalized as unreflected ideologies. I referred in Chapter 5 to the reaction of Adorno and Horkheimer to the Second World War and the holocaust. In their work *Dialectic of Enlightenment,* all the optimism of the beginning of the last century had disappeared. For them, the reality of the Second World War was the final and unavoidable proof of the bankruptcy of the idealistic and universalistic ethics of modernist reason. This reason can, as the holocaust demonstrated, become the victim of its own idealizations. This ethics can prove powerless in challenging the complete instrumentalization of these idealizations. As Adorno points out in writing the *Minima Moralia,* one can see in our everyday language and the stories we tell ourselves whether we are challenging or surrendering to these idealizations. What become large-scale wars of destruction or achievements of creativity can first be seen in the detail of the everyday. It is very important to reflect on what we think this everyday experience is about; whether it is about making sense of our experience as detached observers or whether experience is of its very nature the everyday process of making sense. This is a matter we tend to ignore.

Contrasting time and causality in two theories of experience

We have come to forget in our everyday world that theories about reality are not themselves things. We reify such theories and view them as things that can be used to understand and change our world. In doing this, we change our understanding of the temporal nature of our experience. The temporal quality of the present takes on the reified time of our theories, so that we can use the "past" to change the future. This is of course possible, but Mead argues that we have, over the last two centuries, increasingly lost sight of fact that this is only a small part of what our world is about.

Humans have evolved in a way that makes human experience different to that of other organisms because of a unique temporal structure, referred to in the previous chapter as the movement of the "living present". In this living present, the past and the future are not separate from the present. It is in the present that we are continuously constructing the future on the basis of the enabling constraints developed over time as our past. In other words, because humans have a unique capacity to call forth in themselves the attitudes of others they can know what they are doing. Knowing what one is doing immediately incorporates anticipation and expectation into the action of the present and it also immediately incorporates reconstructions of actions past, or memory, all as the basis of acting in the present. Anticipations and expectations affect what we remember at any point and what we remember at any point affects expectation and anticipation. One acts back on the other, forming the basis of action in the present. In this way, the movement of the living present is experience, having a circular time structure that arises simply because humans have the capacity for knowing what they are doing. In this section I will explore this notion and its implications for everyday social interaction. There is nothing mysterious about any of this but it is made difficult to understand by the prejudice and the "blinding" power of our habit of excluding the future and past from our understanding of the present.

Before going on to contrast different views of experience, it is important to mention at this point that Mead's notion of the present, which I am referring to as the living present, is in no way similar to that to be found in a large number of recent books pressing modern humans to regain a sense of the present. These books have titles appealing to a new focus on the "now" as a liberating power. However, what they mean by the present actually intensifies the exclusion of the past and future from the present. They describe the present as liberation from worrying about the past, which is finished and cannot be changed, and from anxiety about the future, which is unknown. Their most powerful prescription, then, is for people to ignore both the past and the future as a way of attaining freedom from anxiety. Social interaction is understood in terms of autonomous individuals able to choose to forget and so "encapsulate" themselves in the present. It is, however, precisely the exclusion of the past and future from the present that gives a particular diffuse quality to anxiety about the future as the unknown. Because the future is excluded, it becomes potentially much more threatening as a "detached" unknown, increasing the sense of having no control whatever.

It is not surprising that self-help methods to do with concentrating exclusively on being in the present find little support in the business world. There one finds numerous themes dominating interaction in the present that are concerned with attempting to exercise as much control as possible over the future. This is found currently in the focus on vision, simple rules of social interaction, the importance of values in guiding behaviour, the strategic planning function of leadership, and so on. Here, the future is also not included in the present but instead of being split off and forgotten, it is split off and exclusively focused on, so distracting attention from the present. The future is much spoken of in the present, but only in terms of themes of control and intentional change. For this to be achieved the future must be reduced to simple aspects that can be manipulated to determine the present. This is very different to the notion of the living present in which the future, as expectation and anticipation, is in the detail of actual interactions taking place now, as is the past as reconstructions in this process of memory. There is no dismissing the past or the future here, nor is there any distraction of attention from the present of what we are doing together.

This distinction between different ways of thinking about time is of such importance that I would like to examine in more detail the difference between Mead's understanding of time and causality in the present and the understanding that is taken-for-granted in the dominant way we think about everyday social interaction. To do this, I will take up time and causality in Freud's thought as an example of how we tend to reify theories and the influence this has on our understanding of the present.

Contrasting the understanding of experience in Freud's and Mead's thought

Many of Freud's key notions have come into our everyday language to such a degree that those who have studied his thought more rigorously cringe at the vagueness and readiness with which terms such as the unconscious, superego, neurosis, and so on, are used as simple causal explanations of our experience. Freud was aware of the nature of hypothesis and theory and would not himself have reified his terminology in this simple manner. But in comparison with Mead's thought, especially concerning participation and emergence, I would argue that Freud, despite being revolutionary in breaking many taboos, still reaffirmed a causality centred on the concept of the autonomous individual. I am examining it here as an example of how the modernist basis of theories leads to the possibility of easily reifying elements of the theory and thus stopping short of a theory of participative self-organization. This can lead to their being easily subsumed under systemic self-organization, and eliminating the possibility of participative self-organization. In Freud's case, there is the clear example of this in the work of psychoanalytic theorists at the Tavistock Institute (for example, Miller and Rice, 1967) and of family therapists (for example, Campbell *et al.*, 1994) who argue that deficiencies in Freud's thinking about causality can be rectified by an underpinning from systems theory. In effect, they support simple cause and effect science with the formative causality of systemic self-organization. It is important to understand how they have made this move of thinking about organizations as if they were whole systems that can be treated therapeutically using theories developed around individual experience.

In an essay published in 1923, Mead examined an aspect of Freud's thought that might have led him to suggest a kind of emergence. Mead draws attention to the way in which Freud posits:

> a structure in our experience which runs out beyond what we ordinarily term our consciousness: that this structure of idea determines to a degree not generally recognized the very manner of our perception as well as that of our thinking, and yet this structure itself is generally not in the focus of our attention and passes unnoticed in our thought and perceiving.
>
> (Mead, 1923: 229)

He notes that:

> it is one of the valuable by-products of the Freudian psychology that it has brought many people to recognize that we do not only our thinking but also our perceiving with minds that have already an organized structure which determines in no small degree what the world of our immediate and reflective experience shall be.
>
> (ibid.)

Freud's thought, therefore, seems to point toward a concept very close to what might have become self-organization, namely, a structure that is itself unnoticed but is, in some way, organizing experience. However, Freud himself stops short of this and develops his understanding of consciousness in a way that can, all to easily, be reduced to the mechanical thinking of cause and effect. This is what systemic theorists do with the notion of systemic self-organization, for example, when they claim that mental models determine our experience in the self-organizing manner of formative causality, or that we must better understand vision and simple rules, "getting them right" in order to shape the future. This, they argue, reaffirms Freud's insights although he did not have the advantage of the perspective of systems theory.

But Mead goes on to argue that his thought begins where Freud's ends. To explain the "organization" of our thinking and perceiving in terms of *social order,* Freud bases his understanding of the social on his theory of individual consciousness; to do otherwise would call for a type of causality foreign to Freud's thought. This brings him to suggest the theory of consciousness that he does, namely, a consciousness located in the individual, which has been developed in the clash between innate drives and interactions with parents as individuals. The individual is the centre of understanding experience. Freud understood the social in much the same terms as he understood the individual. For him, group phenomena were based on the individual substituting the leader for his or her own superego. The central group experience is the universal one of the primal horde in which the sons murder the father and this mirrors the central individual experience of the Oedipus complex. The group is understood as an individual writ large. Systems theorists drawing on Freud also postulate a "super" individual, the group-as-a-whole, which is determined by the same structures that determine the individual. Self-organization here is the same formative causality as that used by the natural scientists and this is a causality that they themselves have put into the system as a hypothesis.

Mead was aware that we cannot understand the broader question of the emergence of moral and social structures in human interaction if we maintain such a limited understanding of causality. Freud's thinking forms and is formed by the modernist theme of the autonomous, rational individual. Although he expanded on this by introducing elements from biology and included the irrational, his causal thinking remained within the limits of thinking in terms of wholes. When systems thinking is added, the formative causality becomes more sophisticated in understanding the "whole" as a system but reflects the same wholeness of the autonomous individual as the centre of experience. That this is still very much the basis of our thinking today is reflected in the film plot of the utility company contaminating the water of residential communities mentioned above. The actions of "responsible" senior executives are viewed as those of autonomous rational individuals who made choices. Systems thinking has further influenced us to understand the organization also as a whole that is responsible so that we view ourselves as the victims of the culpable actions of "it". We remain blind to the evolving social structures that continue to determine everyday social action.

Mead argued that organized social structures imply a causality that cannot be explained in terms of the individual alone, as Freud did. This meant moving to an understanding of causality in which the future of an individual could not be understood simply in terms of the past, just as the evolution of the structure could not be understood simply in terms of the individual. It is at this point that Mead took up the contrast between cult values and functional values that I introduced in Chapter 4. This distinction, in the light of Mead's theory of time and causality, points to why his thought escapes the tendency to be understood rather mechanically as simple cause and effect and points to another way of viewing causality.

For Mead, values are of key importance in understanding the type of evolving organized social structure that is missing in Freud's thought. Because Freud understood consciousness in terms of the individual, values are then expressions of individuals. Mead, however, differentiated between cult and functional values to draw attention to their social nature:

> The cult value of the institution is legitimate only when the social order for which it stands is hopelessly ideal. . . . There are no absolute values. There are only values which, on account of incomplete social organization, we cannot as yet estimate . . .
>
> (ibid.: 238)

This issue of the meaning of values was key in forming Mead's thinking on the temporal structure of the present. For Mead, the present is being formed by our values because one important *aspect of the present* is that we are continuously constructing our future. Taking cult values as the legitimate social order would mean having to escape to an ideal world of absolutes. But we are forced to do so if we continue to think in the causality of wholes. This causality implies direct cause–effect relationships according to which the values of the "whole" shape the present. In other words, the whole system has inherent values that shape the elements of the system as formative causality. I have pointed this out repeatedly as the key characteristic of systemic self-organization. Mead, however, focuses on the causality of values in terms of "incomplete social organization", that is, a causality that does not shape social interaction in terms of the "whole". This is necessary in order to move to an understanding of what Mead means by participation and what I have been referring to as participative self-organization. To explain this causality of "incomplete social organization", Mead distinguishes between cult and functional values. Cult values "are the most precious part of social heritage" (ibid.: 237) and they are functionalized in ordinary everyday action. In other words, idealized values emerge in the historical evolution of any institution and these are ascribed to the institution. We then remain blind to the evolving social structures that continue to determine everyday social action.

Mead claimed that thinking in terms of the individual and a causality of the whole blinds us to the *emergence* of the "social heritage" of cult values and how that heritage *evolves* as the basis of rules, codes of practice, laws, and so on, which structure everyday social interaction. Idealized cult values become functional values in the everyday interactions between members of the organization. In Chapter 4, I gave the example of the cult value of a hospital that might be to "provide each patient with the best possible care". However, such a cult value has to be repeatedly functionalized in many unique specific situations throughout the day. For example, whether "best possible care" means two doses of medication per day or three, whether a particular procedure is affordable or not. In other words, as soon as cult values become functional values in real daily interaction, conflict arises and it is this conflict that must be negotiated by people in their practical interaction with each other. As participative self-organization this remains "incomplete"; no one can "as yet estimate" all of the results. This is how people are continuously constructing the future. But this does not in any way suggest that they are not acting with intention. Just as they are being formed by the structures, they are also forming intentions on the basis of the cult values they have from their past, "the most precious part of social heritage", in order to shape social action, that is, the constructing of the future in the movement of the present. No matter what others may think, the intentions people form are viewed by them as "good" in terms of what is being negotiated in the present. But of course they are only able to do so as a social act, which means that others are also forming intentions, and what these intentions will mean emerges in the conflictual conversation of gestures and responses as the living present. For this reason, Mead sees conflict not only as unavoidable, but also as the very essence of the movement of thought, change and evolution. This means that cult values and functional values are not in any sense mutually exclusive. To the contrary, they are both paradoxically, simultaneously a part of the movement of the living present.

A note on Mead's use of the term "functional"

Much has happened in the development of sociology since Mead's death. One of the most influential theories over the last century has been the focus on structure and function in theories of social systems. In developing his theory of "value", Parsons (see Chapter 4) equated function with role and he was concerned with social balance and equilibrium (see also Chapter 2). For Parsons the "organization of action elements is, for purposes of the theory of action, above all a function of the relation of the actor to his situation . . ." (Parsons, 1951: 5). Because of his interest in the homeostasis of the system he was interested in the reciprocal expectations and sanctions of the "actor ego" and the "alter ego" which contribute to the on-going homeostasis of the system. Understanding values in this normative sense made them central to Parsons' understanding of social roles as the elements of the structures comprising the systems.

Elias, for example, does not himself use the term "functional" because of the "value judgement" it has taken on from systems thinking:

> The concept of "function" . . . contains an inappropriate value judgement which, moreover, is made explicit in neither interpretation nor use. The inappropriateness of the evaluations is due to the fact that they tend – unintentionally – to use the terms for those tasks which are "good" for the "whole", because they contribute to the preservation and integrity of the existing social system. Human activities which either fail or appear to fail to do that are therefore branded as "dysfunctional".
>
> (Elias, 1970: 77)

Mead, writing of course before Parsons and Elias, is not using the term in this sense. He is interested in the emergence and evolution of structure and wants to understand how it is in the intentional functionalizing of cult values in the movement of intention in the living present that the structures are both sustained and potentially changed at the same time. As mentioned in Chapter 4, Mead turns to the question asked in the tradition of thinking known as teleological causality, that is, how the end or goal toward which we are striving becomes a motivating cause in the present. Here Mead is pointing to what my co-authors and I have called transformative teleology (Stacey, Griffin and Shaw, 2000). It is the key factor in the distinction between participative self-organization and systemic self-organization. Mead argued that in embodied human social interaction it is not useful to focus on the whole because it is "hopelessly ideal" and "absolute". However, the systemic does focus on the whole. Teleology in systems thinking is about the causal process of movement toward ends and goals which are internal to systems only because they have been imputed into the system by observers treating the system from a detached perspective. In drawing attention to cult and functional values, Mead's teleology is quite different.

Sustaining and transforming the social order

There is a story told by Gregory Bateson that may help to illustrate what Mead is getting at in his distinction between cult and functional values. After many years of research and work in differing professions, Bateson ended his public life as one of 25 regents of a Board overseeing state universities in California. He found that he was unable to survive there due to the stifling bureaucratic procedures necessary to try to effect changes and remain in dialogue with students. "I personally had more influence on the processes of education as a senior lecturer than as a regent" (Bateson and Bateson, 1987: 169). Moving to the Esalon Institute he found again that he was unable to survive. There it was due to what other residents and participants made of the ideas he presented. He found the conclusions they drew to support vague New Age ideas and the connections they made to other thinkers incomprehensible and foreign to what he thought he was saying. They found a "soul mate" whereas he found utter confusion. He stayed begrudgingly at Esalon, presumably because he was able to work in solitude, with the occasional escape in conversations with outside friends. Bateson relates the story as one of frustration and disappointment compared to what he had expected would come of his work over the years.

I mention this in the context of Mead's differentiation of cult and functional values because it seems relevant to the source of Bateson's frustration. In bureaucracies, cult and functional values are closely coupled. Increasing size of organizations makes it more and more difficult to functionalize cult value in a way that becomes a cogent argument in the day-to-day conflicts. There are too many persons influencing the present conflicts who are relatively detached from the local interaction. At the same time it becomes correspondingly difficult to argue against cult values presented as more or less direct argumentation because they take on the absolute character which becomes a shield against change or transformation. At the Esalon Institute the case was the opposite extreme. The cult and functional values were so loosely coupled that it was easy for the New Age enthusiasts to believe that the cult values they saw as the consequence of Bateson's theories could be directly made into functional values and so effect large-scale change. In the end this made them no different to cult values so that the social order did in fact become hopelessly idealized.

In his earlier writings, Mead himself did not recognize the paradoxical relation between cult and functional values. As mentioned in Chapter 4, he first formulated the expression "cult value" to explain the negative influence of cults of military strength in different European countries leading up to the First World War. In later writing, he recognized that he was splitting off the negative or destructive aspects, typical of psychologies focusing on the individual. To understand the emergence of cult values, he shifted to a focus on the social order and coined the expression "functional value" to describe how both play a role in sustaining and potentially transforming this order.

This means that both are paradoxically a part of the movement of the living present. This does not imply anything mysterious. Without the paradox of cult and functional values, the experience of the present would feel numbing to us, just as was the case for Bateson when everyday social interaction tended to one extreme or the other. I would like in summarizing this section in Table 6.1 to list some of the characteristics of the two views of experience I have been contrasting – on the one hand experience in terms of causalities of the whole and on the other experience from the point of view of a causality of transformation in an "incomplete social organization".

I am not making this distinction to suggest a simple negation of thinking in wholes. We will of course continue to use the power of reason to

Table 6.1 *Two views of experience*

Experience in terms of the whole	Experience in terms of incomplete social organization
. . . explains experience in terms of causalities of the whole (cause/effect) (formative self-organizing of whole systems)	. . . explains experience in terms of the causality of the process of sustaining and potentially transforming the structures of the social order in everyday interaction
. . . refers to individuals as autonomous and to organizations as wholes	. . . refers to the emergence of persons in local interaction
. . . views identity in terms of the whole as good split off from the bad as dysfunctional	. . . views identity in terms of functionalizing cult values in the present as the conflict of taking the next step
. . . views past, present and future as separate wholes	. . . views the present as including the movement of the past in constructing the future
. . . results in diffuse anxiety about a radically unknown future with a focus on controlling the present	. . . takes anxiety seriously. Anxiety motivates the forming of intention as a contribution to the conflict in which the future is being co-constructed
. . . tends to idealize and reify wholes	. . . deals with the wholes which appear continuously as ideologies to be negated in negotiating the construction of the future

idealize and instrumentalize by creating tools of persuasion and efficiency by which we can achieves our goals. But it is important to remember that in doing so we are literally instrumentalizing our *selves*. We are doing so in the conflictual present in which we are negotiating these aims and goals as the construction of our future. In the next section I look more closely at the way in which we are in the habit of ignoring this living present, which is the theme of ethics. It is in the living present that we emerge as persons.

Cult leadership versus functional leadership: recognizing diversity through conflict

Conflict is at the very core of Mead's theory of ethics. It is through conflict that we are continuously recreating our world and becoming our selves, that is, our identity.

> If we were willing to recognize that the environment which surrounds the moral self is but the statement of the conditions under which his different conflicting impulses may get their expression, we would perceive that the recognition must come from a new point of view which comes to consciousness through the conflict. The environment must change *pari passu* with the consciousness. Moral advance consists not in adapting individual natures to the fixed realities of a moral universe, but in constantly reconstructing and recreating the world as the individuals evolve.
>
> (Mead, 1908: 315)

Elias shared a similar view of the importance of conflict. He pointed to how reluctant people seem to be to explore patterns of conflict in social interaction, preferring to ascribe their difficulties to the advances of technology.

> Despite science fiction nightmares, machines have no will of their own. They can neither invent nor produce themselves, and cannot compel us to serve them. All decisions and activities they carry out are human decisions and activities. We project threats and compulsions on to them, but if we look more closely we always see interdependent groups of people threatening and compelling each other by means of machines. When people blame their uneasiness about life in scientific-technical-industrial societies on to bombs or machines, scientists or engineers, they are evading the difficult and maybe unpleasant task of seeking clearer, more realistic interpretation of the structure of human interweavings and particularly of the patterns of conflict rooted in them. It is this structure which is responsible for the development and use of scientific weapons of war, and for the hardships of life in factories and metropolises.
>
> (Elias, 1970: 24–5)

In distinguishing between idealized cult values and the funtionalizing of intentions in the present, Mead drew our attention to the everyday arena of conflict that we have the habit of ignoring or denying. In participating with each other, people functionalize the ideal in conflict and this is the ethical basis of leadership theory. Leadership theory is also an *everyday* theory of ethics. I am emphasizing "everyday" because we so easily ignore its central importance in the evolution of the groups, organizations and societies we participate in. In the next section I examine more closely the relevance of this distinction between cult and functional in terms of leadership.

The emergence of leadership

As mentioned above, the notion of person combines a duality referring to the mask of actors (inferring roles and changing appearances), on the one hand, and to substance and foundation, on the other. In participative self-organization, where participation means the direct experience of relationship between human beings, the emerging identity in the tension of this duality will have a singular and plural, an "I" and a "we" in the unity of the social act. It is the singular and plural of the same phenomenon: the emergence of persons. The roles emerge in interaction and there is no question of an individual choosing a mask, or role by and for him-/herself. Its emergence and its meaning is social. As groups evolve and develop a past they begin to recognize various members in roles, one of which is leader. The notion of person encompasses personal spontaneity, creativity and ethical responsibility, all of which, however, cannot emerge without the group and the group cannot emerge without the ethical responsibility of persons. Hegel's concept of person, which he developed as an alternative to the concept of the autonomous individual, allows for this paradox since it does not insist on a linear concept of time as beginning and end (see O'Donohue, 1993: 135–44).

We can then move to an alternative to the description of the modernist autonomous individual with which I began this chapter. The "mask", the role, of leader emerges in the interaction and those participating are continuously creating and recreating the meaning of the leadership themes in the local interaction in which they are involved. This is, however, not to say that a leader cannot be appointed. Here the distinction between cult and functional becomes relevant. One could understand the "mask" of the leader as the idealization of leader, the cult leader, whereas the role refers to the functionalizing of the ideals in the everyday conflicts of interaction. The role of leader is very frequently filled by some agreed process of appointment, almost necessarily based on idealized criteria. However, such criteria always require interpretation and begin to shift in conversations during the process of appointment. In other words, the idealized cult leader role is functionalized in the appointment process. However, once appointed, there is a strong tendency for this move from idealization to functionalization to be reversed as the newly appointed leader is idealized by the group, becoming a cult leader – that is, leader of a group of people directly enacting idealized values, cult values, to which they are subtly pressured to conform. This creates a problem for subsequent leadership appointments. It is especially difficult to succeed a charismatic leader who has led a cult of their own personality and the easiest way of dealing with this is to attempt to establish another cult. This obviously blocks the functionalizing of the ideals, which is what an organization needs in order to come alive in the present.

Once appointed, the leader and others in the group together form and are at the same time formed by emergent themes of leadership. In any given situation, but especially in those involving greater numbers of participants, there will be a number of themes of leadership being enacted simultaneously. What are these themes? Where do they come from?

The answer to the second question is perhaps also the answer to the first. Leadership themes emerge in the on-going process of group interaction in which personal and collective identities are iterated and potentially transformed. Leadership themes emerge over time and have virtually unlimited meanings for a group. In ancient Rome, the leadership theme was that of the "man of virtue", representing the virtues that all had. In some religions, for example, the theme of leadership took the form of the priest who represented the people to God in the ritual of sacrifice. With increasingly larger areas of land to protect, military leaders emerged, then aristocracy and monarchs. In the city states of Italy ruthless princes were recognized as leaders because they were the best at conspiring and poisoning wine which seemed to have been a necessary survival tactic as the "rules of the game" emerged. The meanings attached to the term "business leader" have proliferated as the size of corporations has grown. Mafia bosses have emerged, as have criminal leaders, Hitler, political leaders, mayors, presidents, abbots – the list could go on for pages. Also covering pages would be a list of those other roles related to that of leading, for example, pupil, mate, member, servant, employee, partner, and so on.

Why is it that in the theories of leadership dealing with business organizations there is the marked tendency to extol leaders as something exemplary and apart? What I am arguing is that they are by no means apart – they are who they are only in the evolving context of local interaction in which they and other participants are continuously recreating their identity as they construct their future in terms of the enabling constraints of the past. In the work of the management and organization theorists treated in Chapters 2, 3 and 4, there was a central focus on harmony and striving to be a part of a functioning whole. The exception was the work of Pascale who speaks of productive conflict, by which he means conflict that has been instrumentalized to achieve the goals of senior management. This is not the conflict Mead and Elias speak of. Pascale's conflict for the sake of conflict cynically denies identity and recognition, which are the concerns of Mead and Elias. Mainstream literature on leadership amounts to a concerted effort to achieve exactly the opposite of what Mead and Elias are insisting on as the pivotal concern of social interaction. Authors on leadership appeal directly to cult ideals and their systems thinking has the effect of covering over ideologies and splitting off tendencies to challenge power. This is the sense they are recommending be made of the lived present in organizations. By dominating the present with these themes I would argue they are developing only a weak sense of identity, the opposite of what Mead and Elias see occurring when there is recognition of identity through conflict.

Conflict and the recognition of identity

Who are we that we find it so difficult to speak of our conflicting interests, feelings and motives? Why is it that we sense the need to fool even ourselves in what Mead referred to as "hopelessly ideal" illusions of being only good, righteous and exemplary? The fact is that we paradoxically recognize our own selves in recognizing the other and recognize the other in the manner that we recognize ourselves. If we are continuously recreating identity without the struggle of entering into conflict we end up only recognizing the shell of identity we were before. We fool ourselves in fooling others. We fool others in fooling ourselves.

The cycle of recognition is the very meaning of identity. Enacting the themes of the autonomous individual and systemic wholes in organizations enables us to blind ourselves to this experience as the present. As Elias states:

> *But social tensions and conflicts will never be banished from society by suppressing them in theories.* It is easy to see that tensions and conflicts between groups which are losing functions and those acquiring new or increased functions, are a vital structural feature of all development. In other words, it is not just a question of personal, mainly accidental tensions and conflicts, though the people involved usually see them as such. From the viewpoint of the intermeshing groups, they can sometimes be seen as expressions of personal

> animosity, sometimes as consequences of the ideology of one side or the other. On the contrary, however, this is a matter of *structured* conflicts and tensions. In many cases they and their results form the very kernel of a process of development.
>
> (Elias, 1970: 173)

Who are we? This is the key question concerning not only the task, which forms the on-going purpose, but also the roles that evolve over time as the identity of those constructing the future in terms of the constraints of the past. It is the key question and the reason that the role of leader, which embodies this key question, takes on the importance that it has. Who are we? The re-cognition in the themes we enact in the on-going answer to this question create the structures which sustain and potentially transform the group or organization, the social and moral order, the practices, codes, laws and so on: Mead and Elias draw attention to the key factor of conflict. This can take on varying meaning in the living present:

- We can avoid conflict and rotate in a "hopelessly ideal" and empty shell of identity.
- We can seek conflict for its own sake and deny identity.

The two alternatives we encounter most often in our everyday lives are, however, that:

- We can *seek through conflict the active recognition* of difference and thus *at the same time* recreate and possibly transform our identity.
- We can do the opposite and *collude to actively deny* difference and in doing so affirm identity with no possibility of change and no sense that the identity is necessarily real.

There is another possibility, mentioned above in reference to Pascale. One can instrumentalize conflict itself as a form of conflict for the sake of conflict. But as such it is for the sake of conflict *in order to* achieve the goals of some person or persons in the group or organization. Because instrumentalization has currently taken on many different variations and names, it deserves further exploration.

Idealizing and instrumentalizing conflict

It is helpful to return again to the distinction between cult and functional values to understand how instrumentalization itself functions in social interaction. "Conflict" can itself be idealized by removing it from the present and making it hypothetical. It is then a cult value. When conflict is understood in this way as being between two conflicting ideas of what the future might bring, it becomes cult leadership. In other words, conflict becomes the "tool" of leaders. What is then discreetly not talked about is how "we" came to be using this tool and what "we" expect to achieve. But the "we" here is alienated from the "we" of a particular conflictual conversation. From the perspective of complex responsive processes in the living present, the important point is not the "tool" so much as how the goals that the tool is to achieve emerge in conflictual processes. Instrumental thinking deflects attention from this ordinary interactive conflict in a local situation to the idealized possible. Such tools include temporal gap "analysis", such as scenarios, business process reengineering, visioning, and so on, but also new tools, mentioned in Chapter 3, prescribed by those who are reducing complexity theory to a fad. Examples of this are simple rules that "hopelessly idealize" the complexity of the future and "action labs" based on the fantasy that self-organization can be "boxed in" and instrumentalized.

I have developed the concept of participative self-organization in Part II of this book as a basis to argue that if there is any self-organization here it can only be systemic self-organization "playing itself out" in terms of the hypotheses which scientists, or in the above examples others in the organization, have themselves imputed into the system. All the tools mentioned reduce the complexity of how the future is continuously being constructed in the movement of the living present by forming hypotheses of one sort or the other in order to "tame" complexity by reifying it as some sort of hypothesis. Of course we can and do proceed in this manner. The important issue, however, is that in doing so power is exercised in the idealization and deflection involved, and this is being exercised as *participation in the "real" conflict,* that is, in the conflict in the living present of the group involved. Here again the distinction between the ideal and the functional can serve to point to an important perspective on the nature of power.

The cult of power versus the function of power

Power frightens us because it makes us realize that there are situations in which we can be forced to do something. It also fascinates and seduces us because of the possibility of being in the opposite position, that of telling others what to do and in many cases forcing them to do it. Hence the oft-quoted statements of Henry Kissinger that power is an aphrodisiac and of Lord Acton that absolute power corrupts absolutely. Because of the literally awesome aura which power can take on, we can be tempted to shy away from examining and questioning its nature more objectively. What then happens is the idealization of power and the attribution of cult status to it. We easily reify power and locate it in individuals and institutions. This is very real to us, in terms of paying our taxes and obeying other laws of the societies we participate in and following the codes of practice and status positions that can legitimately be reified in organization charts. There can be little doubt that the cult of power is in turn a key factor in the cult of leadership. Elias, however, points out that we can also take another perspective on power, the functional perspective Mead also contrasted to the cult:

> Power is suspect: people use it to exploit others for their own ends. Power seems unethical: everyone ought to be in a position to make all their own decisions. . . . One may say that someone "has" power and leave it at that, although such usage, which implies that power is a thing, leads down a blind alley. A more adequate solution to problems of power depends on power being understood unequivocally as a structural characteristic of a relationship, all-pervading and, as a structural characteristic, neither good nor bad. It may be both. We depend on others, others depend on us. In so far as we are more dependent on others than they are on us, more directed by others than they are by us, they have power over us.
>
> (Elias, 1970: 93)

In the movement of the living present of large organizational operations, there is staggering complexity in the interdependency of which Elias writes. This is all the more so when one considers that any given organization operates in relation to competitors, suppliers and even customers, which are also organizations of comparable complexity. It is astounding that we continue to hold fantasies that single persons or small cliques of persons can steer such complexity to achieve targets that they have set in advance. Leadership and power emerge in the complex processes of relating as thematic patterns, which are the evolving structures that Elias and Mead speak of. These are the visible reality of the emergence of ethics. Each person and his or her actions are as a matter of fact important, but each person emerges as a person in the group, just as the group emerges as persons in interaction. The persons and the themes/structures that are their world are intimately interdependent. As Mead writes: "As a man adjusts himself to his environment he becomes a different individual; but in becoming a different individual he has affected the community in which he lives" (Mead, 1934: 215).

As the themes of interaction/structures become more complex, so also do the evolving figurations of power relationships. These power relationships are, as Elias writes, neither good nor bad in themselves; they are simultaneously the condition for, and the result of, the increasing complexity. Such complexity is related to the task to be done, that is, the on-going purpose of the group or organization. Mead refers to the way in which groups tend to recognize the leader role in those who have acquired a greater spontaneity, a greater ability to deal with the unknown as it emerges from the known context. The on-going purpose or task becomes the "grist to the mill" of the conflictual living present. But the complexity also has to do with embodied human beings with strong emotional themes, which have emerged in their past and constitute the enabling constraints that are the structures of their participation in the living present. Themes of leadership become enacted and these can include mother, genius, grandfather, college football coach, ruthless princess, perpetrator of domestic violence, shepherd, iron lady, czar and so on and on. As the size of a group grows, the number and complexity of these simultaneous patterns also increases, making it impossible to manipulate them. These themes greatly affect power-enacted structures and they are themselves greatly influenced by the structures that are co-created.

My motivation to write this book emerged over the years while working in global companies. I had a growing sense of the complexity and diversity described above, and parallel to that dissatisfaction with the theories of what makes organizations what they are and how they change over time. Such theories have great implications for leadership and power but this connection is usually taken for granted. Theories that remain within systemic self-organization tend to be limited to a common idea of what leadership, diversity and participation in the organization are about. The participative self-organization I have been proposing in Part II offers a significantly different point of view, one that I argue resonates more with our experience in organizations today.

Diversity and the unity of self

I suggested in Chapter 5 that systems thinking has contributed significantly to the growing postmodern argument that we should no longer seek to unify the different worlds that we daily experience. From the perspective of systems thinking, it is a strength to be able to shift in thought between various social systems, participating as a psychic system, and understanding our bodies as systems, but to give up any attempt to unite these systems as a sense of self. Instead, wholeness is sought in all-encompassing wholes, whether mystical or real.

The current multi-faceted concern with diversity in companies reflects this dominance of systems thinking. At a fundamental level there is very little tolerance for difference in modern organizations. Individuals are understood as parts of the system and this means that, in the extreme, difference is understood as the same as dysfunctional. Hence the avoidance of conflict and the focus in sessions and workshops on "diversity training", aimed at getting "the right mix" of diversity and "correctly" understanding political, cultural and religious differences. Again some elements of complexity theory, such as "the edge of chaos", have been construed as a contribution to this effort.

What Mead is getting at in his thinking on conflict and the emergence of the self, which are key elements in his theory of participation, is very different. For him the very essence of leadership is the recognition of actively dealing with difference. The leader acts "with reference to a form of society or social order which is implied but not yet adequately expressed" (Mead, 1934: 217). This is not the idealization of vision but rather participation in conflict in terms of the unknown future being constructed in this participation. For Mead there is no doubt that our participation in various groups is very complex:

> There are parts of the self which exist only for the self in relationship to itself. We divide ourselves up in all sorts of different selves with reference to our acquaintances. . . . There are all sorts of different selves answering to all sorts of different social reactions. It is a social process itself that is responsible for the appearance of the self; it is not there as a self apart from this type of experience.
>
> (ibid.: 142)

It is the ethical structures of the social order that are the condition for the possibility of persons, just as the persons are the condition for the possibility of the ethical structures, the structures of community. This is the emergent person as the organization of self, the unity of self, in which we have a sense of belonging.

> The unity of the self is constituted by the unity of the entire relational pattern of social behavior and experience in which the individual is implicated, and which is reflected in the structure of the self.
>
> (ibid.: 144)

What Mead accomplishes is a theory that combines an ethics of structure in the living present, which is at the same time the continuous construction of the future and the recreation and possible transformation of the past. This is not to say that we do not continue in the tendency to idealize and use power to limit diversity of all kinds – they continue to break through in the conflicts of the living present in order to unleash again the potential of difference.

Summary

In this chapter I have argued that theories of ethics are also theories of leadership. They are both action into the future and, therefore, about the identity of persons who are both changeable and stable. Modernism focuses most attention on the stability aspect of identity and elevates moral codes to do with stability into a theory of ethics. Autonomous individuals, according to this perspective, reason and reflect on the basis of codified practices, rules and laws before they act. It is in external codification and internal reason that the ethical is to be found. Ethical universals are thought of as "fixed realities" against which human conduct is to be judged, apart from and before action with meaning known in advance. Ethical leaders are those who are able to understand the consequences of their actions better than others or have proven themselves worthy of imitation because of the way they keep to the contract. Others, therefore, voluntarily agree to follow them and tend to be lumped together as followers.

The postmodern reaction to this is to declare identity an illusion and ethics purely relative. I propose another response, on the basis of Mead's thought. The ethical interpretation of our experience is then found within the experience itself as new points of view that emerge in the conflictual interaction in which the future is perpetually being created. This view of ethics avoids simply idealizing in a cult manner and focuses on how idealizations are functionalized in the everyday conflicts in which we are always negotiating the future on the basis of the past.

This shift in thinking about the nature of ethics follows from a shift in thinking about time. Instead of thinking about time in a linear way in which the present sinks into insignificance as the "past" is used to change the future, one thinks in terms of the living present having a time structure. It is in the present that we are continuously constructing the future on the basis of the enabling constraints developed over time as our past.

As groups evolve and develop a past they begin to recognize various members in roles, one of which is leader. The "mask", the role, of leader emerges in the interaction and those participating are continuously creating and recreating the meaning of the leadership themes in the local interaction in which they are involved. Groups tend to recognize the leader role in those who have acquired a greater spontaneity, a greater ability to deal with the unknown as it emerges from the known context.

7 Conclusion: articulating the ethics we are living

- **The perspective of systemic self-organization**

In this book I have drawn attention to two fundamentally different ways of thinking about life in organizations. I called the first of these ways of thinking systemic self-organization and argued that it reflects Kant's approach to eliminating paradox by adopting a "both . . . and" form of reasoning. Paradox is eliminated by positing a number of dualisms and then examining first one side of the dualism, followed by the other, in an alternating serial manner. Following this thought procedure, Kant suggested that humans could understand nature in terms of autonomous systemic wholes, hypothesized to unfold pattern already enfolded in them in an "as if" manner. Humans could also, quite separately, understand their own actions in terms of the goals they set themselves as autonomous individuals and the judgements they make as to the ethics of their actions. In making such judgements, they formulate hypothetical imperatives and test actions against them, so discovering the nature of universal categorical imperatives. The procedure is the same, whether understanding nature or human action, and it is that of the objectively observing scientist.

This kind of approach is reflected in most modern theories of management and organization. In particular, I have shown how this approach is evident in modern systems thinking as reflected in the currently popular theories of the learning organization and the organization as a living system. An organization is understood as an autonomous whole. It is reified and intention is ascribed to it by autonomous individuals who manipulate it. This way of thinking immediately leads to a very particular view of leading and leadership. The action of leading is located in autonomous individuals, the leaders, who become the objective observers of organizations as whole systems and the formulators of visions and values which provide the leadership according to which such systems are to unfold their future. Leadership, now split off from leaders, is located in the system. Closely connected to the question of leadership is the question of ethics. Basically, ethics becomes a matter of individuals abandoning their selfishness and submitting to the harmonious whole of organizational culture. Participation is understood as participating in a greater whole. When writers draw on the complexity sciences from the perspective of systemic self-organization, they do not introduce any radical challenge to systems thinking, the learning organization or organizations as living systems. Indeed, they simply reinforce all of these perspectives.

For me, a significant weakness in this whole way of thinking is the manner in which it abstracts and distracts from our ordinary everyday experience of interacting with each other in the living present. Such abstraction distracts our attention from our own responsibility for what we are doing and what happens to us in organizations. It leaves us feeling that we are simply the victims of the system. I have therefore proposed an alternative way of thinking that I have called participative self-organization, where participation does not mean participating in a larger whole, but rather participating in the direct interaction between human bodies. This derives from the reaction of Fichte, Schelling and particularly Hegel to the dualisms of Kant's thought. They countered Kant's dualisms by thinking in process terms and they understood process in paradoxical dialectical terms. Instead of positing an autonomous individual, they proposed that humans know what they know about nature and about themselves through the same process, the social process of interacting with each other. Indeed they become themselves in the process. I have described how this tradition was developed by Mead and by Elias and has been taken up in earlier volumes of this series. Those volumes look for analogies in the complexity sciences from a participative self-organization perspective and form a theory of organizations as complex responsive processes of relating.

Central to this theory is a notion of time that is different to that implicit in systemic self-organization. In systemic self-organization, the implicit notion of time is linear. This can be seen in the prescription for leaders to form a vision of the future to guide the direction of the organization. Implicitly here, the past is factually given because it has already happened and the future is ahead, waiting to be unfolded. In the perspective of participative self-organization, the present itself has a time structure. The past is not factually given because it is reconstructed in the present as the basis of the action to be taken in the present. The past is what we re-member. The future is also in the present in the form of anticipation and expectation. It too forms the basis of action in the present. Furthermore, what we are anticipating affects what we remember and what we remember affects what we expect, in a circular fashion, all in the present as the basis of our acting. In this way, the movement of the living present is experience, having a circular time structure that arises simply because humans have the capacity for knowing what they are doing. This notion of the living present differs from another way of focusing on the present, which is described as liberation from worrying about the past and from feeling anxious about the future by ignoring both. The result is a view of the present in which autonomous individuals encapsulate themselves. This stands in stark contrast to the dominant view in the organizational world where the future is split off and exclusively focused on in the form of vision, simple rules, values and plans, so distracting attention from the present and reducing the future to simple aspects that can be manipulated to determine the present. The notion of the living present is one in which the future, as expectation and anticipation, is in the detail of actual interactions taking place now, as is the past as reconstructions in this process of memory. There is no dismissing the past or the future here, nor is there any distraction of attention from the present of what we are doing together.

This shift in one's way of thinking leads to very different understandings of leadership and ethics. The action of leading is no longer split off from the nature of leadership. Leaders emerge in the interaction between people as an act of recognition. Ethics become a matter of our accountability to each other in our daily relating to each other. What is ethical emerges as themes that organize our experience of being together.

The distinction between systemic and participative self-organization is thus fundamental to the whole argument of this book and in the following sections I provide a fuller summary of what I have been arguing.

The perspective of systemic self-organization

Over two hundred years ago, Kant developed the concept of "systems" according to which he thought of organisms in nature as autonomous self-organizing wholes. Despite his strictures against thinking of human action in systems terms, organizational theorists over the last fifty years or more have done just that and the notion of an organization or a culture as a reified autonomous whole continues to underlie dominant thinking today. The move to understanding organizations as "learning systems", "living systems" and even "complex systems" is fundamentally a reaffirmation of Kant's concern for the autonomy of systems. Autonomy here means unity and wholeness and it is thought that this wholeness can be uncovered and instrumentalized by organizational leaders, just as scientists can supposedly discover and manipulate the wholeness of nature.

Kant's method of looking at a system "as if" it were following the laws of a given hypothesis was taken up by mathematicians and became a theory of modelling. The success of such modelling led to the reification of the systems models, that is, to the taken-for-granted understanding that they were things and the "as if" regulative idea came to be understood as the system's "intention". It came to be thought that in reality a system actually is governed by some regulative idea, such as a vision, and the "as if", hypothetical nature of Kant's thought slipped into the background. In this way of thinking it is still very common to understand an organization in reified terms as having an intention, as following a vision or acting according to values. It is the leader who is thought to be able to manipulate and change the "intention" of the organization according to his or her own goals, purposes, vision and values. Or some democratic grouping of individuals is empowered to formulate the vision and the values for the organizational system. Leaders, or empowered groups of people, are thought of as autonomous individuals observing the system and the system is also understood as an autonomous self-organizing whole, but this is not seen as paradoxical at all. Culture is viewed as an external force that influences the interaction of groups. However, it is then argued that leaders can stand outside of the culture and react when it becomes "dysfunctional".

The reason why beliefs of the kind just mentioned are not seen to be paradoxical flows from the way in which the two kinds of autonomous wholes, individuals and systems, are thought about. They are understood in a serial manner over time, "first . . . then". This is typical of Kantian "both . . . and" thinking that eliminates paradox. However, this very way of eliminating paradox is what many organization theorists are now calling paradox. It is claimed that culture is paradoxical because culture *both* acts on individuals *and* individuals decide what the culture should be. But this is not a paradox because it is stated in serial or alternating terms. There is no notion that individuals form culture while being formed by culture at the same time, implying emergent, evolutionary change acting into the unknown. This simultaneity, and its corollary of emergence and uncertainty, is not recognized when it is held that individuals can change the culture and apply it to others so reducing culture to an instrument leaders can use in the service of their own goals and strategies.

This leads to an ethics that is quite contrary to Kant in that autonomous individuals are required to participate in, submit themselves to, some larger whole or greater good. No longer are the autonomous individuals trying to discover in their actions what the ethical imperatives reflecting the not-to-be-defined whole are. Instead they are required to submit themselves to the visions and values revealed to them by their leaders, or democratically chosen by them as empowered individuals. In doing so they lose their autonomy, except for the occasion on which they choose in an empowered group. Participation then becomes submission to a harmonious whole, variously described as shared values, common purpose, common pool of meaning, transpersonal processes, group mind, collective intelligence, simple rules, and so on. The ethical choice is that of voluntary submission to a larger harmonious whole in which people lose their autonomy.

This way of thinking about ethics and leadership has many consequences. The freedom to choose actions and explore their ethical implications is located primarily in the leader, when in the role of system designer, while the other members of an organization are required to conform to the emerging leadership of the whole, as indeed must the leader in the role of steward and teacher. Again, this is not understood in any way as paradoxical. Any inherent contradiction is simply not noticed. Furthermore, systems thinking provides no explanation of novelty within its own framework. Since the systemic whole is unfolding the given vision of the leader as regulations and practices there is no novelty in the operation of the system. Nor is there any explanation of how the leader comes to design the system or form the vision imposed on the system. Positing a harmonious whole removes diversity and conflict. Since diverse persons, by definition, are not submitting to the whole and so not losing their individuality, there is bound to be conflict but this is either ignored or condemned in the kind of thinking I have described. Theories of the learning organizations and living organizations, as well as most applications of complexity theory to organizations, ignore diversity and conflict and their role in generating novelty.

Instead, these theories tend to present utopian views of human beings harmoniously consenting to the greater good of the larger whole, providing theories of what ought to be rather than what actually is. The result is an abstraction, even distraction from our ordinary, everyday experience of relating to each other. These theories cover up the greed, envy, jealousy, hate and aggression that are as much a part of human life as caring, loving and giving. Also covered over is the matter of power and ideology in the direct experience of human relationships. Those who think of organizations as autonomous wholes often call for a return to ancient wisdom, as a basis for leaders to build more caring communities and also as the basis for countering the global exploitation of the planet. Basing a theory of leadership and ethics on mythology is also a way of moving away from our direct current experience.

By setting up a whole outside of the experience of interaction between people, a whole to which they are required to voluntarily submit if their behaviour is to be judged ethical, this way of thinking distances us from our actual experience and makes it feel natural to blame something outside of our actual interaction for what happens to us. It encourages the belief that we are victims of a system, on the one hand, and allows us to escape feeling responsible for our own actions, on the other. Or it alienates us. We come to feel that our actions are insignificant parts of some greater whole and that there is nothing much we can do about it, especially when management becomes a matter of changing *whole* organizations.

An ethics based on autonomy, of the individual or of a systemic whole, is an ethics based on universal moral principles, which do not depend upon social or natural contingencies. They do not reflect the present context in which people are interacting with their particular life circumstances, aspirations and motivations. This is an idealized view of ethics in which autonomous leaders exercise their freedom independently of the contingencies of nature and society. Management becomes the formulation of visions for an organization, independently of nature and the society in which the organization operates. In the Kantian sense of autonomy, the endorsement of the vision statements of top management by others is in effect the surrender of their autonomy. Participation becomes participating in the leadership of the leaders. If their actions are to be ethical, from this perspective, then individuals are required to be "connected to the world" and "committed to the whole". When social and cultural systems are thought of as wholes, with humans as the individual agents, there is no other possibility than to attribute some sense of ethical responsibility and stability to the organization as a "whole". There is but a short step from this view to some kind of mysticism based on wholes and on a view of ultimate forms of learning being inexplicable. The result is various appeals, from New Age spirituality, mythology, oriental wisdom and ancient tribal understandings of belonging, to transcendental or all-encompassing "wholes" that influence, even determine our actions. These approaches have in common the appeal to escaping the "selfish" aspect of the autonomous individual and the "grasping self". As soon as one understands participation as individuals participating in self-organizing wholes outside of ordinary interaction, it follows that each individual is split into "good" and "bad". An individual is "good" to the extent that he or she participates in the overriding values of the self-organizing whole and "bad" or "selfish" to the extent that he or she does not conform to the overriding values. Ethics becomes the voluntary giving up of individual, selfish and egoistic inclinations in order to participate in the self-organization of the system.

Mead argued that individualizing a collective and treating it "as if" *it* had overriding motives or values, amounted to a process in which the collective constitutes a "cult". The actions of members of such "cults" are driven by the cult's values. A cult provides a feeling of enlarged personality in which individuals participate and from which they derive their value as persons. "Cult values" are an idealization of the collective, experienced as an enlarged personality that is often taken as a justification for the terrible actions people take. The idealization functions to divert people's attention from the ethics of their daily actions. This diversionary function of cult values follows not only from negative ideals but also from positive ones, the most precious part of our heritage, such as family values and democracy. Idealized values emerge in the historical evolution of any institution, to which they are ascribed, and they become functional values in the everyday interactions between members of the institution. For example, the cult value of a hospital might be to "provide each patient with the best possible care". However, such a cult value has to be repeatedly functionalized in many unique specific situations throughout the day. As soon as cult values become functional values in real daily interaction, conflict arises and it is this conflict that must be negotiated by people in their practical interaction with each other. Functional ethics is this negotiation.

In stressing functional values, Mead was alerting us to the dangers of focusing on the cult values themselves, on the values of the personalized institution or system, and directly applying them as overriding universal norms, conformity to which constitutes the requirement of continuing membership of the institution. This is the usual understanding of a "cult", namely an idealized group that is thought of as having values to which individuals must conform and if they do not they are judged to be selfish or sinful, which raises questions about their continued membership of the group. When organizations are said to be caring, or to have a soul, then they are being idealized as cults. Instead of focusing attention on the daily, necessarily conflictual functionalization of cult value, this idealization of the organization involves the direct application of the cult values as universal norms abstracted from daily life and people are said to be selfish when they do not conform to them. Cults are maintained by the technique of presenting a social situation free from the obstacles that prevent an institution being what we want it to be.

The use of visions and value statements in modern corporations is a striking example of this technique. Leaders are supposed to set out a vision, that is, an idealized future for the organization, and then empower people, that is, drive leadership down through the hierarchy. Participation becomes participation in an idealized systemic whole. Those proclaiming organizations to be living systems then link such systemic wholes to the forces of nature, sometimes using the complexity sciences to justify the link. Participation in turn becomes participation in this living whole, often understood as a kind of mystical union. The ethical and moral responsibility of individuals is related to this mystical whole rather than to the everyday contingencies of ordinary life in organizations. Culture comes to be thought of as an overriding, autonomous, harmonious whole to which "good" people must conform. The notion of participation as ordinary interaction between people and the notion of ethical and moral behaviour as our accounting to each other tends to be lost.

The perspective of participative self-organization

Organizations are not things at all, let alone living things, but rather they are processes of communication and joint action. Communication and joint action as such are not alive. It is the human bodies communicating and interacting that are alive. This immediately focuses attention in the communicative interaction between the living human bodies that are an organization. This is the basis of the alternative perspective of participative self-organization as the process sustaining and potentially transforming identity directly in participating in ordinary interaction between people. Participation is that of the embodied human beings with each other rather than the modernist concept of the autonomous individual. Experience can be understood not in terms of the individual alone but rather in terms of a world in which the individual plays an active part. Individuals come to an understanding of themselves in the continuity of their action, in the world in which they play an active part, and this is a social self-organizing process. Knowing and knowing selves are social processes. Drawing on the analogy provided by the complexity sciences, interaction of this kind has the intrinsic capacity to form patterns; when the interaction is between diverse human beings, those patterns may be genuinely novel so that the world becomes a different world through the amplification of difference. Humans collectively change the world in their acting and, at the same time, this changing world changes them. Novelty is not necessarily some large change, but it is necessarily unpredictable. In other words, novelty is that which is not simply determined by the past. This is a point of major significance in thinking about organizations. Most people nowadays seem to think that it is necessary to manage novelty by first formulating values and simple rules that create the "right conditions" in which people will act to produce novel outcomes. However, since novelty is unpredictable, it is impossible to specify in advance any rules, simple or complicated, that will lead to the kind of future novelty anyone may have decided upon in advance.

The move to the perspective of participative self-organization is a complete contradiction of systemic self-organization and as a theory of action it has implications for understanding leadership. Leaders emerge in the interaction between people as an act of recognition. Effective leaders tend to be those who have, in the course of their lives, developed more spontaneity and ability to deal with the on-going purpose and task of interaction. Leaders are individuals who have enhanced capacities for taking the attitudes of the other members of the group. They enhance communication within and between groups.

Leaders act and leadership is action. This immediately means that a theory of leadership is also a theory of ethics. Ethical values emerge in interaction as a reflection of the emergence of leaders. Large-scale organizational and cultural events emerge in everyday social interaction through participation in local events. Values, both cult and functional, are sustained and passed on in this ordinary social interaction, as themes that pattern our actions only in terms of local interaction. The cult values that seem to transcend this local interaction do not do so in any real sense, but only in an ideal sense which can only become real in the functional reality of the living present. Experience is interaction and it is "in the present". The ethics of reason and idealism to be found in those who take the perspective of systemic self-organization, with its appeals to universals and wholes, has failed to prevent the atrocities of instrumentalized, large-scale genocide and the destruction of the planet. Taking a participative self-organization perspective leads to a "minimal" ethics as opposed to the edification implied in the "greater" ethics of idealized universals. We find such an ethics in the smallest detail of our everyday lives, especially in language. Adorno argued that "the whole is that which is not-true" and that the foundations of fascism lie in a fascination with that which is, in and of itself, the "whole" in which people find their identities as "parts". It is in this fascination with the idealized whole, and peoples' identification of themselves as parts of it, that ethics fails. This happens because there is no questioning of the whole as such, only the instrumentalizing and optimizing of "selves" as parts in service of the whole. Local interaction is then alienated from a genuine living present because it is in the service of a whole that is not part of the experience of the present. To retain the emphasis on sustaining the whole one must impose a preconceived meaning on local interaction. This in turn results in understanding the "present" in a detached way because it has, in a very real sense, been predetermined. The whole is clearly predetermined even when it is defined as a vision of the future, as was the case with the utopian future for an idealized human community put forward by both fascism and communism.

Mead's view of the emergence of the person in social process, as one who can know, one who is self conscious in the form of an "I–me" dialectic, retains the responsible person with the freedom to choose as the basis of ethics. This perspective moves away from the autonomous individual but in so doing does not radically deny the individual or posit the existence of a transcendent whole. Instead the paradox of individual responsibility in a social process is retained.

Thinking about ethics and leadership

Theories of ethics and leadership are both concerned with the future, specifically with action into the future, and this means that they both have to do with "who" is acting into the future, a matter of identity. The underlying concern in both has to do with persons and the notion of person combines two opposite aspects, namely changeability and stability. This combination of transformation and continuity is at the core of what identity is about and therefore at the core of what ethics and leadership are about.

There used to be a distinction between ethics and morals. The former stressed the change aspect, seeing identity as the capacity to deal with change. The latter tended to refer to the stability and substance at the core of identity and was concerned with moral codes. In modernism, it is the latter aspect of person and the connected aspect of moral codes to do with stability that has been elevated to become the theory of ethics. Modern ethical theory, and associated leadership theories, tends to ignore the changeability of persons and the ethical aspects of dealing with change.

The modernist theory of ethics assumes that we are autonomous individuals, each of whom is capable of making rational decisions based on reflection apart from and before action itself, weighing the consequences of the outcomes and deciding whether to proceed or not. In other words, it is assumed that people "have" experience and are also able to detach themselves from it in order to manipulate and change it through thinking. That thinking, or reflection on action prior to implementation, if it is to be ethical, is to be done on the basis of a "contract" between individuals according to which each will be held responsible for their acts. Through history, the contract becomes codified as practices, rules and laws to be referred to in the reflection before action. Should the individual not be able to find a clear reference for a proposed action in such codes, it is nevertheless believed that he or she can use reason in the light of the "contract" with others to decide on any proposed action. The basis of ethical reflection, then, is referral to the codes and rational decision making. Ethical leaders are those who are able to understand the consequences of their actions better than others or have proven themselves worthy of imitation because of the way they keep to the contract. Others, therefore, voluntarily agree to follow them and tend to be lumped together as followers.

Ethics, then, has come to be regarded as the stable pole of universal principles and it is complemented by theories such as that of leadership, in effect ethical theories of "everyday" interaction, that are also concerned with the stability of identity. The paradox of stability and change at the core of the notion of identity is resolved so that we no longer notice it.

One possible reaction to this emphasis on the stable pole in theories of ethics and leadership is postmodernism. The paradoxical tension of stability and change in understanding the person and identity, and therefore ethics and morals, is declared illusory. However, there is another way of moving from thinking about ethics and leadership entirely in terms of stability, without concluding that they are illusory. One can avoid thinking in terms of ethical universals as "fixed realities" against which human conduct is to be judged, apart from and before action with meaning known in advance. Instead one can think of ethics as the interpretation of action to be found in the action itself, in the on-going recognition of the meanings of actions that could not have been known in advance. Motives then do not arise from antecedently given ends but in the recognition of the end as it arises in action. The moral interpretation of our experience is then found within the experience itself as new points of view that emerge in the conflictual interaction in which the future is perpetually being created. This view of ethics avoids simply idealizing in a cult manner and focuses on how idealizations are functionalized in the everyday conflicts in which we are always negotiating the future on the basis of the past. It avoids detaching from the everyday present of social interaction and instrumentalizing ideologies that go unnoticed and unchallenged.

In other words, instead of escaping to an ideal world of absolutes, idealized cult values, I am suggesting a focus on the functionalization of those cult values in the everyday interactions between members of the organization. In bureaucracies, cult values and functional are so closely coupled that it is difficult to argue against them. They take on the absolute character of a shield against change or transformation. In some other kinds of organizations, cult and functional values are so loosely coupled that it is easy for the New Age enthusiasts to believe that they can be directly applied as functional values and so effect large-scale change. Both tight and loose coupling mean that there is no difference between cult and functional values. However, in everyday experience, it is in the arena of conflict, in participating with each other, that we functionalize the ideal.

Here there is a difference between the meaning I attach to conflict in the process of functionalizing values and the way many other writers use it. Those who speak of productive conflict are instrumentalizing it *in order to* achieve the goals of senior management – conflict becomes the "tool" of leaders. In this way, "conflict" is idealized and becomes a cult value. From the perspective of complex responsive processes in the living present, the important point is not the "tool" but how the goals that the tool is to achieve emerge in conflictual processes. Instrumental thinking deflects attention from this ordinary interactive conflict in a local situation to the idealized possible.

The role of leader

As groups evolve and develop a past they begin to recognize various members in roles, one of which is leader. The "mask", the role, of leader emerges in the interaction and those participating are continuously creating and recreating the meaning of the leadership themes in the local interaction in which they are involved. One could understand the "mask" of the leader as the idealization of leader, the cult leader, whereas the role refers to the functionalizing of the ideals in the everyday conflicts of interaction. The idealized cult leader role is functionalized in the appointment process but once appointed, there is a strong tendency for this move from idealization to functionalization to be reversed as the newly appointed leader is idealized by the group. The leader then becomes a cult leader, that is, leader of a group of people directly enacting idealized values, cult values, to which they are subtly pressured to conform. This creates a problem for subsequent leadership appointments. It is especially difficult to succeed a charismatic leader who has led a cult of their own personality and the easiest way of dealing with this is to attempt to establish another cult.

Leadership themes emerge in the on-going process of group interaction in which personal and collective identities are iterated and potentially transformed. Leadership themes emerge over time and have virtually unlimited meanings for a group. Mafia bosses have emerged, as have criminal leaders, Hitler, political leaders, mayors, presidents, abbots and so on. However, these are not the only roles. There are many other roles related to that of leading, for example, pupil, mate, member, servant, employee, partner, and so on. This tends to be forgotten in the theories of leadership that extol leaders as people who are exemplary. In this way, power is idealized power and acquires the attributes of cult status. The cult of power is in turn a key factor in the cult of leadership. What is then lost sight of is how all participants are continuously recreating their identity as they construct their future in the living present in terms of the enabling constraints of the past.

Groups tend to recognize the leader role in those who have acquired a greater spontaneity, a greater ability to deal with the unknown as it emerges from the known context. But the complexity also has to do with embodied human beings with strong emotional themes, which have emerged in their past and constitute the enabling constraints that are the structures of their participation in the living present. Themes of leadership become enacted and these can include mother, genius, grandfather, college football coach, ruthless princess, perpetrator of domestic violence, shepherd, iron lady, czar and so on and on. As the size of a group grows, the number and complexity of these simultaneous patterns also increases, making it impossible to manipulate them. These themes greatly affect power-enacted structures and they are themselves greatly influenced by the structures that are co-created.

There is staggering complexity in the interdependency of people in a large organization in the movement of the living present. This is compounded by similar complexity in the many other organizations it interacts with. It is astounding that we continue to hold fantasies that single persons or small cliques of persons can steer such complexity to achieve targets that they have set in advance.

To conclude, the purpose of this book has been to explore in detail the way of thinking that produces what has become the dominating view of ethics, of leaders and of leadership in organizations today. I have argued that this way of thinking is fundamentally split in the form of a "both . . . and" dualism between the autonomous individual and the autonomous "whole" as a system called "common pool of meaning", "group mind", "organization", "culture" or "values". These take the form of missions, visions and simple rules articulating universal, ethical principles, often mysteriously linked to the whole universe or ancient wisdom. They amount to the hopeless idealizations typical of cult values. On the other side of the dualism, it is the role of the leader, which could either be the charismatic individual or the democratic group of autonomous individuals, who has the role of defining these idealized or cult values. These are to be applied directly to conduct and through many subtle and not so subtle means, persons are pressured into conforming to them – the very essence of a cult. This cult ideology is hidden in the "pseudo-scientific" language of systems and systemic self-organization. Such hidden ideology makes current power relations feel natural and so sustains them. This is the basis of our social arrangements in which a few heads of large corporations receive disproportionately large salaries supposedly justified by their special role as visionaries and crafters of values. The problem is that the cult idealization of such leaders is never far away from the flip side of denigration. With astonishing rapidity people can turn on idealized leaders, blame, punish and imprison them. Furthermore, because of the idealization involved, disillusionment is never far away. Those who believe in the cult values are repeatedly disappointed and so withdraw from organizational and political processes.

What this way of thinking, and the idealized leader roles it sustains, does is to distract attention from the functionalization of roles and values emerging in everyday interaction. It also lumps all other roles together as "followers" giving a highly simplistic view of interaction, while reducing differentiation and thus meaning. In the process, this way of thinking covers over conflict.

In this book I have proposed another way of thinking about ethics and leadership. This focuses attention on everyday interaction between people in their local situation in the living present. It is in these interactions that ethical interaction emerges and it is also therefore in this interaction that roles emerge, including the roles of leaders. Leadership emerges in the recognition of leaders by others. I am not going to add to the idealized generalities about leadership to be found throughout the literature on organizations. Instead I would like to refer the reader to other books in the series of which this book is one. Streatfield (2001), Fonseca (2001) and Shaw (forthcoming) all provide detailed accounts of experience in the living present of local situations in which leadership roles emerge in the recognition of interaction between people.

Bibliography

Adorno, T.W. (1969) *Minima Moralia*, Frankfurt am Main: Suhrkamp.

Argyris, C. and Schon, D. (1978) *Organizational Learning: A Theory of Action Perspective*, Reading, MA: Addison Wesley.

Ashby, W.R. (1952) *Design for a Brain*, New York: Wiley.

Bateson, G. (1973) *Steps to an Ecology of Mind*, St Albans: Paladin.

Bateson, G. and Bateson, M.C. (1987*) Angels Fear: Towards an Epistemology of the Sacred*, New York: Macmillan.

Bednarz, J. Jr. (1988) "Autopoiesis: the organizational closure of social systems", *Systems Research*, 5, 1: 57–64.

Bohm, D. (1965) *The Special Theory of Relativity*, New York: W.A. Benjamin.

—— (1983) *Wholeness and the Implicate Order*, London: Routledge (ARK).

Bohm, D. and Peat, F.D. (1989) *Science, Order and Creativity*, London: Routledge.

Bowie, N. (2000) "A Kantian theory of leadership", *The Leadership and Organization Development Journal*, 21, 4: 185–93.

Campbell, D., Coldicott, T. and Kinsella, K. (1994) *Systemic Work with Organizations: A New Model for Managers and Change Agents,* London: Karnac.

Capra, F. (1983) *The Turning Point: Science, Society, and the Rising Culture,* New York: Bantam.

—— (1996) *The Web of Life: A New Scientific Understanding of Living Systems*, New York: Anchor.

Coe, M.D. (1999) *The Maya*, London: Thames & Hudson.

Dennett, D.C. (1978) *Brainstorms*, Montgomery, VT: Bradford.

—— (1991) *Consciousness Explained*, Boston: Little, Brown and Co.

Elias, N. (1970) *What is Sociology?* New York: Columbia University Press.

—— (1989*) The Symbol Theory*, London: Sage Publications.

Fonseca, J. (2001) *Complexity and Innovation in Organizations*, London: Routledge.

Frederick, W.C. (1995) *Values, Nature, and Culture in the American Corporation*, New York: Oxford University Press.

Gadamer, H.G. (1960) *Wahrheit und Methode,* Tuebingen: J.C.B. Mohr.

Gay, P. (1970) *The Enlightenment: An Interpretation*, London: Wildwood House.

Geertz, C. (1979) "From the native's point of view: on the nature of anthropological understanding", in P. Rabinow and W.M. Sullivan (eds), *Interpretive Social Science*, pp. 225–41, Berkeley: University of California Press.

Gell-Mann, M. (1994) *The Quark and the Jaguar: Adventures in the Simple and the Complex*, London: Abacus.

Gleick, J. (1988) *Chaos: The Making of a New Science*, London: Heinemann.

Golembiewski, R.T. (1989) *Men, Management, and Morality: Toward a New Organizational Ethic,* New Brunswick: Transaction Publishers.

Goodwin, B. (1997) "Complexity, creativety and society", LSE Seminar Series Paper, to be published.

Habermas, J. and Luhmann, N. (1971) *Theorie der Gesellschaft oder Sozialtechnologie*, Frankfurt am Main: Suhrkamp.

Hampden-Turner, C. (1994) *Corporate Culture,* London: Piatkus.

Harth, E. (1993) *The Creative Loop: How the Brain Makes a Mind*, London: AddisonWesley.

Hayek, F.A. (1941) "The Counter-revolution of Science", *Economica* 8: 127.

—— (1943) "Scientism and the study of Society, II", *Economica*, 10.

Heidegger, M. (1958) *The Question of Being,* New Haven, CT: College and University Press.

Holland, J.H. (1995) *Hidden Order: How Adaptation Builds Complexity*, Reading, MA: Helix Books, Addison-Wesley Publishing Co.

Horkheimer, M. and Adorno, T.W. (1947) *Dialektik der Aufklärung*, Amsterdam: Suhrkamp.

Hunt, J.G. (1996) *Leadership: A New Synthesis*, Newbury Park: Sage.

Husserl, E. (1960) *Cartesian Meditations: An Introduction to Phenomenology*, London: Allen & Unwin.

Jantsch, E. (1980) *The Self-Organizing Universe*, Oxford: Pergamon.

Jaspers, K. (1957) (Original German edition 1931) *Man in the Modern Age*, Garden City: Anchor Books.

Judson, H.F. (1987) *The Search for Solutions*, Baltimore, MD: Johns Hopkins University Press.

Kant, I. (1786) [1956] *Grundlegung zur Metaphysik der Sitten*, Gesamtwerke Band 6, Wiesbaden: Insel.

—— (1790) [1987] *Critique of Judgement*, trans. W. S. Pluhar, Indianapolis: Hackett.

Kauffman, S. (1995) *At Home in the Universe: The Search for the Laws of Complexity*, London: Viking.

Kroeber, A.L. and Parsons, T. (1958) "The concepts of culture and of social system", *American Sociological Review*, 23: 582–3.

Lewin, R. and Regine, B. (2000) *The Soul at Work*, London: Orion Business Books.

Lovelock, J.E. (1988) *The Ages of Gaia*, New York: Norton.

Luhmann, N. (1967) "Soziologie als Theorie sozialer Systeme", *Kölner Zeitschrift für Soziologie und Sozialpsychologie*, 19: 615–44.

—— (1995) (Original German edition 1984) *Social Systems*, Stanford, CA: Stanford University Press.

Mainzer, K. (1997) *Thinking in Complexity*, 3rd edition, Berlin: Springer.

Marais, E.M (1937) *The Soul of the White Ant*, London: Methuen.

Marion, R. (1999) *The Edge of Organization: Chaos and Complexity Theories of Formal Social Systems*, Thousand Oaks, CA: Sage.

Maturana, U. and Varela, F. (1987) *The Tree of Knowledge*, Boston, Shambhala.

McCarthy, J.C. (2000) "eLeadership for the net economy", *The Forrester Brief*, 16 October: 1–4.

McCulloch, W.S. (1965) *Embodiment of Mind*, Cambridge: MIT Press.

Mead, G.H. (1908) "The philosophical basis of ethics", *International Journal of Ethics*, XVIII: 311–23.

—— (1914) "The psychological bases of Internationalism", *Survey*, XXIII: 604–7.

—— (1923) "Scientific method and the moral sciences", *International Journal of Ethics*, XXXIII: 229–47.

—— (1934) [1970] *Mind, Self and Society*, Chicago: University of Chicago Press.

—— (1936) [1972] *Movements of Thought in the Nineteenth Century*, Chicago: University of Chicago Press.

—— (1938) [1967] *The Philosophy of the Act*, Chicago: University of Chicago Press.

Miller, E.J. and Rice, A.K. (1967) *Systems of Organization: The Control of Task and Sentient Boundaries*, London: Tavistock Publications.

Mingers, J. (1995) *Self-Producing Systems*, New York: Plenum Press.

Minsky, M. (1985) *The Society of Mind*, NewYork: Simon and Schuster.

Nicolis, G. and Prigogine, I. (1989) *Exploring Complexity: An Introduction*, New York: W.H. Freeman and Company.

Nonaka, I. (1988) 'Creating organizational order out of chaos: self renewal of Japanese firms', *California Management Review*, 30/3: 57–73.

O'Donohue, J. (1993*) Person als Vermittlung: Die Dialektik von Individualität und Allgemeinheit in Hegel's 'Phänomenologie des Geistes'*, Mainz: Matthias Grünewald.

Parsons, T. (1951) *The Social System*, New York: The Free Press.

—— (1966) *Societies: Evolutionary and Comparative Perspectives*, Englewood Cliffs, NJ: Prentice Hall.

Parsons, T. and Shils, E.A. (eds) (1951) *Toward a General Theory of Action*, Englewood Cliffs, NJ: Prentice Hall.

Pascale, R.T. (1985) 'The paradox of corporate culture: reconciling ourselves to socialization', *California Management Review*, 27, 2: 26–41.

—— (1990) *Managing on the Edge: How Successful Companies Use Conflict to Stay Ahead*, London: Viking Penguin.

Pascale, R.T., Millemann, M. and Gioja, L. (1997) "Changing the way we change", *Harvard Business Review,* November/December: 127–39.

—— (2000) *Surfing the Edge of Chaos: The Laws of Nature and the New Laws of Business*, New York: Crown Business.

Prigogine, I. (1997) *The End of Certainty*, New York: The Free Press.

Prigogine, I. and Allen, P.M. (1982) 'The challenge of complexity', in Schieve, W.C. and Allen, P.M. (eds) (1982) *Self-Organization and Dissipative Structures: Applications in the Physical and Social Sciences*, Austin Texas: University of Texas Press.

Prigogine, I. and Stengers, I. (1984) *Order Out of Chaos: Man's New Dialogue with Nature*, New York: Bantam Books.

—— (1985) *Order Out of Chaos: Man's New Dialogue with Nature*, London: Fontana Press.

Rawls, J. (1971) *A Theory of Justice*, Cambridge, MA: Harvard University Press.

Reynolds, C.W. (1987) "Flocks, herds and schools: a distributed behavior model", Proceedings of SIGGRAPH "87", *Computer Graphics*, 21, 4: 25–34.

Schein, E.H. (1992) *Organizational Culture and Leadership*, 2nd edition, San Francisco: Jossey-Bass.

Senge, P. (1990) *The Fifth Discipline: The Art and Practice of the Learning Organization*, New York: Doubleday.

Sennett, R. (1998) *The Corrosion of Character: The Personal Consequences of Work in the New Capitalism*, New York: W.W. Norton.

Shaw, P. (forthcoming) *Changing the Conversations in Organization: A Complexity Approach to Change*, London: Routledge.

Shotter, J. (1993a) *Conversational Realities: Constructing Life through Language*, London: Sage.

—— (1993b) *Cultural Politics of Everyday Life*, Buckingham: Open University Press.

Sidgwick, C. (1988) "The Kantian conception of free will", *Mind*, 13.

Simon, H.A. (1960) *The New Science of Management Decision*, New York: Harper and Row.

Slater, P. (1970) *The Pursuit of Loneliness: American Culture at the Breaking Point*, Boston: Beacon.

Stacey, R.D. (2001) *Complex Responsive Processes in Organizations: Learning and Knowledge Creation*, London: Routledge.

Stacey, R.D., Griffin, D. and Shaw, P. (2000) *Complexity and Management: Fad or Radical Challenge to Systems Thinking?*, London: Routledge.

Stewart, I. (1989) *Does God Play Dice?*, Oxford: Blackwell.

Streatfield, P. (2001) *The Paradox of Control in Organizations*, London: Routledge.

Varela, F., Thompson, E. and Rosch, E. (1995) *The Embodied Mind: Cognitive Science and Human Experience*, Cambridge, MA: MIT Press.

von Bertalanffy, L. (1968) *General Systems Theory: Foundations, Development, Applications*, New York: George Braziller.

von Foerster, H. (1992) "Ethics and second-order cybernetics", *Cybernetics and Human Knowing*, 1, 1: 9–19.

von Krogh, Georg and Roos, J. (1995) *Organizational Epistemology*, London: Macmillan.

Waldo, D. (1948) *The Administrative State*, New York: The Ronald Press Company.

Waldrop, M.M. (1992) *Complexity: The Emerging Science at the Edge of Order and Chaos*, London: Penguin.

Wheatley, M.J. (1992) *Leadership and the New Science: Learning about Organization from an Orderly Universe*, San Francisco: Berrett-Koehler.

—— (1999) *Leadership and the New Science*, revised edition, San Francisco: Berrett and Koehler.

Wilber, K. (1995) *Sex, Ecology and Spirituality: The Spirit of Evolution*, Boston: Shambhala.

Wittgenstein, Ludwig (1980) *Remarks on the Philosophy of Psychology*, vols I and II, Oxford: Blackwell.

Index